Colour Painting
Using the Full Palette

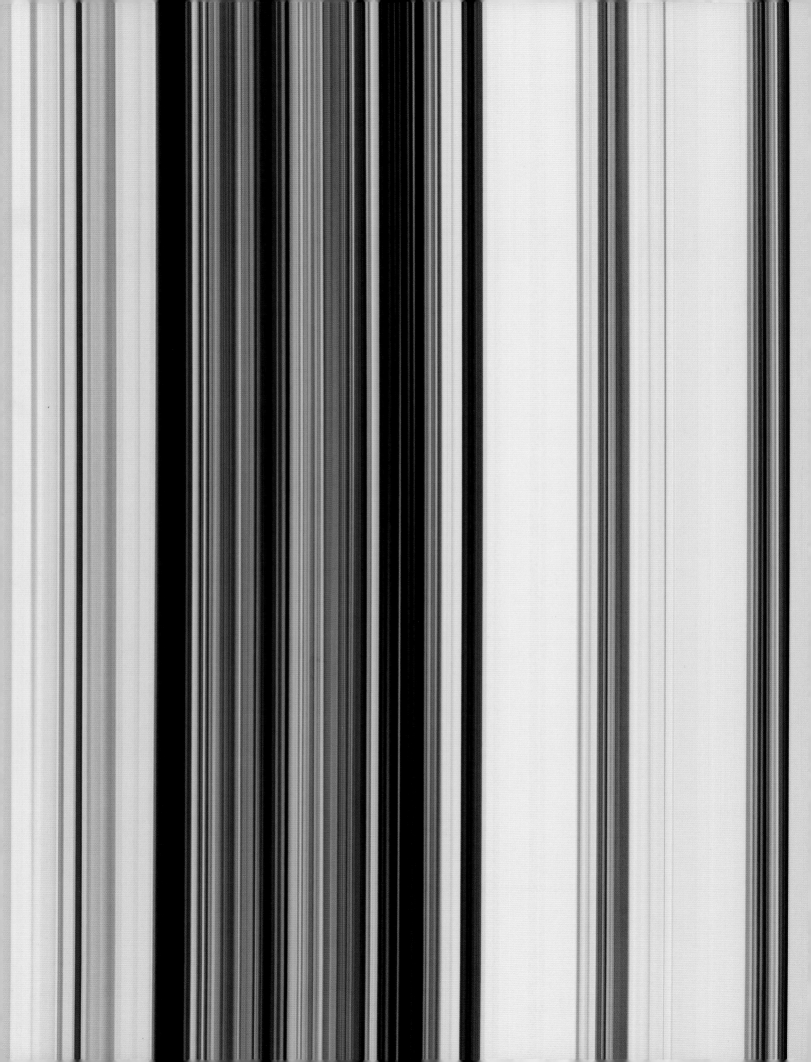

Diane Edison

Colour Painting
Using the Full Palette

Laurence King Publishing

Dedication
To Daphne Blackburn and my daughter
Rebecca, whose unwavering support,
encouragement, and love made this book
possible, and in memory of my mother Davie
and sister Mary, who are in my thoughts daily.

LAURENCE KING

Published in 2008 by
Laurence King Publishing Ltd
361–373 City Road
London EC1V 1LR
United Kingdom
Tel: + 44 20 7841 6900
Fax: + 44 20 7841 6910
e-mail: enquiries@laurenceking.co.uk
www.laurenceking.co.uk

A catalogue record for this book is available
from the British Library

ISBN-13: 978 1 85669 551 0

Design: Roger Fawcett-Tang, Struktur Design
Picture research: Julia Ruxton and Diane Edison
Printed in China

Front cover: Designed by Roger Fawcett-Tang from
an original design by David Zoellick, and painted
by Meredith Lachin

Contents

Preface

The human desire to embellish, imprint and record has survived from the earliest times to the present day, while techniques of painting have constantly evolved as new materials were discovered and put to use. Prehistoric cave dwellers would decorate walls with paint made from dirt or charcoal, mixed with spit or animal fat, before they realised that pigments taken from iron oxide deposits in the earth were more reliable. As early as the ancient Egyptians, the technique of fresco painting, in which water-based colour is painted on a prepared wet plaster surface, made huge wall commissions possible. The advent of wood panels around 1100, followed by canvas stretched over panels or a frame, ushered in portable works of art. This new portability, along with the patronage of the arts by wealthy benefactors, helped to increase the role of the artist as a professional. And despite the limitations imposed by the preferences of patronage—frequently for portraiture, scenes of great battles and religious themes—the individual personality of the artist often shines through in early oil paintings. Patronage continues in the guise of museums, galleries and collectors, but today's artists are highly individual, often highlighting personal causes at the same time as honoring commissions.

Artists today use a variety of surfaces to paint on—paper, metal, glass and whatever other surface will hold paint. Computer-generated images have helped young artists to reconsider and stretch their subject matter. An understanding of the rigour involved in learning to paint, however, strengthens such experimentation. When teaching an advanced painting studio, I find that the very definition of what a painting can be is regularly challenged in unexpected ways. Yet for a challenge to be successful, the basics must be in place—rather like a pianist learning to play the scales before going on to master improvisation.

Idelle Weber
Gutter II (Land O'Lakes)
1979
Oil on linen
48 ½ x 71 ¼ in.
(123.19 x 180.98 cm)
Courtesy Idelle Weber and
Bill Massey

In *Land O'Lakes*, Weber treats us to a different interpretation of garbage. Using classic realism, chiaroscuro shading and brilliant colour, she leaves us to ponder the question of beauty in art. The claustrophobic crop brings the viewer almost too close for comfort.

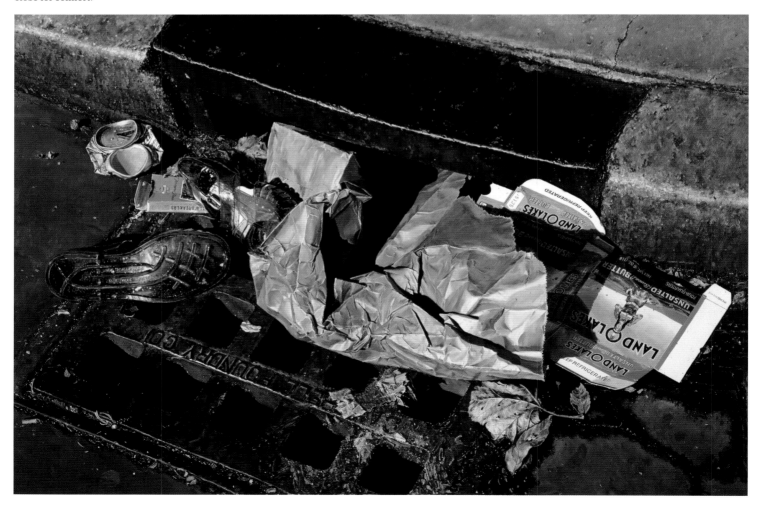

My philosophy of learning to paint is twofold: I want to illustrate what I view as a natural bridge between seeing and painting colour, while at the same time challenging beginning students with complex ideas surrounding painting. For many, drawing is considered the most direct medium from the mind to the hand; it is also an artistic discipline in itself, transcending its perceived service as primarily a preparatory instrument for art. Beginning students, however, do not always make the connection that drawing is an art form, which accounts for the fact that they seem to forget how to draw when they begin painting. This lack of connection is troubling, since it tends to interfere with the intuitive ease of the transition from drawing to painting.

With this book, I propose a different approach from the traditional practice of starting painting courses with monochromatic colour schemes, thereby circumventing the problem of "drawing" with the paint rather than spreading paint as a liquid; instead, *full-range colour painting* is the centrepiece of instruction. Full-range colour is the use of a comprehensive colour palette that originates from direct observation of colour in an environment. By seeing and understanding colour and colour value, this way of painting can become as direct as a drawing. This text will provide painting students with the tools and techniques to work in full-range colour using oil or acrylic media, and in so doing will present them with a context for appreciating the value of colour theory and design. The comprehension of these relationships in tandem with the physical application of the paint is the crux of why I view this text as a bridge. I am attempting to advance the intuitive quality ordinarily associated with an easeful transition from drawing to painting.

Over the years, I have consistently challenged beginning students in ways they were not expecting. It is at this point in their educational careers that they are the most approachable and least cemented in the conceit of what an artist is supposed to be, thus making this an ideal time for influencing their attitudes toward painting and art in general. The issue at hand is how to encourage beginning painters to think the way they did in grade school—perhaps before some well-meaning instructor told them that what they had created did not resemble what they intended it to look like, an experience that can mark the end of visual interpretation. Experimentation, risk and a love of making a mess are gradually discouraged in the pursuit of perfection in the style of working from observation alone that tends to begin in middle school and peak in high school. I intend that this book should enable students to recover that fearlessness and freedom so necessary to making art.

Even at this early stage of painting it is important that students are given instruction on integrating content and narrative throughout the planned assignments. The painting philosophy expressed in my text encourages an appreciation of traditional materials and techniques while simultaneously presenting students with opportunities to branch out and experiment—to "break the rules," so to speak. I believe it is just as important to teach students to find a personal style and provide an opportunity for new ideas as it is to help them to master technique.

I begin the book with a discussion of design and the visual elements of design in Chapter 1. These are the building blocks for composition that students will need to learn in order to create and edit paintings. In Chapter 2, we go on to explore the other element for composition;colour. Students will learn to understand colour and how to create and use it while making their own colour wheels using paint, the first opportunity in the book to learn about palette preparation and paint mixing. In the next three chapters, three painting techniques are described in detail: wet on wet, or alla prima painting, wet on dry and scumbling and, finally, the

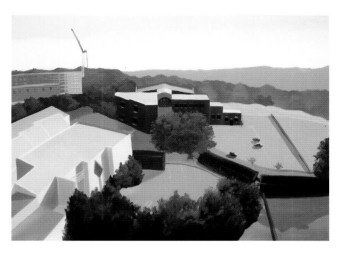

Laurin Ramsey
Oil on canvas

Beginning student Laurin Ramsey's landscape oil painting is a panoramic view of the changing cityscape of Athens, Georgia. Her strong composition and subtle colour mixing provide good examples of creating natural light and atmospheric perspective.

Venetian painting technique of glazing in layers. In Chapter 6 there is a chance to bring all these painting techniques together in a study of subject matter and content, including portraiture, landscape and abstract painting. The book ends with sections on self-critique and health and safety, and includes a glossary and list of further reading.

Throughout the book, step-by-step sequences demonstrate techniques, while the text is illustrated with examples of finished work by a wide range of artists. Feature spreads pick out such subjects as palette preparation, building a stretcher frame, stretching and priming the canvas, choosing and using brushes, and also cleanup and preparation for the next day's painting.

Acknowledgements

Thanks to Laurence King Publishing: to Lee Ripley, Publishing Director, for her active help and support with her offer of a contract—her faith in me was my greatest encouragement; to Anne Townley, whose patience helped me gather my knowledge of painting into a clear and concise manuscript, while asking all of the right questions; and to Melissa Danny, whose questions and commentary have helped me to sharpen my writing. Thank also to Eric Himmel, Editor-in-Chief at Harry N. Abrams. I am also grateful to the reviewers who provided useful feedback at various stages of the manuscript. In particular I would like to thank Clare Marie Goldsworthy and James Xavier Barbour. My thanks to the following: Irina D. Costache for introducing me to Helen Ronan, who invited me to submit a proposal; Dana Vannoy, who edited my proposal and was a constant source and support for my writing; Robin Dana, my book photographer, for the wonderful suggestions, ideas and collaboration; George Adams, of the George Adams Gallery, who has represented me as an artist for fifteen years—his support and encouragement of my art and the writing of this text have been immeasurable; Carmon Colangelo, director, colleague, adviser and friend; Clarence Morgan and Arlene Burke Morgan, who have been my colleagues from afar and up close, for their support over the years; Rylan Steele for additional photography; Thomas Manley, whose hard work as my studio assistant will always be appreciated; Judson Duke, my invaluable research assistant and builder of painting surfaces; Lesley Dill, gallery mate and friend; Carol May, a true friend for over two decades; Ellen Levy and Joan Marter, with whom I served on the board of the College Art Association; Joseph Wiley and Brandon Williams, for all their technical and IT support—they kept my upgrades coming. I am also very grateful to the strong support of my colleagues at the Lamar Dodd School of Art, University of Georgia Athens: Radcliffe Bailey, James Barsness, Scott Belview, Stefanie Jackson, Margaret Morrison, Joseph Norman, Judy McWillie, Martijn Van Wagtendonk and Troy Duane Wingard; and to all of my beginning painting students for their wonderful art, some included in this book, and for continuing to teach me how to teach.

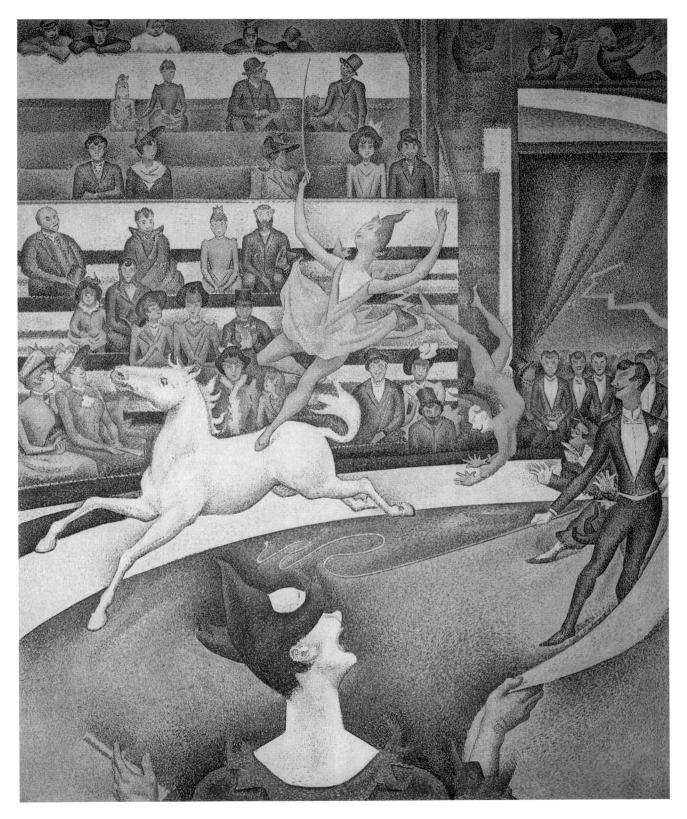

Georges Seurat
Le Cirque
1891
Oil on canvas
73 x 60 in. (185.5 x 152.5 cm)
Musée d'Orsay, Paris

Seurat, known for his style of painting called pointillism, creates a swirling movement with a series of performers in the centre stage of a circus. This technique uses small dots of pure colour that merge in the eye of the viewer, bringing luminosity and warmth to the scene.

Chapter 1:
Design Principles and the Visual Elements

In this chapter we will explore the concept of design and its practical use in composing paintings. The importance of basic design knowledge cannot be overemphasised. The utility of design is often overlooked or disparaged for fear that too much concentration on design principles may impede creativity. I believe that, on the contrary, an understanding of design strengthens and empowers the new painter. As for the danger of impeding creativity, I will always counsel a new painter first to master the rules and then choose to break them later. Design is about planning and organizing. It is useful, when painting from observation, in providing both a blueprint and a template to organise the illusion of three-dimensional space on a two-dimensional plane (the flat space of the canvas or paper in front of you), and it is crucial to understanding visual phenomena. You need a strategy to make sense of what you are seeing, which will then help you to make decisions about what to include in your painting. Design is but one of many ways to edit your paintings.

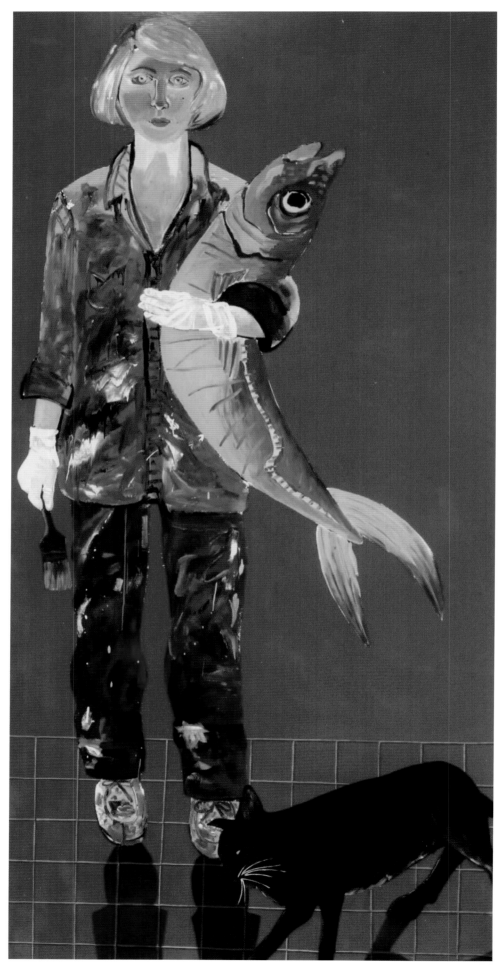

Joan Brown
Self-portrait with Fish and Cat
1970
Enamel on Masonite
96 x 48 in. (243.8 x 121.9 cm)
Courtesy of George Adams
Gallery, New York, and Gallery
Paule Anglim, San Francisco

Joan Brown's self-portrait is an
example of dramatic colour
usage. The painting is
deceptively simple yet elegant
in line. Colour and value are
used to great effect in the use of
bright red in both the foreground
and the background. The yellow
of the fish is made even more
dramatic by comparison. The
chromatic neutral greys in the
clothing help create the illusion
that the figure is moving from
front to back on the picture
plane. Because of the high
contrast, the blue-black
colouring of the cat creates a
silhouette that keeps it front and
centre. It is the placement of the
strong colours that affects the
composition, which itself has a
very economical use of line.
Although Brown's painting is
figurative, the space is
imaginary and symbolic and, in
the case of the background and
foreground, creates a sense of
figure/ground ambiguity, where
it is hard to decide what is figure
and what is the background.
The use of simultaneous
contrast in the placing of
complementary colours of
similar brightness—red and
green and yellow and blue—
conveys a sense of movement.
It is also a strong example of the
use of chromatic neutrals to
create grey (see p. 51).

Design Principles and the Visual Elements

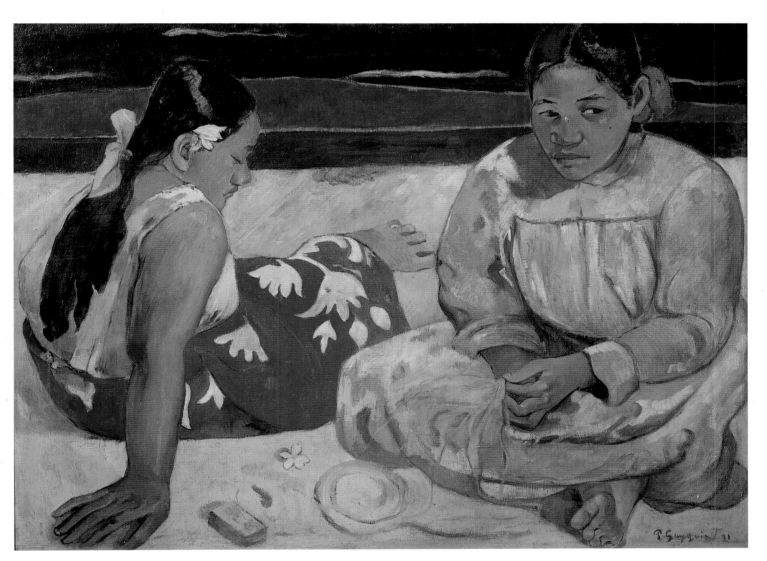

Paul Gauguin
Tahitian Women: On the Beach
1891
Oil on fine-weave canvas
27 x 35 in. (69 x 91 cm)
Musée d'Orsay, Paris

Gauguin's *Tahitian Women* shows the effect of scale and proportion within a composition. By placing the figures in the foreground and making them large, the background is automatically diminished and the illusion of distance is created. The space between the figures and the way the hand and one foot are cropped off the paper create interesting pockets of negative space (see p. 76). The sense of balance is achieved by equality of the visual weight of the figures and the negative space surrounding them.

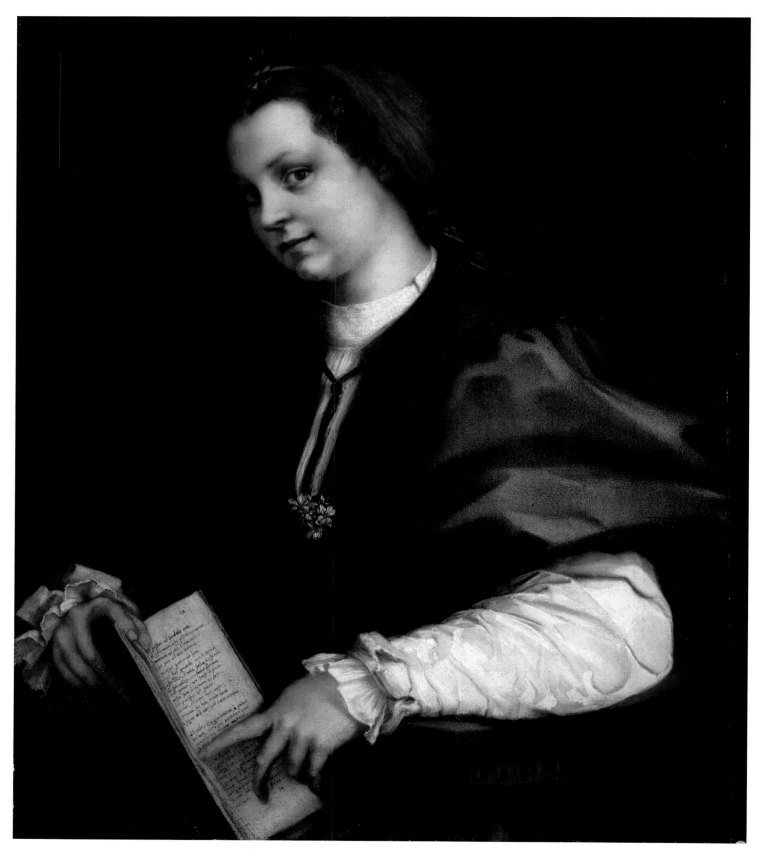

Andrea del Sarto
Portrait of a Woman with a Book of Petrarch's Poetry
c. 1526–28
Oil on panel
33 x 27 in. (84 x 69 cm)
Uffizi Gallery, Florence

In portraiture, one often speaks of the gaze, the relationship between the sitter and the viewer. Andrea del Sarto's subject is all awareness, with a knowing nod to the viewer. Compositionally, she is framed by a series of triangular shapes, starting with the blue of her cloak on her left shoulder, followed by the length of the sleeve of her left arm. Her emergence from darkness is a strong example of the chiaroscuro painting technique following the tradition of Caravaggio (see p. 78).

Design is also about problem solving, though in art and painting there is no single right answer. It may help to think of design in art as a bag of visual tricks composed of a series of elements and principles that can be used to create the illusion of space. How you use these visual tricks is up to you, but you should be aware of these underlying processes. The elements of design can be broadly described as dots and lines, shape and depth, texture, space, value and colour. How you go about designing or composing your image using these elements is usually governed by various principles, including harmony, balance, economy, scale and proportion, dominance and focal point, and rhythm and movement. We will explore these elements and principles in this chapter, and each will be illustrated in the accompanying contemporary, historical and student images.

Most professional artists produce paintings in a very intuitive manner, which tends to be reflective of their knowledge both of the role of design as a creative tool and of art history. It is always worth studying works by historical and contemporary artists. Once you understand how and why they created their images, you will be able to use the lessons you learn to help you plan and organise your own paintings.

Beginning students need only refer to Kako Ueda's *Vanitas* (p. 18) to gain an idea of the breadth and variety of the design elements and principles being used in creative contemporary art. Here, the design elements of repetition and similarity coexist in the same painting. Repetition, combined with colour and scale, helps achieve an overall sense of balance. These collected patterns form the core of a painting that leads the viewer through the composition. Ueda's use of shaped cut paper and paint explores the definitions of what a painting can be.

When we begin to create a painting, we are faced with a flat surface (the paper, the canvas and so on). This is known as the picture plane. Beginning painters will usually start with a painting surface that is either rectangular or square, and are thereby dealing with an area that has four right angles. Not unlike a window, the outside shape of your canvas is what will frame your subject matter. The design challenge is how to create an image that is equally interesting in all four corners and not just focused on the centre of the canvas. This is where the design elements and principles can be brought into play.

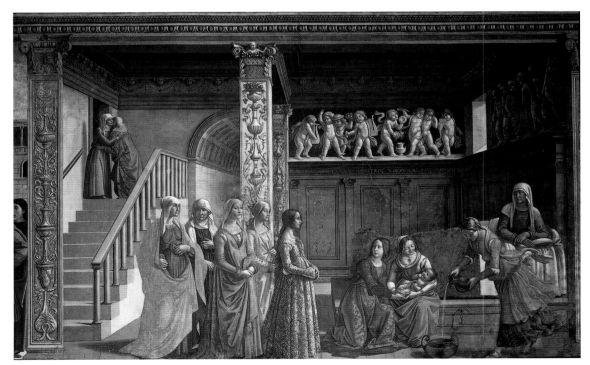

Domenico Ghirlandaio
The Birth of the Virgin Mary
1486–90
Fresco
Cappella Tornabuoni, Santa Maria Novella, Florence

This fresco illustrates the use of one-point perspective (see p. 22), in which the lines and figures converge on a single vanishing point at the eye level of the artist. If you used a ruler and traced the lines, you would see this quite clearly. The vanishing point here is slightly above the head of the standing woman in the gold gown (fifth figure from the right).

Design Elements

Dots and Lines

The dot can be described as the most basic mark. Lines can either stand alone or be connected. A line can follow the general outline of a subject. Lines can also have different qualities; they can be thick or thin, light or dark, free-flowing or rigid. Richmond Teye Ackam positions lines and dots to create a cohesive image in his painting *Red and Black*, below.

Shape

We can create a shape by joining several lines together. The shape can also be referred to as the **figure**—whether it is an object or a person—and the space between the shapes and on which the shapes rest is called the **ground**. The relationship between the figure and the ground, known as the **figure/ground relationship**, is important in the composition of the whole image. In Rogier van der Weyden's *Portrait of a Lady* (p. 19), the use of a dark background mirroring the dark tones of the costume serves to accentuate the paler, more ethereal qualities of the face, neck and veil.

There are occasions, however, when it is useful to blur the distinction between the figure and the ground, and this is known as **figure/ground ambiguity**. Joan Brown's *Self-portrait with Fish and Cat* (p. 12), demonstrates this, where both the background and foreground of the image are painted in red, achieving an imaginary and symbolic space.

Richmond Teye Ackam
Red and Black
2003
Acrylic on vellum
11 in. (28 cm) diameter
Courtesy of the artist

In this work, the subtle basic shape of dot, line and form gives way to a fully realised painting. The size, shape and colour of the individual forms help define the focal point, or the area that the viewer's eye is most drawn toward: the yellow, which stands out in contrast to the green. The black arch in the background comes in and out of our view, an example of figure/ground ambiguity. The ambiguity arises out of the sense that the figure and ground are at times visually indistinguishable. The slightly larger circles in front give the illusion of deep and shallow space (foreground and background). The image appears deceptively simple. As you see, abstract or nonrepresentational art is by no means exempted from the requirement of design fluency.

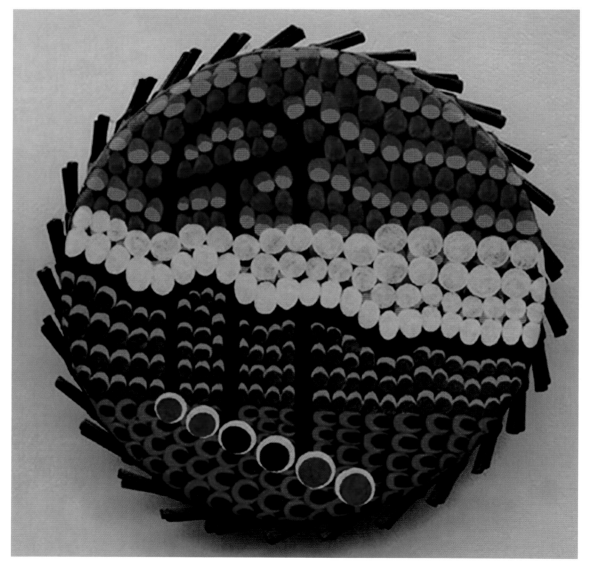

Similar to the concepts of the figure and the ground is the design element of **negative space** (see also p. 76). If you consider a mark on the picture plane as a positive shape, then the area surrounding it is negative space. The tendency of new artists to view the outside lines that form objects or figures as the most important often gets in the way of understanding their relationship to the negative space. One way to demonstrate negative space is to attempt to draw the negative space first, such as the inside lines of a picket fence. What remains is the fence itself. The term negative space is not meant to be disparaging; it is a means of visually separating the figure from the ground.

Like figure/ground relationship, negative space is important in terms of composition on the square or rectangular surface. A successful composition will be one where the shapes of the negative space are also considered as part of the design. Beginning painter Kelly Smith's *Fruits and Vegetables* painting (right) is an illustration of effective and inventive overall use of negative space. Here the negative space is formed by the pale blue material on which the fruit and vegetables are placed, and the shapes created as a result are as interesting as those of the objects in the still life arrangement itself. Together, the fruits and vegetables and the pale blue of the negative space create a dynamic composition.

Smith's painting also shows the effective use of **cropping** to create a visually interesting composition with a sense of continuation. Here the edges of the picture plane have been considered as a frame to the image, allowing a carefully chosen portion of the still life arrangement to be included within it, as is demonstrated by the cutting off, or cropping, of some of the fruits and vegetables. Cropping the image through composition is also illustrated in van der Weyden's *Portrait of a Lady*.

Texture

Texture in a painting can be both tactile, through the tactile nature of the paint, and visual, in the rendering of textures such as feathers or fur. It can be created through the use of **repetition**. In design, this is a mark or shape that is repeated throughout the image. A checkerboard is a good example. In nature, this phenomenon is called **similarity**. An example is a field of grass in which each blade appears to be exactly the same, but in reality they are all different. As we have seen, Kako Ueda's *Vanitas* (overleaf) shows both repetition and similarity. The repeating of shapes and colours in this image also creates a **motif**.

A motif occurs when visual elements are combined and this new combination is repeated, creating a pattern, which becomes a visual theme. A motif can be in the form of strict repetition, or it can merely suggest similarity.

Almost the opposite of repetition is **variety**, where many dissimilar shapes form the core of the design. More of a random quality is conveyed, as demonstrated in Norman Rockwell's *Shuffleton's Barbershop* (p. 27), where all the pieces of furniture and objects in the room combine to create one cohesive whole. Most designs and artwork employ a combination of repetition and variety.

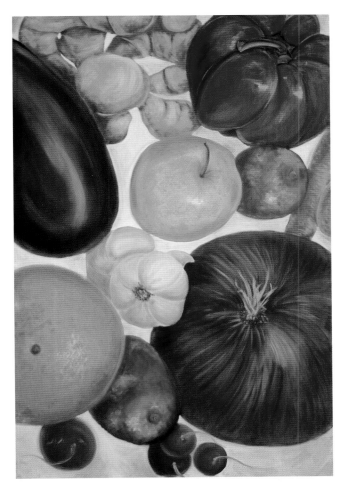

Kelly Smith
Oil on canvas

Beginning painting student Kelly Smith's fruit and vegetable painting is an inventive illustration of the overall use of negative space. For the sake of simplicity, view the pale blue material on which the fruit and vegetables are placed as negative space—negative only as a way to describe the difference between the objects and the space or air around them. Arranging your still life and allowing for interesting abstracted shapes with this space creates a dynamic viewpoint. This picture is a very open composition, with the edges cropped from all sides.

Space and Depth

Creating a sense of space and depth in a painting is all about creating an illusion of a three-dimensional space on the two-dimensional plane of a flat piece of paper. Space can be **deep** or **shallow**. In deep space we look far into the distance, as in Richmond Teye Ackam's *Red and Black* (p. 16), but we can also look into shallow space, which seems much more limited and is also suggested in the foreground of Ackam's painting by the use of larger dots to define a more cramped area.

Artists use a variety of different visual tricks. The most basic is to place a larger object next to a smaller one. Of course, a sense of proportion comes into play. If one of those objects is a house and another is an adult person then we might assume that both are a similar distance away from the viewer. But if one is a large cup and the other a small cup, then we might assume that they are actually of a similar size and that the larger one is nearer to us and the smaller one farther away.

Kako Ueda
Vanitas
2004–5
Hand-cut paper with watercolour
18 x 19 in. (45.7 x 48.3 cm)
Courtesy of George Adams Gallery, New York

Ueda's *Vanitas* shows repetition and similarity coexisting in the same painting. An overall sense of balance is achieved by repetition, colour and scale. The repeating shapes and colours create a motif.

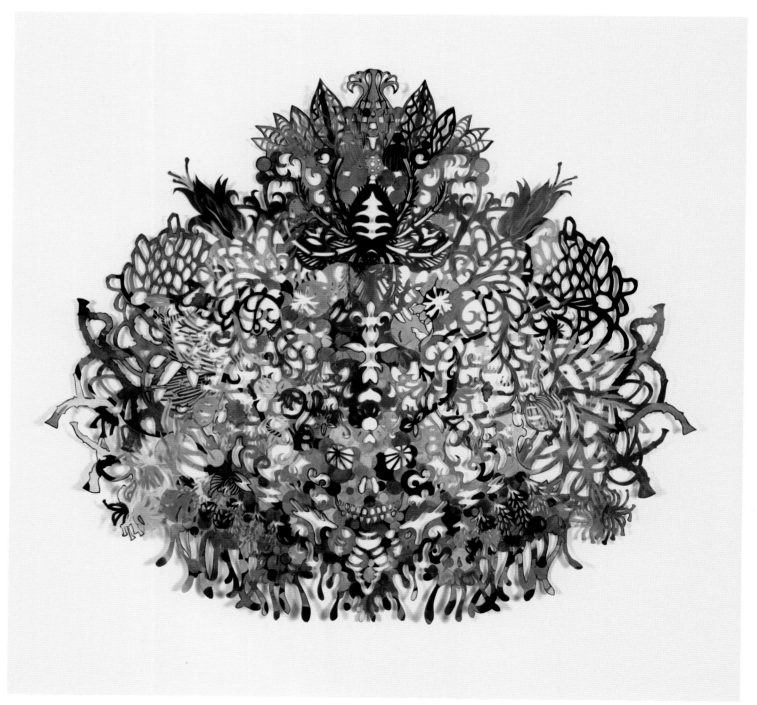

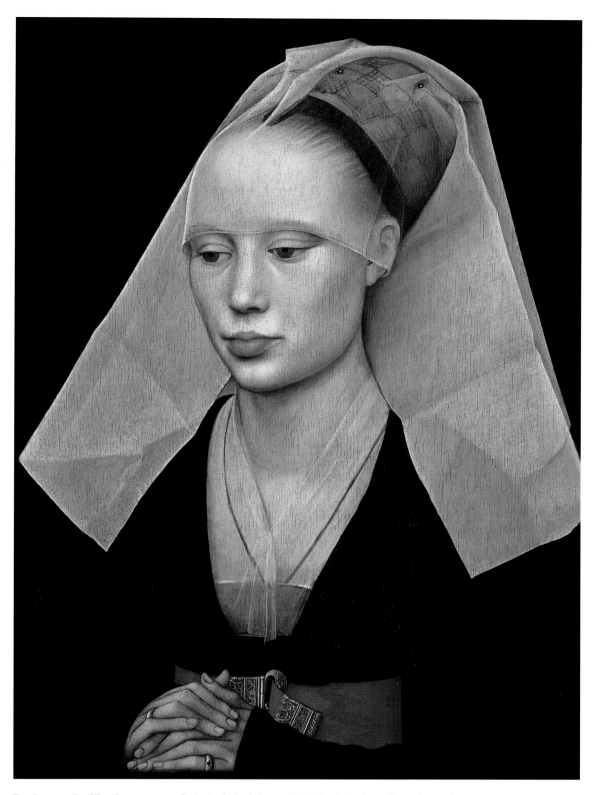

Rogier van der Weyden
Portrait of a Lady
c. 1455
Oil on oak panel
14 ½ x 10 ⅜ in. (37 x 27 cm)
National Gallery of Art,
Washington, D.C.
Andrew W. Mellon Collection

Portrait of a Lady has a distinctive interplay of figure/ground relationships. The dark background tones behind the figure echo the dark clothing, creating drama in the pale skin tones. The painting illustrates cropping of the image through composition. It also employs repetition, with a triangular shape recurring throughout, starting with the veil being cropped off at the edges, thereby allowing the background to repeat this shape. The red band tied high above the waist becomes a sort of focal point by way of its isolation: It simply stands out. And the triangular shape continues at the neck, and even in the subtle shape of the wrinkles in the veil.

Another trick is to overlap objects, where the objects that are overlapped will appear farther away. In his image of *Tahitian Women* (p. 13), Gauguin overlaps the two central figures so that the figure on the left appears to be farther away from the front of the canvas.

Artists have traditionally used **linear perspective** as a way of depicting distance in paintings and drawings. Linear perspective describes a visual point of view. A scene itself remains the same: What changes is the viewpoint from which we choose to see or depict it. Viewpoint changes according to where we stand, our height and how we hold our heads. (Think of the different ways in which a small child and a full-grown adult would see and describe the same scene.) Linear perspective consists of one-, two- and three-point perspective. The perspective is determined by the original viewer of the scene—that is, the painter—and once the painting is painted, the perspective is fixed (wherever the viewer stands, the viewpoint depicted in the painting stays the same).

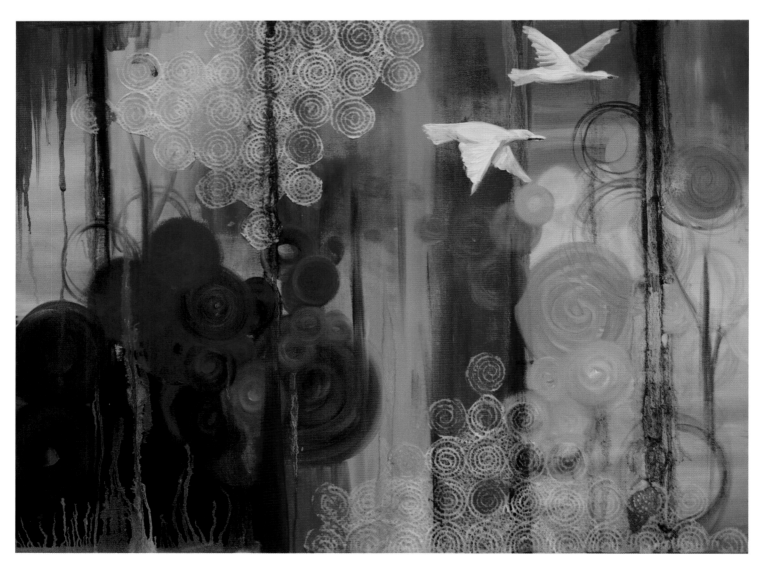

Jessica Schramm
Oil on canvas

Beginning student Jessica Schramm's painting combines abstract shapes and imagery with realistic birds, thereby creating an imaginary world. She has combined wet on wet painting, glazing and scumbling to good effect.
(See pp. 156–163 for more examples of abstract painting.)

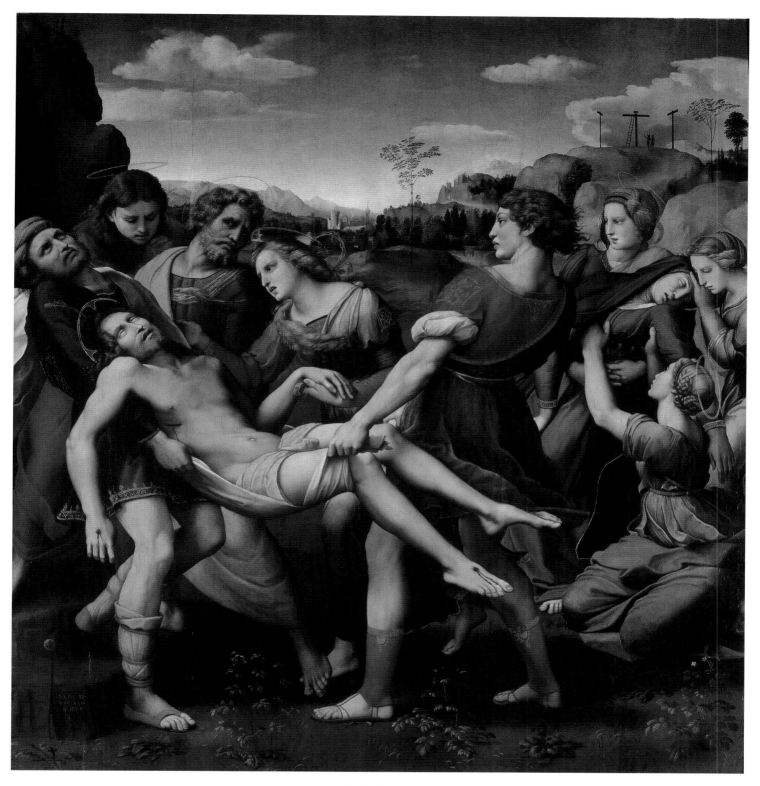

Raphael
The Entombment
1507
Oil on wood
72 ⅔ x 69 ⅛ in. (184 x 176 cm)
Borghese Gallery, Rome

Raphael's *The Entombment* is an example of one-point perspective. In this painting there is a single point where the lines and figures converge to a vanishing point, just over the shoulder of the middle woman helping to carry the Christ figure.

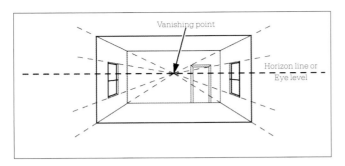

One-point perspective

In **one-point perspective** there is a single point at which the lines and figures converge to a vanishing point. This vanishing point changes depending on the height of the person viewing a scene; everyone will see the horizon line differently. The vanishing points converge at the horizon line. Imagine staring down railway tracks with the tracks directly in front of you: If you are standing and then decide to sit down, the horizon line and vanishing point will change. In Ghirlandaio's *The Birth of the Virgin Mary* (p. 15), the vanishing point is just to the right of the head of the figure in the background, and in Raphael's *The Entombment* (p. 21), it is just over the shoulder of the middle lady.

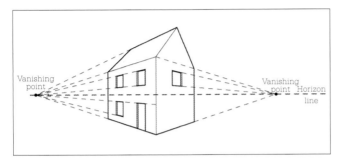

Two-point perspective

In **two-point perspective** the viewer (the artist) is standing to either the left or the right, at an angle, and the lines will converge toward two vanishing points, both on same horizon line. Imagine a room in which you are standing over on one side. Two-point perspective often seems a more natural point of view, because we tend to enter environments casually, without heading for the absolute centre. I usually advise my students to compose as they naturally come upon a view. Andrea del Sarto's *Portrait of a Woman with a Book of Petrarch's Poetry* (p. 14) is an example of two-point perspective, in which the vanishing points are at elbow height and off each side of the painting.

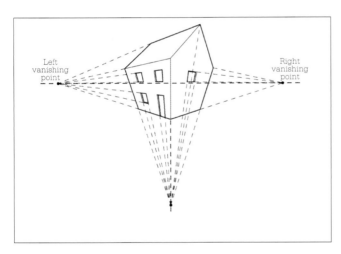

Three-point perspective

Three-point perspective takes into consideration a view looking up or down. The horizon line is near the bottom or top or off the page itself. In François-Auguste Biard's *Four O'Clock at the Salon* (opposite), three-point perspective is used as part of the composition to add to the sense of an upward view. Both we, as viewers of the image, and the figures in the foreground of the painting are looking up toward a vanishing point that is off the top of the picture, while the horizon line is off the bottom of the painting. The other two vanishing points are off the picture to the left and right.

In nature, **atmospheric perspective** is created by such atmospheric effects as dust or clouds combined with distance, such as in a landscape painting. This creates a hazy, soft-edged effect, an effect that also changes the colour strength and tone, with objects that are closer to the viewer appearing clearer and harder-edged. The overlapping of objects as they recede in space also heightens this phenomenon.

Value and Colour
Value can be defined as the relative lightness or darkness of a visual space. Value in colour is defined as the relative gradations between the darkest and lightest tones. Adding white **tints** a colour lighter, whereas adding black creates a darker **shade**. There are combinations of colour patterns that produce various optical results. Most artists use these intuitively. In *Pistia Kew* (p. 24), Idelle Weber contrasts blue with its complementary colour orange to create a dramatic visual. Having an understanding of how colour works will help you to design your painting much more quickly.

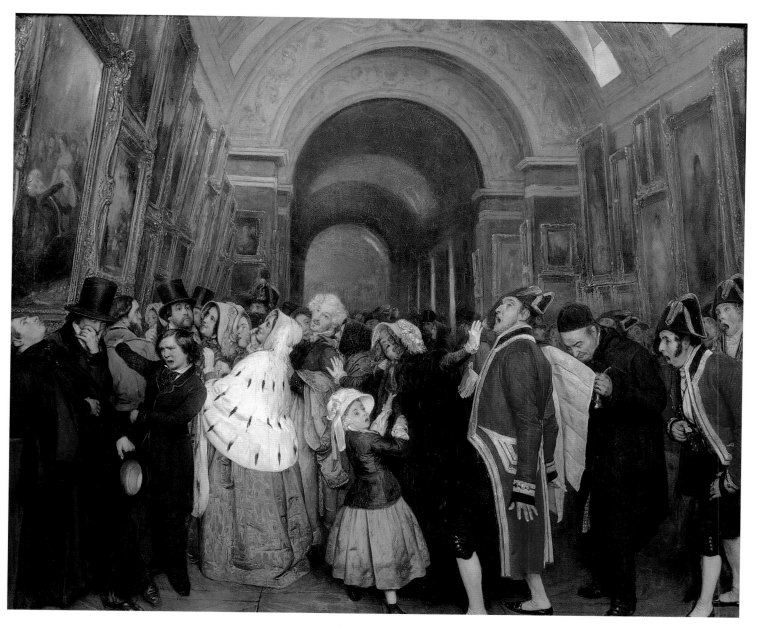

François-Auguste Biard
Four O'Clock at the Salon
1882
Oil on canvas
22 ⅜ x 26 ½ in. (57.5 x 67.5 cm)
Musée du Louvre, Paris

Four O'Clock at the Salon is an example of three-point perspective, with the viewer looking upward toward a vanishing point and the horizon located off the bottom of the painting.

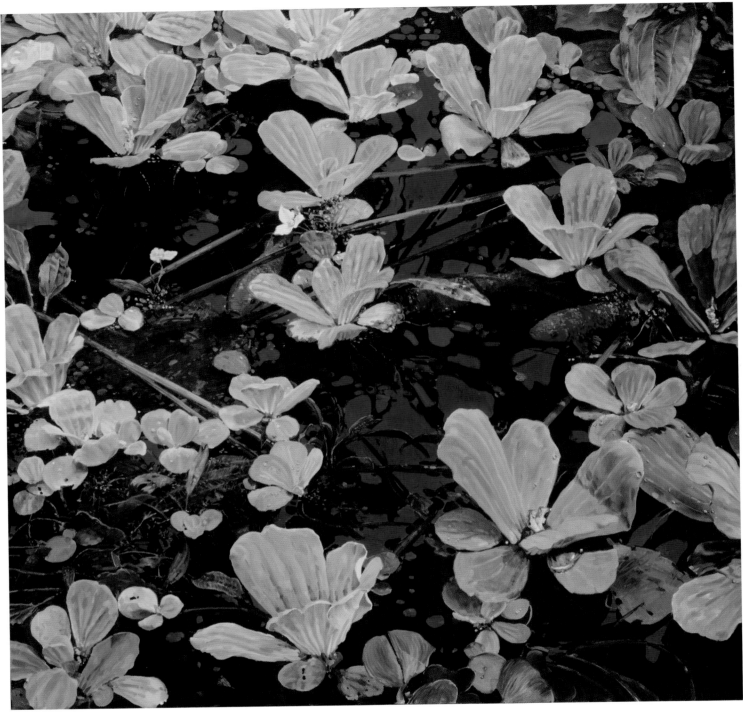

Idelle Weber
Pistia Kew
1989
Oil on linen
58 x 59 in. (147.3 x 149.9 cm)
The Nelson-Atkins Museum
of Art, Kansas City, MO
Courtesy Idelle Weber and
Bill Massey

In *Pistia Kew*, the sense of balance that Weber
achieves is a combination of figure/ground
ambiguity, motif and dramatic colour usage. The
cropping of the image serves to create the sense
of continuous space with its open composition.

Principles of Design

Harmony

Harmony is about bringing all the design elements together in the right proportions so as to create an image that is easy to view. Liz Wright's *Tidal Wave*, below, demonstrates harmony of colour where no one colour is predominant. Repetition can also be used to create harmony, as shown in Wright's repetitive use of abstract circular shapes, and Ueda's *Vanitas* (p. 18), where the repetition of shape draws the image together.

Balance

In artwork, we refer to the visual **balance** of the composition. For example, a small, dark, filled-in circle and a larger circle drawn with a thin line placed next to one another will be perceived as having equal balance. Colours can also be balanced, as in van der Weyden's *Portrait of a Lady* (p. 19), where the dark tones of the background and the sitter's dress are balanced by the lighter tones of her face and veil. Gauguin's *Tahitian Women* (p. 13) demonstrates balance in the equality of the visual weight of the figures with the visual space surrounding them.

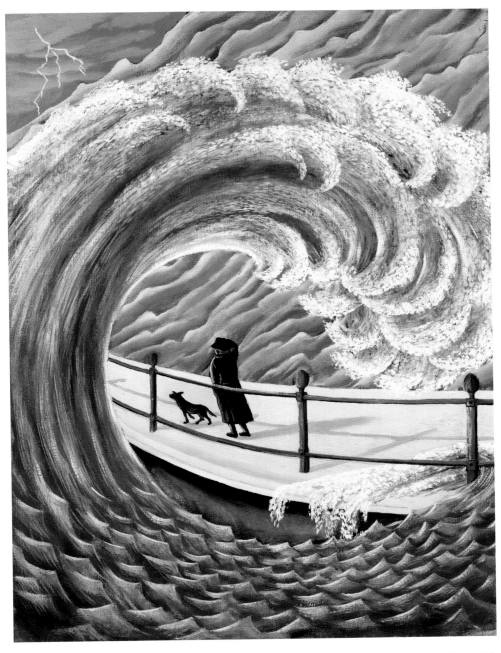

Liz Wright
Tidal Wave
1993
Oil on panel
16 x 12 in. (40.7 x 30.4 cm)
Private collection

Liz Wright's *Tidal Wave* is at once beautiful and foreboding. The concentric sweep of the wave creates a frame within a frame, and in so doing allows the figure and dog to compete visually with the power of the wave. They are almost in silhouette, creating a high-contrast focal point.

Economy

Using economy in design involves being disciplined about using only what is needed to create an image without clutter. Liz Wright uses the minimum of objects in *Tidal Wave* (p. 25), combined with a minimal use of colour, to create her composition.

Scale and Proportion

Scale and **proportion** relate to size, and thus to the creation of depth in an image. Size is relative in the sense that a small object placed next to a larger one will create the illusion that the smaller object is farther away. With context, however, you will have a frame of reference to judge its size—for example, if you photograph a small piece of jewellery next to someone's hand. Scale and proportion in a painting are usually demonstrated by means of the design elements used to show space and depth.

Dominance and Focal Point

In design, the way in which the viewer perceives certain areas of a composition is controlled by placement. Some parts of the design will stand out and become the focus because they **dominate** visually. This can be achieved through colour. In Richmond Teye Ackam's *Red and Black* (p. 16) the **focal point** is the yellow, which stands out in contrast to the green. He invites you into his painting by the concentric patterns on the outer edge of its surface, which create a drumlike effect. This is again emphasised by the repetition of the circle. In *Shuffleton's Barbershop* (opposite), Norman Rockwell uses dramatic lighting to create a focal point and draw the eye into the picture and through into the room at the back where a game of cards is taking place.

Jane Deakin
The Sacred Snake
1994
Oil on canvas
47 ¼ x 47 ¼ in. (120 x 120 cm)
Private collection

Jane Deakin's *The Sacred Snake* uses colour to literally snake the imagery throughout her composition. The chromatic greys of the background serve to bring forward the centre space that engulfs the snake, yet the highly detailed body of the snake still moves further out. These decisions lead to an interesting level of figure/ground ambiguity.

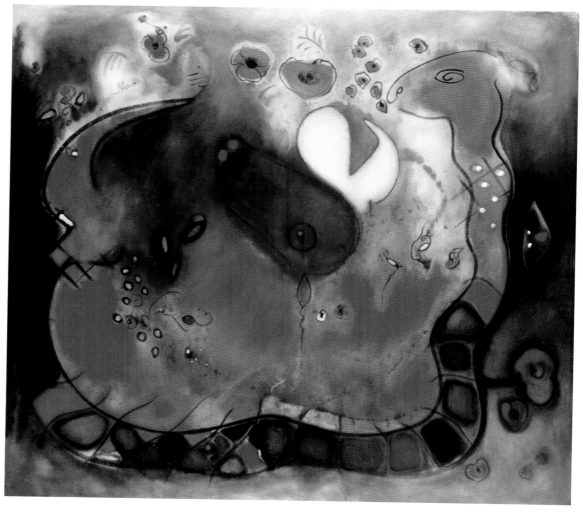

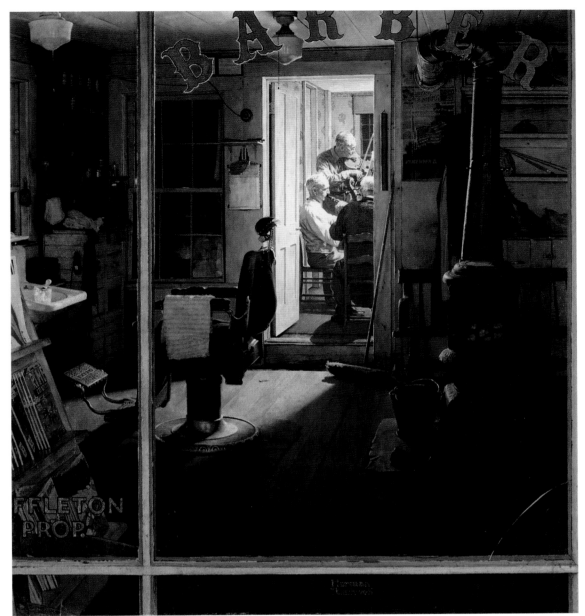

Norman Rockwell
Shuffleton's Barbershop
1950
Oil on canvas
46 ¼ x 43 in. (117.5 x 109.5 cm)
Berkshire Museum, Pittsfield,
MA. Printed by permission of
the Norman Rockwell Family
Agency. © 1950 The Norman
Rockwell Family Entities

Rockwell's composition pulls the
viewer from an outside stance
into the deep space of the card
game in the background. By
using dramatic light for the
background, Rockwell shows
the concept of focal point and
dominance. In this painting,
you really understand how the
outside edges of the rectangle
are taken into account to create
both deep and shallow space.
Through these visual devices,
Rockwell presents examples
of proportion, balance, variety,
harmony and economy.

Rhythm and Movement

Colour can be used to create visual **rhythm** in an image, as in Richmond
Teye Ackam's *Red and Black* (p. 16), in which he uses different shades and
tones of colour to create a wave effect. **Simultaneous contrast** is another
way of using colour to create movement in an image. This phenomenon
occurs when two complementary colours (colours opposite each other on
Itten's colour wheel—see p. 35), such as bright red opposite bright green
or bright blue opposite bright orange, are used to create an even brighter
reaction. Comic book illustrations use this knowledge to dramatic ends. The
spacing of these colours can create visual movement, as demonstrated in
Joan Brown's *Self-portrait with Fish and Cat* at the beginning of this chapter.

Chapter 2: Understanding Colour through Paint Mixing

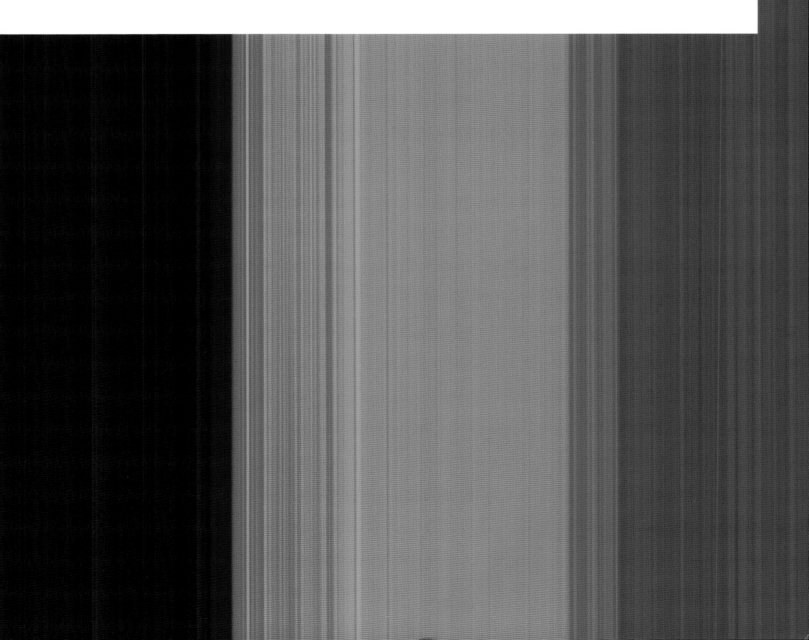

In this chapter, we begin to examine colour theory using the colour wheel and a chromatic colour chart, and we will create our own colour wheels and charts using paint in order to explore colour in a very practical way. This will introduce us to the process of colour mixing and the application of paint to a prepared surface. Full-range colour as a method of painting emphasises a full-colour palette right from the start of a piece of work. Learning to see colour in all of its combinations, from the more obvious to the subtle, is the first step in painting from life. Later, when you begin your first painting from direct observation (see p. 70),

you will discover that your colour choices soon become more nuanced and comprehensive as you become more skilled at representing the colour in your subject matter.

Although it is possible to purchase a variety of colour wheels and charts, constructing your own teaches you about colour through trial and error. You will also learn how to prepare a palette, how to choose your preferred type of paint and medium, and how to mix your own paint colours. The colour wheel and chart that you create here will help you in your observations and choices of colour in the discussions throughout the rest of this book.

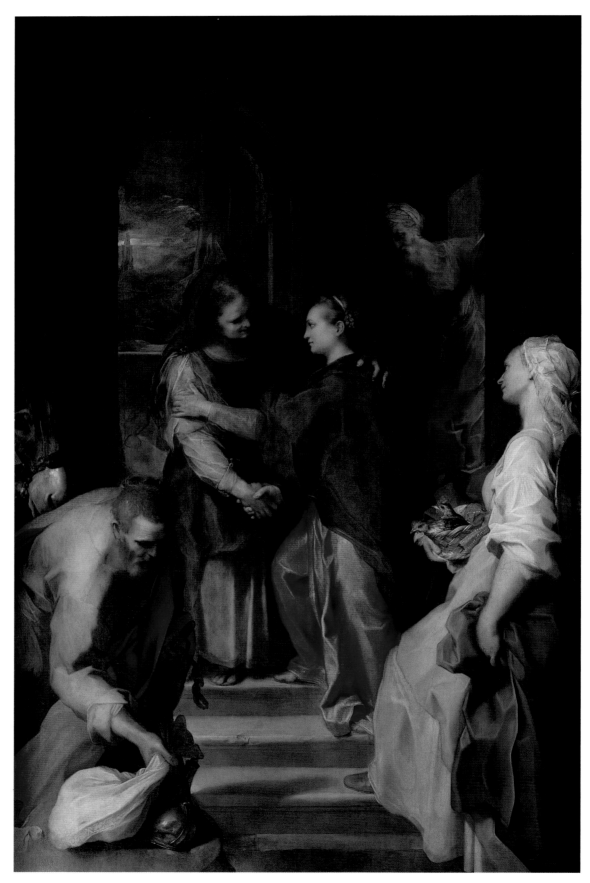

Federico Barocci
Visitation
1584–86
Oil on canvas
82 x 70 in. (208 x 180 cm)
Cappella Pozzomiglio, Santa
Maria in Vallicella, Rome

In the *Visitation*, warm primary colours form a
triangular shape in the foreground; darker, cooler
colours are used to render the background,
allowing it to recede from the foreground.

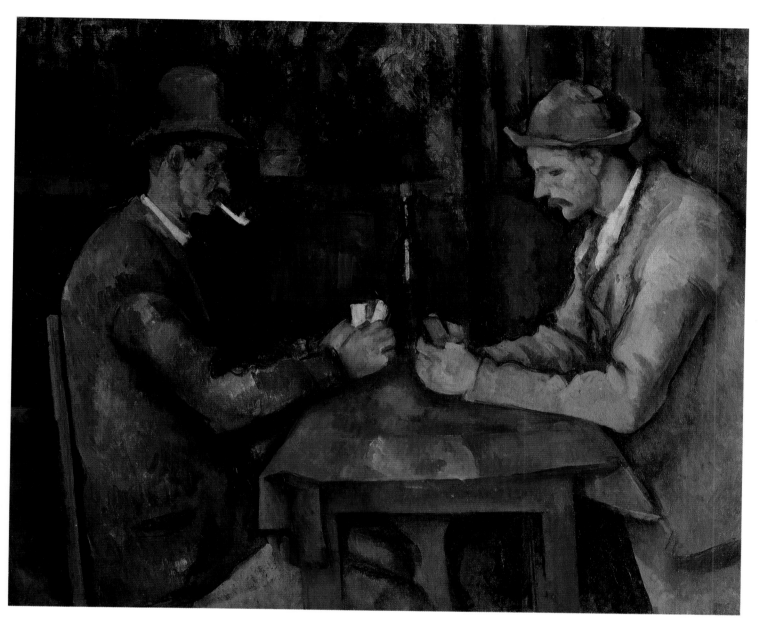

Paul Cézanne
Les Joueurs de Cartes
(The Card Players)
c. 1890–95
Oil on canvas
18 ¾ x 22 ½ in. (47.5 x 57 cm)
Musée d'Orsay, Paris

Cézanne's *The Card Players* illustrates the way in which warm and cool colours can be used to create a sense of composition. The warm colours appear to advance, while the cool colours seem to retreat into the background. This is an intimate study of a game being taken seriously; its warmth offsets the intensity of the subject matter.

Colour Wheels and Chromatic Charts

In this chapter you will:
— prepare a palette for colour mixing;
— choose either oil or acrylic paints and the appropriate mediums for each;
— mix your paints for making a colour wheel;
— make a colour wheel using paint with black and white tone and tint sections;
— make a chromatic colour chart using paint;
— clean up and prepare for the next day's painting.

Colour wheels are systems designed to explain the behavior and properties of colour. In this book, we will use the colour wheel system created by the Swiss artist and designer Johannes Itten (1888–1967); this is one of the most widely accepted of the colour wheel systems and, in my experience, is the most intuitive (see p. 35). Using it, we will create one colour wheel and one chromatic colour chart.

Colour wheels provide a way to compare and contrast colour appearance and to observe the effect of a given colour on adjacent colours. Armed with this basic understanding, we can begin to view and examine colour phenomena. Most beginning painters will have a tendency to think of colour in limited ways: Apples are red and lemons are yellow. But by doing so, they are considering only local colour—that is, colour unaffected by light and dark. It would be hard to imagine when that might occur. When I tell my students to paint all of the colours they see reflected in a pot, they find that the supposed grey or silver of the pot is actually comprised of all the colours of the fruits in the still life, and there is no silver or grey as such.

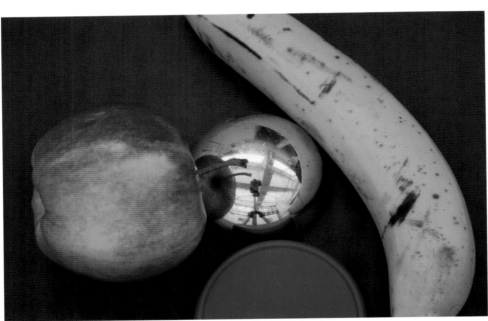

Images showing colour reflected in a shiny object

If you were to paint a round, shiny object, such as a ball, with a bright red apple and a banana placed beside it, the ball would show colours reflected from the fruit (above).

If you changed the colour of the surface that the fruit was placed on, you would get a different set of colours in the reflections (right).

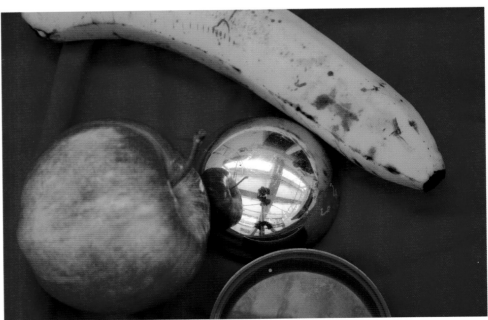

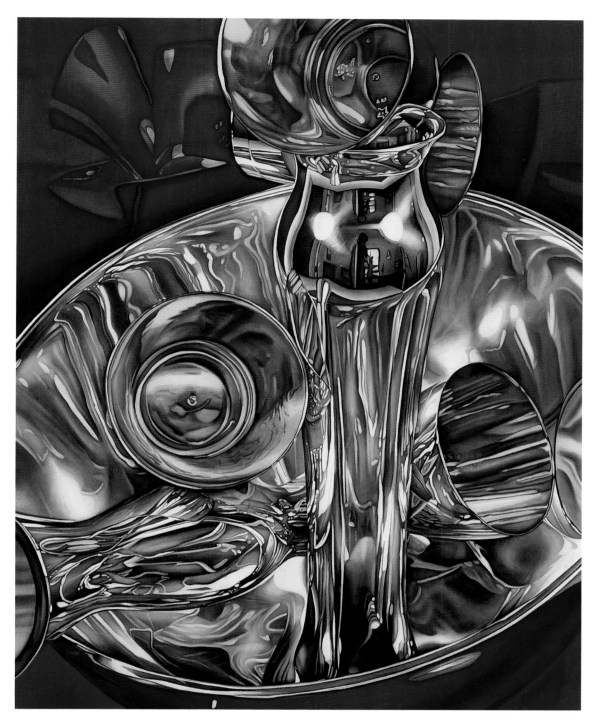

Jeanette Pasin Sloan
Balancing Act XIII
1999
Oil on linen
28 x 22 in. (71.1 x 55.9 cm)
Private collection

In this rich and varied painting by Jeanette Pasin Sloan, her choice of highly reflective surfaces, and therefore reflected colour, results in imagery whose abstracted shapes create a sense of tension and the possibility of movement.

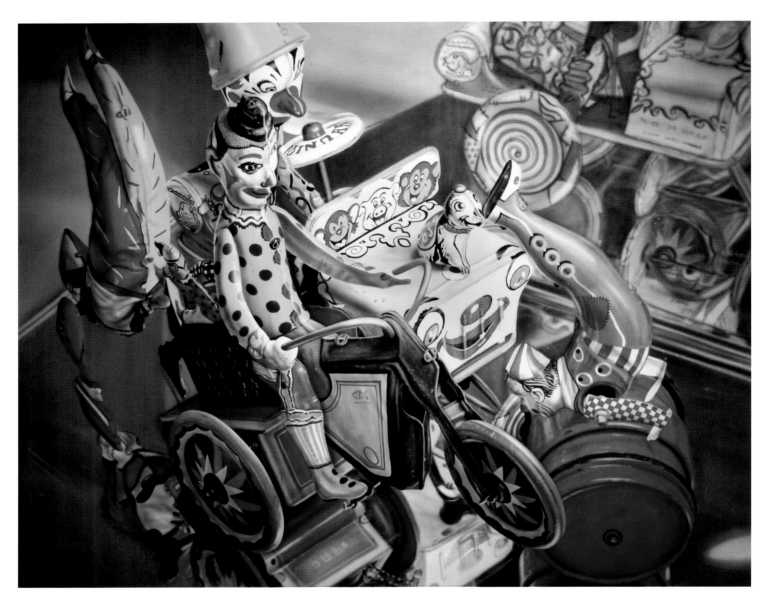

Cesar Santander
A Group of Performing Clowns
Date unknown
Acrylic on Masonite
24 x 30 in. (66.9 x 76.2 cm)
Gallery Henoch, New York

Cesar Santander combines strong colour and rich value in his *A Group of Performing Clowns*. With heavy use of unmixed primary colours and chromatic greys, the muted colours of the walls and floor make the red, blue and yellow colours seem brighter by comparison. It is the darker tones that create this contrast.

Colour wheels also aid us in judging value, which is the relative lightness or darkness of a visual space. Value in colour refers to the relative gradations between the darkest and the lightest tones, for example dark blue or pale blue. The way we view colour is relative and depends on adjacent colours. Colour is not viewed in a vacuum. As we move through this book, you will better understand the possibilities of colour mixing.

The three primary colours that form the basis of the colour wheel are red, yellow and blue. These three colours are taken straight from the tube, because you cannot mix any other colours together to create them. When you mix pairs of the primary colours, three secondary colours are formed: orange, green and violet. When you mix each primary colour and its adjacent secondary colour, you form the six intermediary colours. These colours are red-orange, red-violet, yellow-green, yellow-orange, blue-green and blue-violet. Together these twelve colours make up Itten's colour wheel. Colours opposite each other on Itten's colour wheel are known as complementary colours. At the end of this chapter, you will learn how to create a chromatic chart. This chart helps you to see how many complementary colours can be mixed to produce chromatic greys, rather than relying on the mixing of black and white alone.

Once you have created your colour wheels and chromatic charts, you will have a set of tools to refer to when you begin your first paintings. As you paint you will begin to see that generally the chromatic chart will be the most useful in terms of normal colour usage. This is not to say that the three primary colours are less prevalent; rather, variations of these three colours are harder to recognise at first.

Itten's colour wheel
Johannes Itten's colour wheel is one of many colour systems and is widely used. The traditional colour wheel is usually round, but you will see from the student examples on the following pages that different styles also work well.

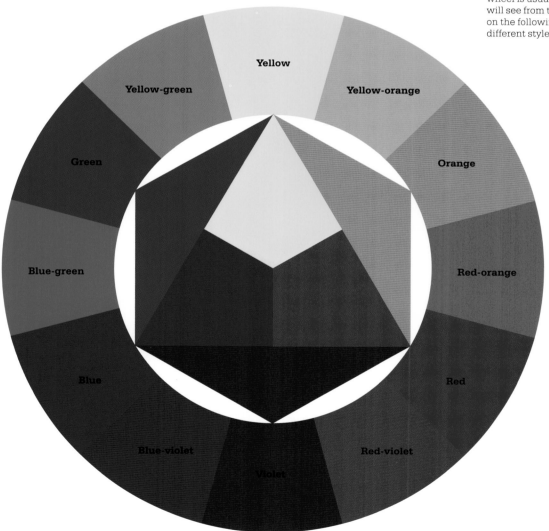

Using Black and White

With a clear understanding of the ways in which they affect colour, black and white can be quite useful. It is important to remember that there is also colour in black and white objects—when you look at an object that you think is black or white, try looking again more closely. Black, for example, may be quite bluish in nature, while white may have more of a pinkish or a yellowish tone. By adding white and black to the colours in Itten's chart, you will learn how to work with tint and shade—tint being the addition of white and shade the addition of black. It is wise to be cautious to begin with, so as to not dull or muddy the colours.

Note that there are no bad colour mixtures—just results that you might not want to use at the moment. The term "muddy" generally refers to colour that is unclear or has a greyish or brownish tone. Muddy colour is simply a form of a chromatic neutral grey. (See pp. 50–53 for a discussion of chromatic greys.)

Colour wheel painted by student Ashley Buzzy showing the results of tint and shade. The twelve colours of Itten's colour wheel have been shaded (i.e., black added) in the inner circle and tinted (i.e., white added) in the outer circle.

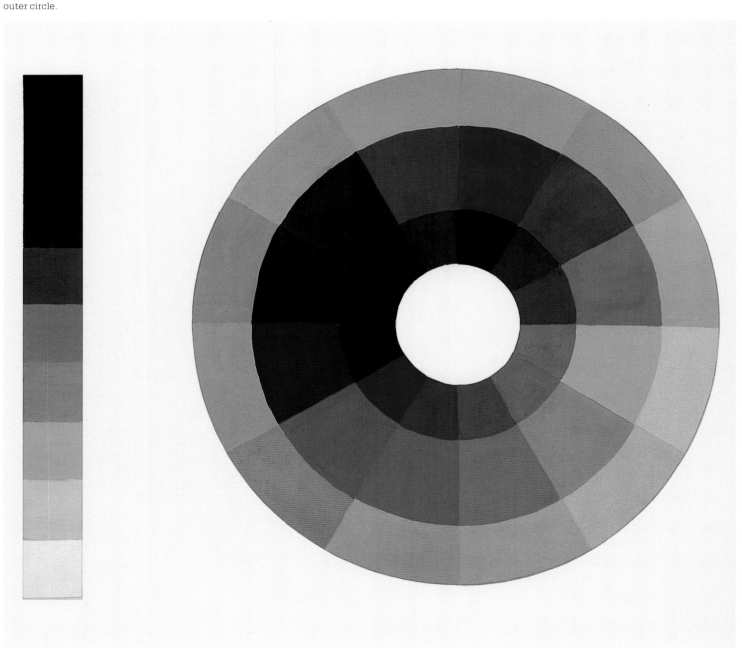

Warm and Cool Colours

Generally speaking, the warm colours on the colour wheel are yellow, yellow-orange, orange, orange-red, red and red-violet. Used in a painting, such colours give the appearance of advancing forward, of coming out toward the viewer.

The cool colours are yellow-green, green, green-blue, blue, blue-violet and violet. These colours appear to recede in a painting, away from the viewer.

Many different effects can be created by working with this temperature theory, combining warm and cool colours in subtle or less subtle ways. Refer to the colour wheel to see the transition from the warm of yellow to the cool of violet, bearing in mind that there are also warm and cool shades within each colour, such as warmer yellow and cooler yellow.

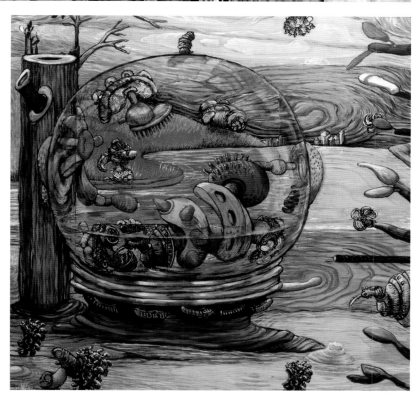

Sandy Winters
Devil's Haircut
2006
Oil and collage on wood
48 x 48 x 2 in. (122 x 122 x 5 cm)
Courtesy of George Adams
Gallery, New York

In Sandy Winters' *Devil's Haircut*, we are treated to an imaginary world that is both contained and open. The outside environment of floating images reflected on the surface of the globe exaggerates the transparency and distortion that is created by the reflections from inside the globe.

Preparing a Paint Palette for Colour Mixing

Materials:
— **11 x 16 in. (30 x 40 cm) glass [alternatives to glass: ceramic tray, paper palette pad, white butcher's wrapping paper]**
— **White paper**
— **Duct tape**
— **Firm piece of board or wood**

A palette is a flat surface on which to mix your colours. You will need to use a palette to mix your paint for all painting projects. The dimensions of your painting palette will generally be based on the size of the given area requiring paint coverage. For example, for a large landscape painting, you will need to mix larger amounts of colour to fill the size of the canvas; for this, a large palette allows for more room. For the purpose of these charts, the size of your palette should be approximately 11 x 16 in. (30 x 40 cm). There is a variety of surfaces to choose from when selecting a palette: glass, a ceramic tray, a paper palette pad, or the inexpensive alternative of plain white butcher's wrapping paper. I prefer

glass, because of its smooth surface, which makes paint mixing relatively easy and cleanup fairly simple. I highly recommend the heavy-duty glass used for furniture tops, which is designed to be unbreakable with normal use.

Whichever surface you choose, you need to prepare it for use as a painting palette. Since the surface you are painting on will be white, you should have white as the colour of your palette. If you are using glass there are two ways of achieving this: by painting the underside of the glass white, or by placing a sheet of white paper under it. You should then tape the glass down to a firm surface such as wood, being careful to tape over any sharp edges. Duct

tape is the best for this, given its flexibility and ease of tearing; it also sticks well and generally does not lose its adhesive qualities if it comes into contact with wet paint.

Ceramic trays are both smooth and white, so serve well as palettes, the only drawback being the possibility of chipping the ceramic surface when using a paint scraper.

Paper palette pads, bound like drawing pads with a cardboard backing, make good palettes since their waxy surface encourages the paint to stick, as does butcher's wrapping paper—a cheaper alternative that needs to be attached to a firm surface like cardboard.

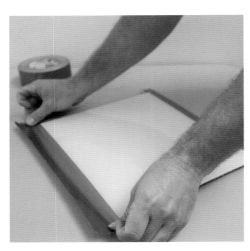

4 Repeat this procedure on the opposite side, again placing a piece of duct tape on the front edge of the glass.

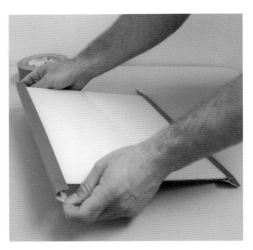

5 Fold the duct tape under all three layers.

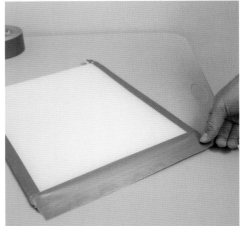

6 Lay duct tape on the edge of the front surface of the third side of the glass.

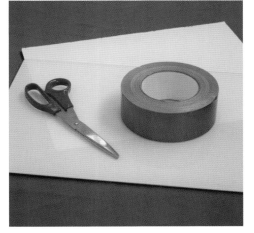

1 To prepare a glass palette, you will need scissors, duct tape, a white sheet of paper and a firm piece of board or wood.

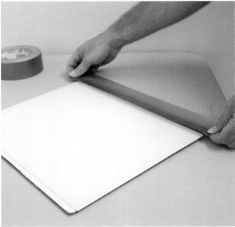

2 Place the white sheet of paper under the sheet of glass and attach to the board. Lay a strip of duct tape on the edge of the front surface of the glass.

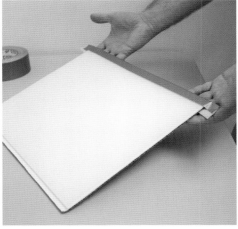

3 Take the duct tape and very carefully fold it under all three layers.

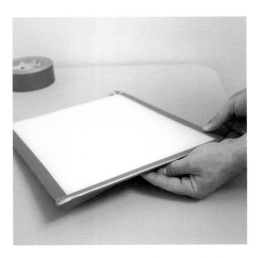

7 Fold this third piece of tape under all three layers.

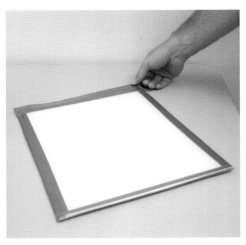

8 Follow the procedures above to complete the fourth and final side.

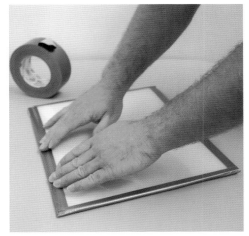

9 In this final step. make sure all sides are smooth and secured to all three layers.

Paint Preferences: Oil Paint or Acrylic?

With its long and rich history, oil paint is often perceived as preferable to or better than water-based media such as acrylic. Yet acrylic offers the painter choices and techniques that are not possible with traditional oil paint. In the end, the choice comes down to the desired style for your painting and the way in which you prefer to apply the paint. Where oil paint requires several measures to prepare the painting surface, acrylic paint can adhere to most surfaces with little or no preparation. Be sure to choose oil paint or acrylic paint: Never mix acrylics and oils together or use the same brushes for both types of paint.

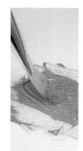

Acrylic Paint

Acrylic paint is a water-based painting medium noted for its quick drying time. It uses an acrylic polymer emulsion as a binder. It creates a clear, strong and flexible paint surface. It is waterproof once dry and not as toxic as oil paint, although it can never be considered totally nontoxic (see pp. 168–69). Acrylic paints adhere to most surfaces and the brushes clean up with water and soap (although once dry, the paint will not come off the brush completely). This ease of cleanup makes it attractive to many painters. Owing to its quick drying time, users can rapidly paint over sections and start again, and this, I believe, is the main drawback of acrylic for the beginning student—being able to abandon sections of a painting can quickly create a situation where painters do not learn from their mistakes.

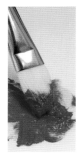

Oil Paint

Oil paint is made with pigments that are ground and mixed in oil. Linseed oil has historically been used for this purpose and is still used today along with other oils such as poppy seed, safflower and walnut. Oil paint is slow-drying, dries with a hard film and maintains its brightness of colour. The lack of change after drying, together with the possibility of both transparency (allowing light to pass through a layer of paint so that other layers may be revealed) and opacity (resistance to light so that images cannot be seen through the layers of paint) in one painting, makes this medium highly desirable. Oil paint is my paint of preference, thanks to its smooth application and its slower drying time, which means that I do not have to worry about my palette drying out too fast while painting. However, many oil paint pigments are toxic, as are the solvents necessary to paint with and clean them. Therefore, there is always a slight risk attached to the use of oil paint, whether from ingestion, inhalation, or skin contact (see pp. 168–69).

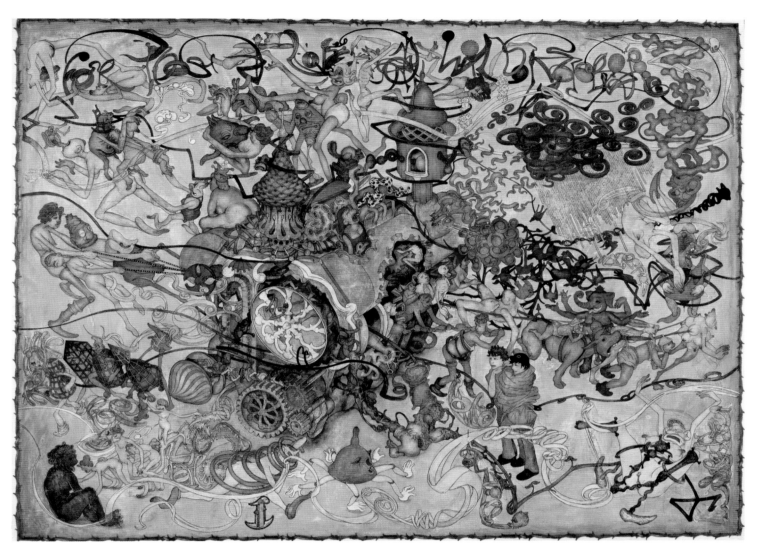

James Barsness
Engine
2005
Acrylic and ink on paper,
mounted on canvas
51 ¾ x 69 in. (129.5 x 175.5 cm)
Private collection. Courtesy
of George Adams Gallery,
New York

The figures within this imaginary world by
James Barsness are captured in a tableau of
entanglement, relentless movement and colour.
The colours consist mainly of warm hues, which
keep the narrative to the fore. The seductiveness
of this painting lies in the tension between its
sense of playfulness and the underlying intensity
of the spectacle. While the curvilinear shapes
guide you through the painting, its myriad details
are only absorbed after multiple viewings.

Painting Mediums

The function of painting mediums is to aid the spread of paint on a surface. They are mixed with the paint and used to control it and affect its behavior. Depending on their individual properties, mediums can change the gloss, the drying time, the level of transparency and the consistency of the final film (layer of colour) of the painting. Acrylic mediums come prepackaged, while oil painting mediums need to be mixed up from various ingredients by the artist.

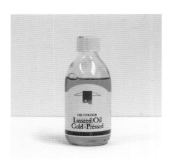

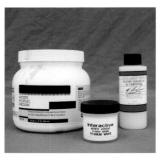

Acrylic Painting Gel Mediums

Gloss medium: Adding this medium creates a shiny surface and can create a transparent effect if you allow one layer of colour to dry, coat the medium over it, then repeat this process with another colour.

Matt medium: This helps in the spread and flow of the paint on the painting surface and leaves a neutral, flat appearance.

Masking fluid: This clear fluid is painted over specific, dried areas of a painting in progress to protect them from colours being applied in another area. When the new section of the painting is dry, the masking fluid can be removed to reveal an untouched area. This method is often used for highly detailed work.

Retarder: This is added to acrylic paint to slow down the drying time.

Oil Painting Mediums

Oil painting mediums help the flow of the paint by lessening the drag of the brush and they also speed up the drying time. I recommend using a medium consisting of one part cold-pressed linseed oil, one part linseed oil, one part stand oil and one part gum turpentine. You can use odourless turpentine, which has similar properties, as an alternative to gum turpentine, but for the purist, gum turpentine is a must; I have used both to good result.

Liquin: "Liquin" is the trade name for a Winsor Newton product that I will use here, but other companies have similar products—Galkyd, for example, which is made by Gamblin Artists Oil Colours. The addition of Liquin helps to create a smooth, glossy surface and to thicken oil paint. Mix a single drop into each of the individual mixed colours of paint on your palette just before applying to the painting surface. Liquin is also a paint drier, so keep in mind that you should not use too much, as you do not want your colours to dry out over the course of a painting session. This is true for both the beginner and the more experienced painter. If your paints dry out too soon on the palette, you will need to mix a new set and try to match the original colours.

Pacita Abad
An Eternity Ago
2004
Oil, acrylic, printed paper and
Mylar collaged on handmade
paper
53 x 27 ½ in. (135 x 70 cm)
© 2004 Pacita Abad Art

An Eternity Ago takes the basic
motif of the circle and combines
it with a dizzying array of colours
and patterns, producing a rich
tapestry. The variety of mediums
and surfaces that Pacita Abad
uses compounds this feeling of
movement and detail.

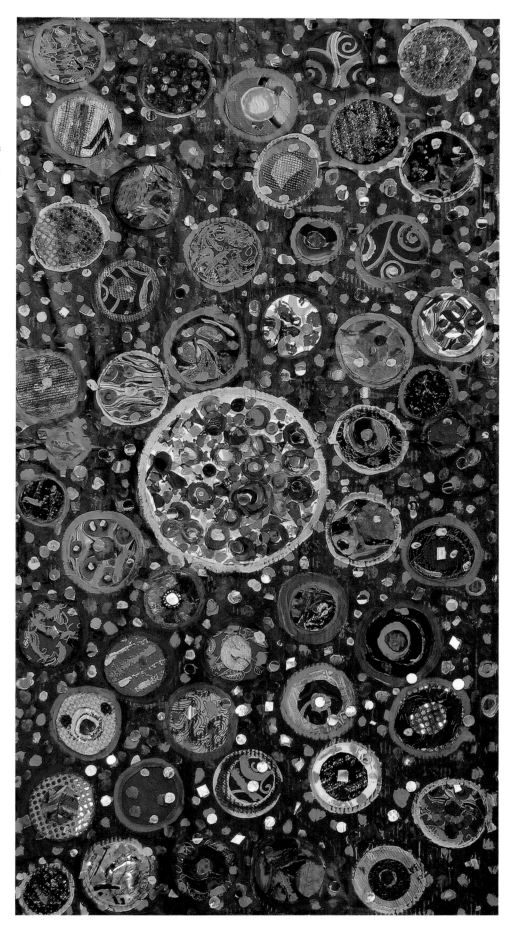

Making Your Colour Wheel

Tools and equipment
— Gesso hardboard panels (we will use the more permanent board so that we have a handy and sturdy reference tool), or firm cardboard or any other flat surface
— Chalk pastel pencil or chalk
— Circle compass, 10-in. (25-cm) diameter capacity (the compass will be used only if your wheel requires perfect circles; other designs may be used instead)
— Filbert brush
— Palette
— Palette knife
— Cotton rags
— Brush-cleaning containers
— Palette cups
— Plastic plant spray filled with water (for use with acrylic paints only)

Paint colours
— Cadmium yellow light
— Permanent red
— Ultramarine blue deep
— Titanium white
— Black

Finally, we begin working with paint, as we prepare a painting palette to create a colour wheel.

The colours listed to the left make up a palette of the three primary colours that can be mixed together to form all the other colours on the wheel, plus black and white. The wheel you will create is based on Itten's colour wheel. You will add a shade using black and a tint using white. This will enable you to understand the effects of black and white on colour.

You will find that different paint manufacturers will use different names for each colour and so you may need to search through the paints supplied by several manufacturers to find the colours you want.

Instructions
Begin with an 11 x 14-in. (28 x 35-cm) gesso board, which can be purchased with gesso already painted on the board. Using a light-coloured chalk pastel pencil and a compass, draw a circle and divide it into twelve equal parts. (Alternatively, you can choose to make a different design, but you will still need to start with twelve equal parts. See the examples on pp. 46–47.) The shape of these sections may follow any design you choose, though it is best to draw each section with the same shape. You may choose to use as large a circle as the dimensions of the board allow or one that is smaller. (Remember to save some space in your design, both inside and out, so that you can use the black paint to shade your twelve colours and the white to tint them.) Using a filbert brush (see p. 86), your aim is to paint each section on your wheel with these colours in this order, moving counter-clockwise: yellow, yellow-green, green, blue-green, blue, purple-blue, purple, red-purple, red, red-orange, orange and orange-yellow.

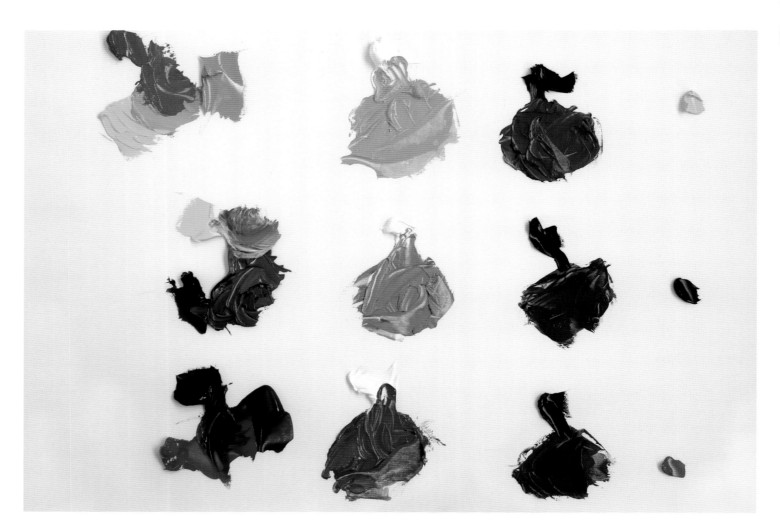

Using your choice of either oil or acrylic paints (see p. 40), mix your colours on your palette (see pp. 38–39 for palette preparation). You will need to mix enough paint for both the colour wheel and the tint—these wheels will only be successful if you mix enough paint to have the same mixtures each time.

Start by squeezing out approximately a 3-in. (7.5-cm) wide and 1-in. (2.5-cm) deep amount of paint from the red, yellow and blue tubes. Place these colours about 2 in. (5 cm) apart from each other on the palette. These are the three primary colours and should come directly from the tube: You cannot mix any other colours to make these three. Using your palette knife, mix together the yellow with the blue (see pp. 48–49). The result will be green. The tone of the green will depend on how much of each colour has been applied. Yellow is the lighter colour: More of it will lighten the green. Conversely, more of the blue will make it darker. For the purpose of these charts, a deep green leaf colour will work the best. Using the same steps, mix red and yellow to make orange. The best orange colour to aim for would be somewhere between an orange and a pumpkin. Finally, mix red and blue to get violet. Violet is the trickiest to mix and may take more time.

You have now created your secondary colours. You may find that you are not able to make these mixtures at first try, but you should continue to mix different proportions until you have the colours you need.

Now, using the secondary colours of orange, violet and green, you will make the intermediary colours, which are created by combining a primary and a secondary colour, using the same steps as described above.

I often have my colour students take notes about the paint colours and proportions they have used on the colour swatches they make, which creates what I call a colour diary. Repeated attempts to achieve the desired colour should not be cause for concern: They are not mistakes, but rather practice exercises. The finished result makes up your twelve-step chart of primary, secondary and intermediary colours.

Opposite below
The colours mixed here were created using red, yellow and blue.

The left examples on each row show a mixture of two colours before white and black is added. Top row far left shows red and yellow mixed to create orange; second row shows blue and yellow mixed to create green; final row shows blue and red mixed together to create violet. The middle examples in each row were tinted with white paint, and the right-hand examples were shaded with black paint.

Below
Table showing how the three secondary colours (green, violet, orange) mixed with the three primary colours (yellow, blue, red) combine to form intermediary colours.

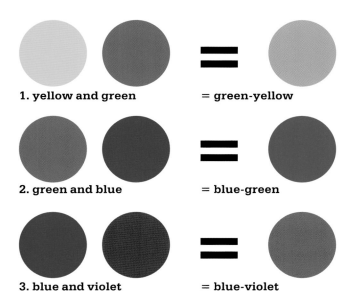

1. yellow and green   **= green-yellow**

2. green and blue   **= blue-green**

3. blue and violet   **= blue-violet**

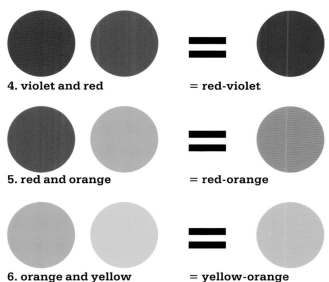

4. violet and red   **= red-violet**

5. red and orange   **= red-orange**

6. orange and yellow   **= yellow-orange**

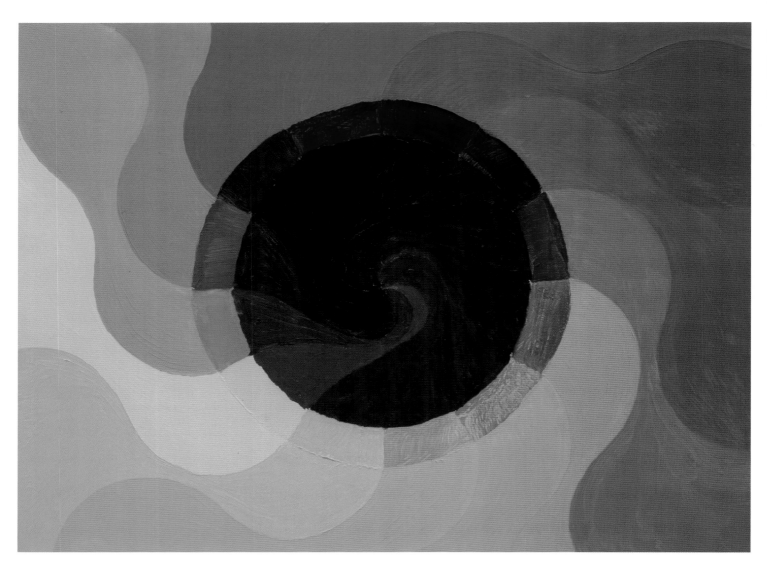

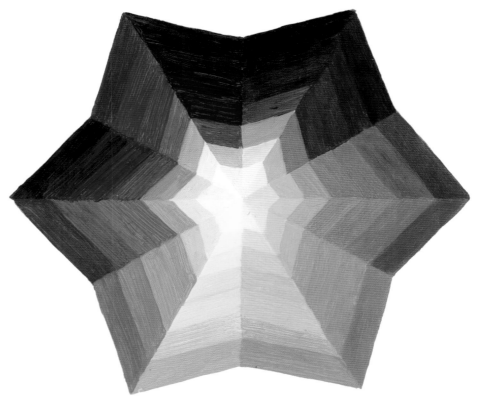

Understanding Colour through Paint Mixing

As the examples show, you may be as creative as you like in your layout. Whatever shapes you choose to use, they should be clear to you. As you make your charts, you should ensure that the colour is carefully mixed so that the chart can be used as a tool as well as a visually pleasing wheel.

When you have completed your colour wheel, you should clean up your palette and your brushes, in preparation for your next painting session (see pp. 56–57).

Washing Brushes During a Painting Session

Brushes may be cleaned over the period of a painting session as needed. This is not to be confused with the final cleanup with soap and water (see pp. 56–57). Work with at least three separate brush-cleaning jars. It is better to clean brushes of similar paint tones in the same jar during a painting session. With oil paint, swishing the brush in the brush-cleaning jar works well enough. Acrylic paint must never be allowed to dry on the brush, so you must clean it off with water as you go along. It is good idea to have several brushes to work with, as the bristles get saturated over the course of a painting session and tend to dilute the paint more toward the end.

Opposite above
Student David Zoellick's colour wheel is an inventive take on the circle, where the swirling darker shades merge into the centre of the wheel.

Opposite below
Star-shaped colour wheel created by student Kimberley Perry. This design clearly shows the effects of the white tint on the inside star and the black shade on the outer edges.

Below
This colour chart by student Krista Franks is a very nontraditional take on the colour wheel, but no less effective as a result. She has her twelve colours in the centre line slightly larger than the others, with the effects of the white tint going from the centre to the bottom, and the effects of the black shade from the centre to the top.

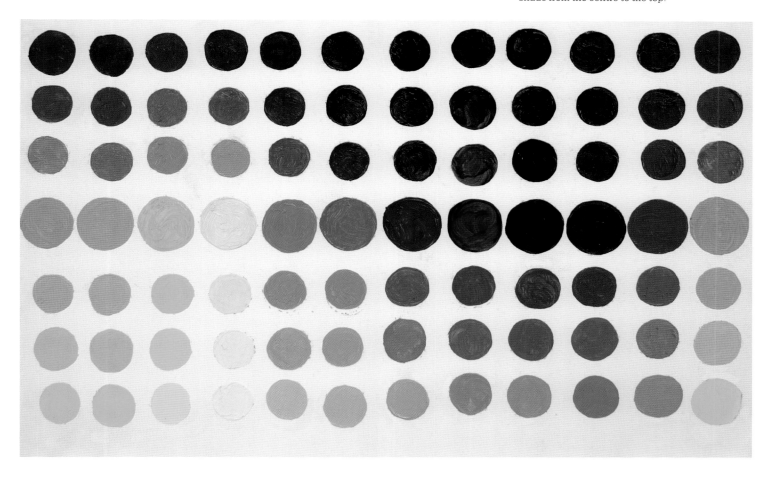

Colour Mixing: Oils and Acrylics

Materials:
— **Tubes of paint**
— **Palette**
— **Palette knife**
— **Painting mediums for oil**
— **Painting gel gloss medium for acrylic**

Arrange your paints and painting mediums. Your painting mediums should be placed in containers similar to shampoo bottles—plastic containers with tops. This protects the medium from getting dirty and muddying the colours. You can also use anything left over later.

Squeeze out enough paint for the day's task from your paint tubes. Lay out your palette with your colours on the left-hand side if you are right-handed and the reverse if you are left-handed. You will find it easier to mix your colours if you do not try to mix them straight from the tube. Place these colours about 2 in. (5 cm) apart from each other on the palette.

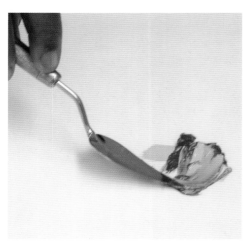

1 Squeeze out some yellow oil paint from the tube to the palette.

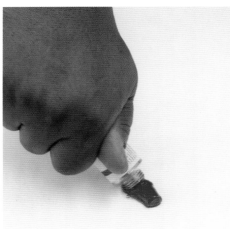

2 Squeeze out a similar amount of red oil paint from the tube to the palette.

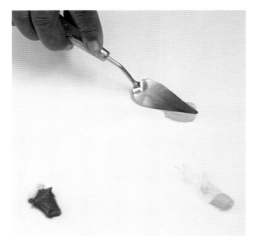

3 Using your palette knife, move a small amount of yellow paint over to the other side of the palette.

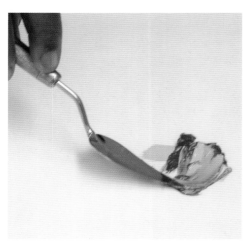

7 Using a sideways motion with the flat bottom of the palette knife, as if you were decorating a birthday cake, begin to mix the yellow and red together.

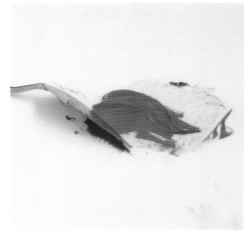

8 Once all the streaks are gone and a solid colour remains, see whether this is the colour you want. If you need to add more colour, repeat the procedure.

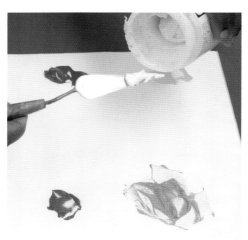

9 If using acrylic paint, add some acrylic gel gloss medium to the newly mixed orange paint.

Controlling the Drying Time of Acrylic Paints

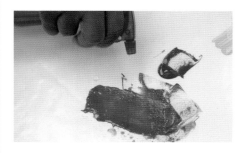

Acrylic paint dries rather rapidly as the water evaporates from the paint, and so may present more challenges than oils. As with oil paints, there is first a drying time, when the paint feels dry to the touch, and then a curing time, during which it dries fully. Hot, moist environments will slow down the drying time of both acrylic and oil, although the effect is more marked with acrylic. A hot and dry or windy environment will speed up the drying time.

For acrylic paints, there are products on the market you can apply while the paint is still wet to slow the drying time considerably, such as retarders. Spraying water periodically over your palette using a plant spray will also slow down the drying time. A note of caution: Too much water will dilute the chroma (brilliance of colour) or the hide (covering ability) of the paint, causing acrylic paint to perform more like transparent watercolour.

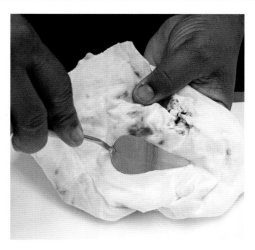

4 During the mixing, stop and wipe your palette knife. This will help you to control the colour. As you are mixing, keep track of the changing colour.

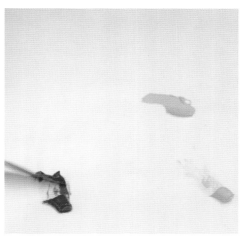

5 Scrape up a little of the red paint that you wish to mix in.

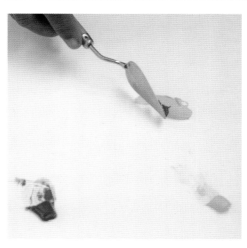

6 Place the red colour on top of the yellow.

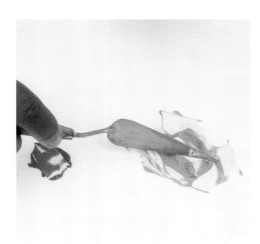

10 Mix the acrylic gel medium into the orange paint.

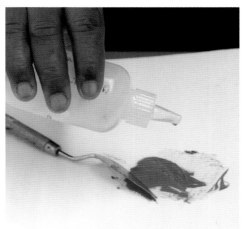

11 If using oil paint, add a drop of Liquin to the orange to speed up the drying time and give it a glossy look.

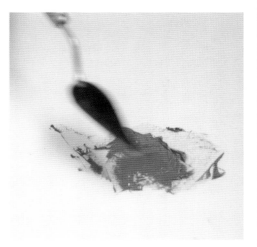

12 Mix the Liquin into the mixed orange paint.

Making Your Chromatic Chart

Tools and equipment
— Gesso hardboard panels or firm
cardboard or any other flat surface
(we will use the more permanent board
as a handy and sturdy reference tool)
— Chalk pastel pencil or chalk
— Filbert brush
— Palette knife
— Cotton rags
— Brush-cleaning containers
— Palette cups
— Plastic plant spray (for use with acrylic
paints only)

Paint colours
— Cadmium yellow light
— Permanent red
— Ultramarine blue deep

The colours listed above comprise the three
primary colours that can be mixed together
to form all the other colours on the
chromatic colour chart. Painting mediums
will not be necessary for the colour chart.

In the earlier discussion, you learned how to use white for tinting and
black for shading (see p. 44). When students begin to think of how to
create the colour grey to add value (relative lightness or darkness), what
immediately comes to mind is some combination of black and white. Yet it
is important to remember that colour is to be found everywhere within our
environment. It may not be that bright and unadulterated colour you find
in colour wheels, but it is a form of colour nonetheless. When students rely
solely on black and white for their grey tone when creating value, they end
up with a monochromatic grey, when in fact grey contains colour, just as
we saw that black and white do earlier. Using monochromatic grey would
be no different, for example, from painting an apple using red and adding
white to make it lighter and black to make it darker: The painting would
appear indistinct, chalky and rather dull; the colour would not look natural.

To create greys that contain colour, we mix together the complements
(the colours directly opposite each other on the colour wheel). The grey
tones achieved in this way are called chromatic neutrals. Now that we
have finished the first step of creating a colour wheel, we can use the
twelve colours to make a chromatic chart. Think of the chromatic chart as
a series of greys created with colour from the colour wheel.

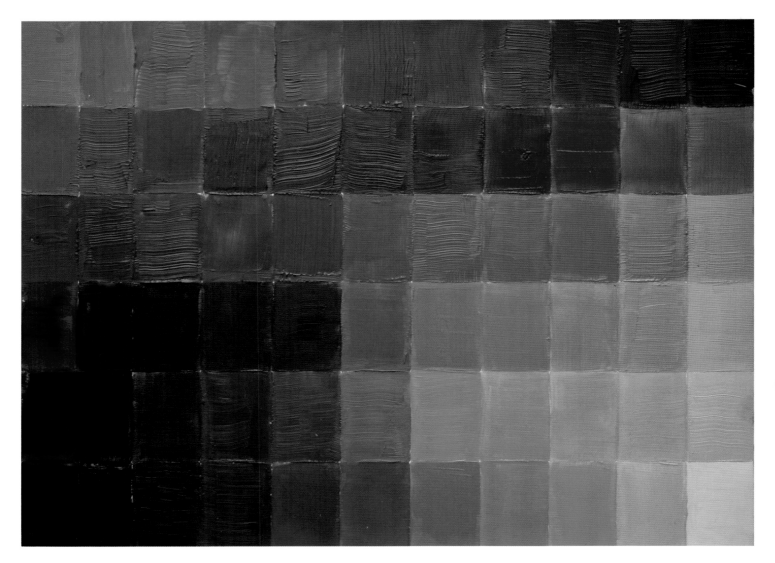

How to Make a Chromatic Grey

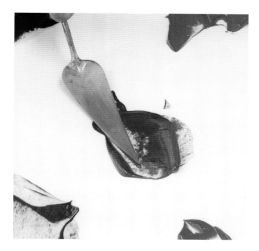 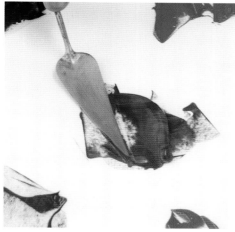 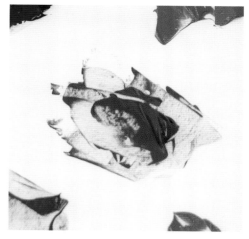

1 In these first three steps you will see how to make a chromatic grey using red and green—complementary colours on the colour wheel. Place green paint onto the red.

2 Mix the green paint into the red with your palette knife.

3 Here is the result: a chromatic grey formed by mixing red and green.

How to Make a Monochromatic Grey

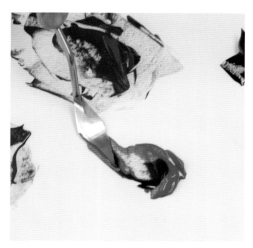 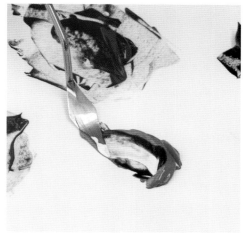 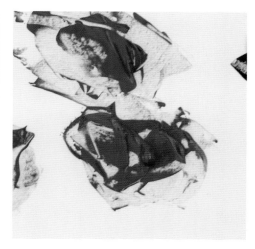

1 A monochromatic grey is formed by the addition of black and white (instead of mixing complementary colours, as in the three steps above). Add black paint to your red.

2 Next, add white paint to the black and red mixture, and mix up with the palette knife.

3 As you can see, this monochromatic grey mixture you have created (bottom) is very different from the chromatic grey colour (top).

Opposite
In this chart by Zeke Paull, the paint strokes are quite evident, yet the chart is still very effective. How one decides to place paint on the surface becomes a personal choice after exposure to a variety of painting techniques.

Instructions

You can use many different designs for chromatic charts, but in order to paint the design below, take a chalk pastel pencil and start by drawing a grid with six columns and twelve rows. Then, using either oil or acrylic, follow the instructions for mixing your paints on pp. 48–49 (for reasons that will become clear, please make plenty of each of the colours you mixed to obtain your colour wheel, pp. 44–45). Paint the following colours in the following order across the top row of the grid, starting at the left:

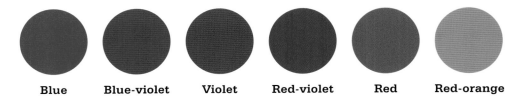

Blue **Blue-violet** **Violet** **Red-violet** **Red** **Red-orange**

Next paint the following colours in the following order across the bottom row of your grid, starting at the left:

Orange **Yellow-orange** **Yellow** **Yellow-green** **Green** **Blue-green**

Below
This chromatic chart was painted by student Laurin Ramsey. The number of steps it takes is not as important as learning how to create the greys. An interesting-looking chart will help when it is referred to while painting.

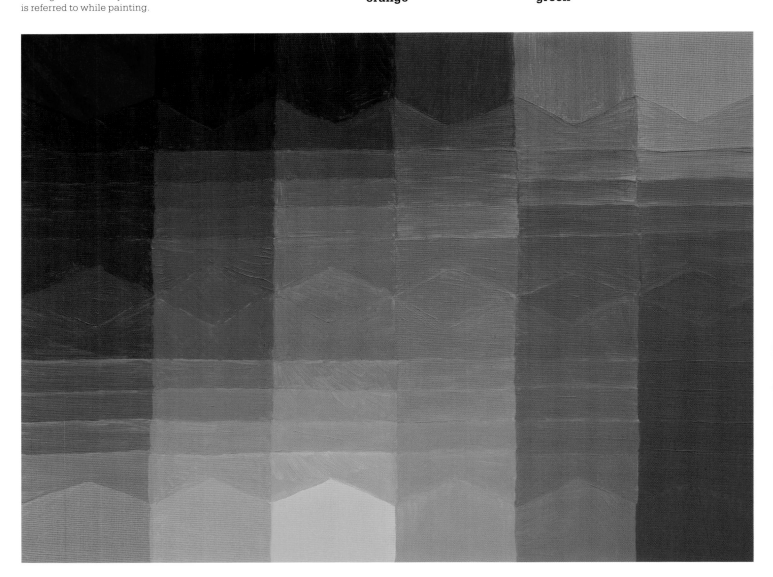

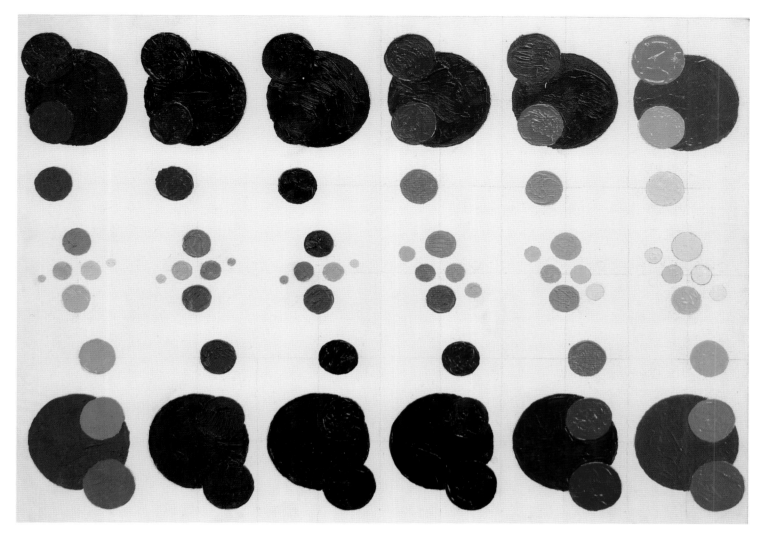

You will then complete this chart by mixing the two colours that face each other across a column into the intervening cells. Let us take, for example, the fifth column from the left, which has red at the top and green on the bottom. Move some red down into the second row of that column, then mix in green taken from the bottom. Do the same for the other end—move some green up from the lowest row into the cell above and mix in some red. Continue to add red to the green shades at the bottom moving up, and likewise, green to the red colour down from the top, moving together into the centre of the column. Gradually, you will end up with a chromatic neutral colour in the middle. As you aim for the most neutral tone, notice the colour bias (the emphasis of one colour over another depending on the amounts of colour added while mixing). The resulting greys will not be those of black and white but, rather, chromatic grey hues.

In six steps, as in this example of a chromatic chart, you end up with a fairly colourful grey. When done in only three steps, the grey would be extremely colourful, whereas in ten steps or more, you end up with colours that have much less chroma (brilliance of colour). Of course, you do not need to use a grid of squares. You can choose any format you like, as you can see from the other examples shown.

When you have completed your chromatic chart, you should clean up your palette and your brushes, ready for your next painting session (see pp. 56–57).

Above
The results of student Alexander Shute's assignment were unplanned but very instructive. By allowing some of his colours to sit on top of others, he has discovered one of the hardest things for new students to understand: that colour is relative. As you can see with the top yellow—when it is placed on the green-yellow it appears very bright, yet on the white board it takes on a different tone.

General Painting Supplies

When buying your painting supplies, it is important to have the best quality within your budget. Student-grade art supplies are cheaper, but should be augmented with professional-grade wherever possible. It is worth buying professional-grade versions of your three primary colours; you can always then mix these with various grades of secondary colours. Although Internet shopping is invariably the cheapest option and provides the greatest variety, I encourage my students to shop locally and try to support the merchants in town when possible. In terms of hardware—hammers, staplers and drills—there is no valid reason to go cheap here. Go to a hardware store and ask questions. You must not skimp on safety.

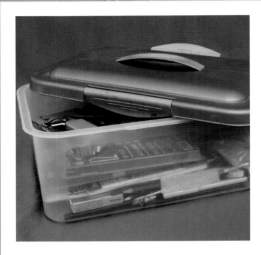

Tackle box: An essential storage and carrying case, tackle boxes are inexpensive, usually plastic with a handle, and can be purchased with either one or two compartments.

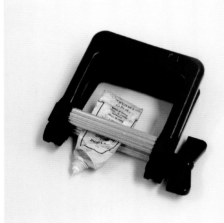

Paint tube squeezer: This handy tool will literally push out every last drop of paint from a tube. A less effective but cheaper alternative would be a metal or wooden dowel.

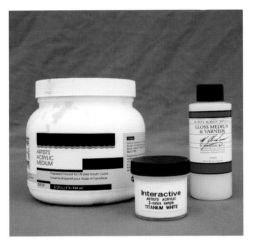

Gesso and acrylic mediums: Gesso—used to prime most painting surfaces—is least expensive when purchased in large containers as shown here. Acrylic mediums can be found in every art shop.

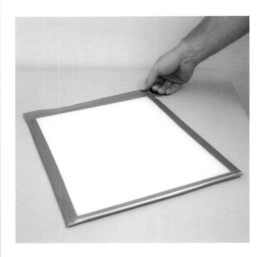

Glass palette: A properly prepared glass palette provides one of the best surfaces on which to mix paint. The duct tape serves the dual purpose of covering the sharp edges of the glass and taping to it a sheet of white paper and a firm surface (see pp. 38–39).

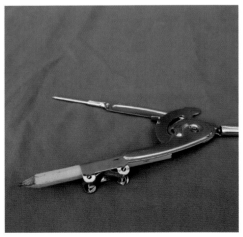

Circle compass: If used carefully, the compass will give you a perfect circle and is essential for creating a colour wheel.

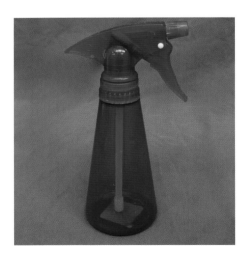

Plant spray: For those choosing to work in acrylic or other water-based media, the spray will keep your palette moist. It also helps to shrink a loose canvas to a more taut stretch.

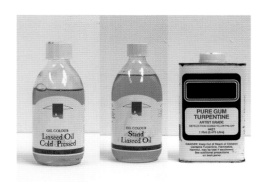

Oil painting mediums: As in so many art products, you will find the larger containers will be much cheaper in the long run than the tiny jars that tend to be pushed in art stores.

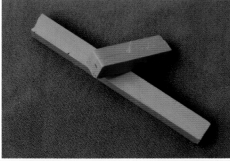

Pastel sticks and pencils: Using a light-coloured pastel pencil (above) or stick (top) for preliminary sketching is preferable to lead pencil as it mixes easily with the oil of acrylic paint. You will need a dark enough colour to be legible.

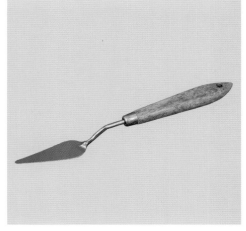

Palette knife: This invaluable tool should be chosen carefully. This example shows the blade in a stair-step fashion that keeps your hands out of the paint. The handle is generally made of wood (plastic-handled versions are cheaper but not recommended).

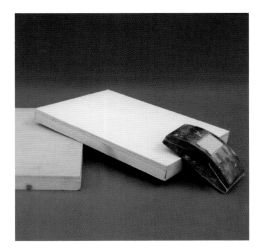

Prepared gesso hardboard panels: These work well for small paintings and colour wheels; they are preprimed and require nothing more than perhaps a light sanding to give them extra tooth.

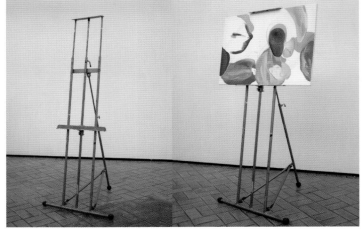

Easel: This metal adjustable easel has the advantage over wood in terms of durability and weight. It will take a large-size painting and adjusts from both ends. As you can see from the right-hand example (painting by Zeke Paull), the easel allows for the height of the individual artist—you need not bend or reach if you adjust it properly.

Cleanup and Preparation for the Next Day's Painting

Materials:
—Tubes of paint
—Painting mediums
—Plastic containers with tops
—Palette knife
—Palette
—Liquin

There are many ways to save paint that you have mixed on your palette for the next day's work. The palette cup can be used to collect and save paint. Another inexpensive alternative is to leave the paint on the palette and cover it: Before covering it, use a paint scraper to remove all the paint that has dried out and perhaps mix together any patches of paint that are very small, as paint tends to dry more quickly in smaller amounts. You will find that the random leftover colours end up being used for something. After you have separated your colours, you can put baby-food jars over each patch, or you can put plastic wrap over the whole palette.

Alternatively, if you wish to clean up the palette completely, it is much easier to do so while the paint is still wet, when you can simply rub it off with a cotton rag. Once the paint becomes tacky or dried out, a paint scraper is required.

To clean your brushes, use a paintbrush-cleaning container filled with odourless turpentine for oils or plain water for acrylic to remove excess paint before washing each brush in warm soapy water. You can make such a container from a glass jar by placing a piece of metal or plastic screen (similar to what you find on a screen door) near the bottom, about two fingers up. This protects the brush from going into the mix of old paint and solvent.

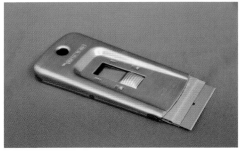
Palette cups have airtight tops to preserve paint.

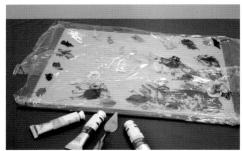
A palette scraper is invaluable for cleaing glass.

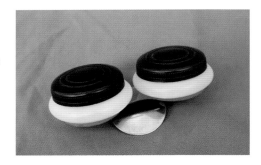
Overturned jars are another simple, cheap method of protecting your premixed paints on the palette.

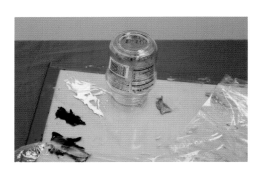
Clear plastic wrap has the advantage of covering all the paints at once, with minimal expense.

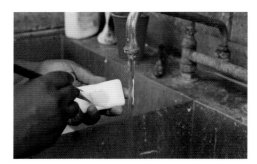
After soaking brushes (see opposite), wash them thoroughly with soap and warm water.

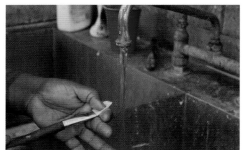
Although it may not look as though you need this extra soapy water rinse with acrylic paint, squeeze the brushes to remove any stubborn remainders.

Care of Brushes

Never leave your brushes in the cleaning jar with the brush facing down. This will bend and ruin your brushes. If for some reason you need to soak them, make sure they are elevated, not resting against the bottom, with just the bristles in the solution.

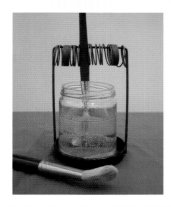

Example of a damaged brush allowed to sit in jar of turpentine, alongside the proper way to suspend a brush in a cleaning solution.

After you have cleaned your brushes with odourless turpentine, you must wash them out with soap under warm running water. This will take off the oil paint and solvents, which break down the brushes over time. Acrylic brushes should also be washed out with soap under warm running water.

Another way to clean your brushes is to use baby oil, which is nontoxic and can be used to wash both your hands and your brushes. Generally I put the baby oil on the brush and rub my finger through, using a cotton cloth to clean off the excess. Afterwards, you should use warm, soapy water to get the oil out, as described above, and then wipe it on a clean cotton rag.

After washing your brushes, it is a good idea to wrap them part in newsprint to help them keep their shape. If you can be this disciplined, your brushes will last for years.

The next time you prepare to start painting, take all of the old turpentine and old paint sludge that has settled to the bottom of your glass jars and pour off the clearish mixture into a new jar to be reused. By reusing your turpentine, you will save money. With acrylic paints, simply use fresh water.

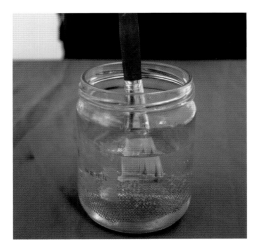

Clean acrylic paint from a brush using clean water with soap.

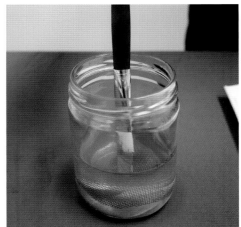

Clean oil paint from a brush by placing it into a container of turpentine. The mesh inside here (and in the previous image) is to prevent your brush from mixing with old paint and solvents that may gather at the bottom of the jar.

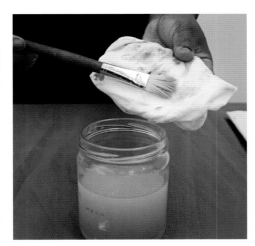

Dry all your brushes with a clean cotton cloth.

Chapter 3:
First Painting:
Wet on Wet

In this book, we will look at three basic methods of painting: wet on wet (alla prima painting), wet on dry and scumbling, and Venetian painting in layers. This is not an exhaustive list of painting techniques, but rather something with which the new painter can begin. It is not unusual for all three methods to be combined in one painting.

For our first painting, we will use the wet on wet, or alla prima, method. This is a rapid style of painting in which the paints are first mixed on the palette and further colours are then created on the painting surface by mixing the wet colours together. With this technique, there is only one layer of paint. It uses full-range colour and is often completed in one session, working with wet paint blending into wet paint. A whole painting, or a section of a longer project, can be completed from start to finish in a single day.

First, however, we need a painting surface. Unlike the preprepared gesso board we used in the colour wheel projects, we will now prepare and prime our own surface for painting.

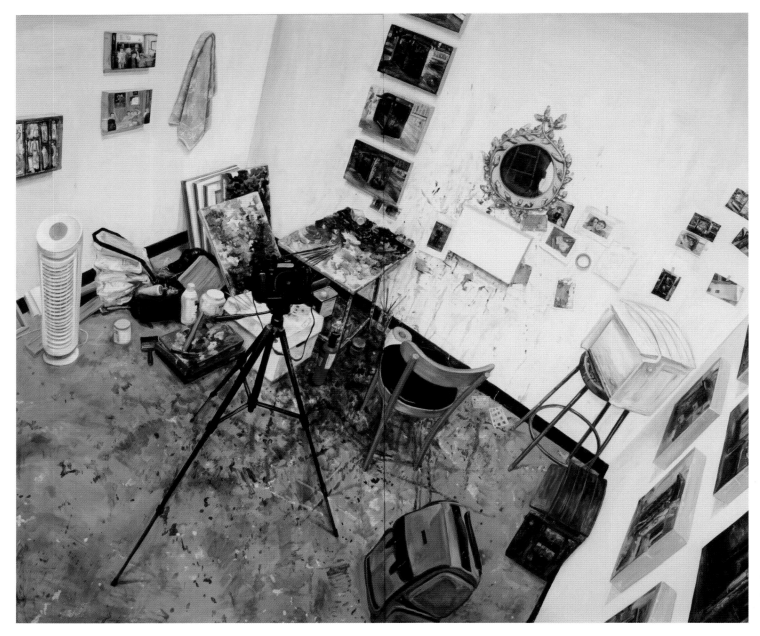

Amer Kobaslija
*Con Te Partiro
(Time to Say Goodbye)*
2006
Oil on panel, diptych
74 ¼ x 85 ⅞ in. (188.6 x 218.4 cm)
George Adams Gallery,
New York

Kobaslija's painting of his studio is a glimpse into the working life of an artist. He provides us with a personal point-of-view that is over his shoulder and into the room. The life-size scale adds to this feeling of intimacy.

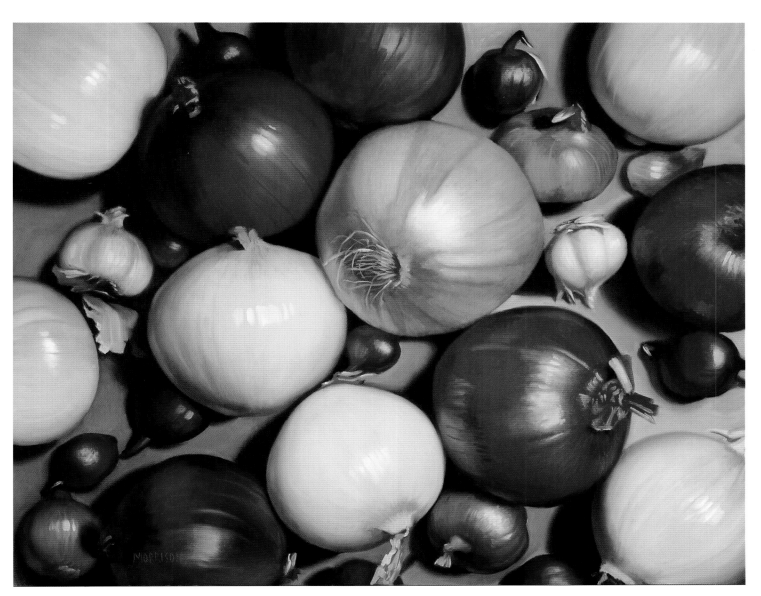

Margaret Morrison
Onions
2005
Oil on canvas
24 x 30 in. (60.9 x 76.2 cm)
Courtesy of the artist and the
Woodward Gallery, New York

Margaret Morrison's "portraits" of or "odes" to onions take the subject matter out of a limited set of perceptions. This still life is rich in colour and depends on the dramatic use of the chiaroscuro technique (see pp. 78–79) to create a sense of volume and immediacy. It is this kind of still life that we are going to try in this chapter.

Painting Support and Canvas Preparation

In this section you will:
— **assemble your premade stretcher bars;**
— **stretch your canvas;**
— **prime your canvas with gesso.**

Alternatively, you can use preprepared canvas or wooden panels.

Artists can, and do, paint on a variety of surfaces, limited only by what the paint will adhere to. The beginning painter has at his or her disposal the firm yet flexible stretched canvas—a woven material stretched over a wooden frame until it is taut enough to paint on. Professional artists may use prepared wooden panels, metal, glass and any flat surface that meets the needs of their imagery. Historically, wood panels were some of the first firm, transportable surfaces used for painting. Over the years, I have painted on both canvas and wooden panels to good effect. The choice of a painting surface is a decision based on experience and preference. Ease of application is usually at the top of the list. For example, a surface with tooth (that is, a surface with a slightly rough texture) creates what we call a drag on the brush, which simply means that the brush has to move over a slightly uneven surface. The downside of too much tooth is that it requires the painter to load up the brush with paint more often. There is no right or wrong surface, just one that works for the individual. In this book, our aim will be to create a smooth surface, and we will concentrate on wooden stretchers with canvas and wood panels.

For ease and speed, we will start with premade stretcher bars and proceed to prepare them with the gesso ground; priming a canvas with gesso creates a uniform surface for acrylic or oil paint. If, on the other hand, you would rather make your own stretcher bars, see pp. 68–69 for a demonstration of stretcher building using lumber and cutting tools.

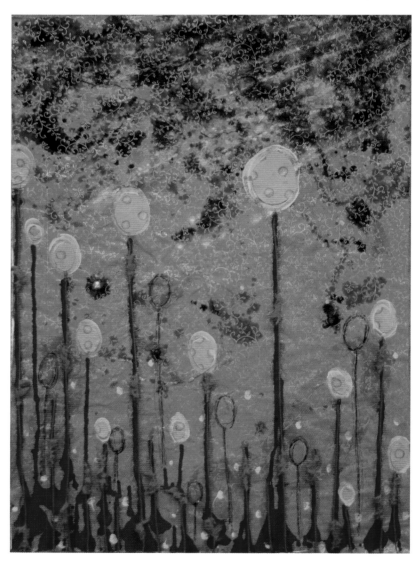

Kelly Smith
Mixed media on Masonite

Kelly Smith's abstract painting combines a variety of mixed media to create both tactile and illusory texture. The red swirling lines moving upward are created using a shiny red fabric. The yellow and orange round-shaped tops are slightly warmer in tone than the red, which has a bit of purple in its mixture, thereby making it cooler. As a rule, warm colours move forward, so the yellow tops seem closer to the viewer. It is this combination that makes for an exciting composition.

Wood Panel Preparation

Materials:
— Wood panels
— Sandpaper
— Gesso
— Lumber for framing
— Wood glue
— C-clamps

Painting on wood has a long tradition and is every bit as common as canvas stretched on a frame. In some cases, artists prefer to stretch the canvas to a wooden panel, as this gives a firm surface to paint on. If you follow this method, you need to prime the surface with gesso in a similar fashion to the way in which you apply it to the stretched canvas (see pp. 66–67).

I prefer to put the gesso directly on sanded wood, rather than applying canvas on top, to provide a smooth, firm surface. Wooden panels are generally about 1 in. (2.5 cm) thick, and it is a good idea to attach a frame to the back of the board to prevent the wood from warping. You can easily make a frame using wood glue and C-clamps.

When applying the gesso, I use three to five coats. Careful sanding in between each coat makes the wood more uniform and adds tooth so that the gesso adheres better.

The choice of surfaces is down to personal preference. Wood panels can be purchased inexpensively at hardware stores or can also often be found discarded at construction sites. Another inexpensive alternative is tempered Masonite ("hardboard" in the UK). The tempering of Masonite involves a process that infuses oil into the board to make it water-resistant. I have found that tempered Masonite, with its dark brown colouring and slippery smooth surface, is much more tedious to prime than other wood. If choosing Masonite, it is a good idea to attach wooden support beams to the back to prevent too much flexibility (see p. 69 for stretcher support beams).

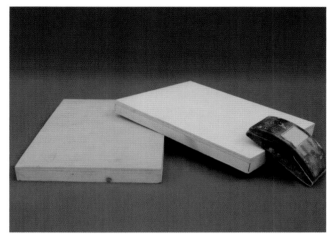

Primed and nonprimed boards: It is not an absolute rule that you must paint on primed wood, but for ease of application without the paint seeping into the surface, priming is superior. Some artists consider the boxlike quality to be reminiscent of religious three-dimensional icons.

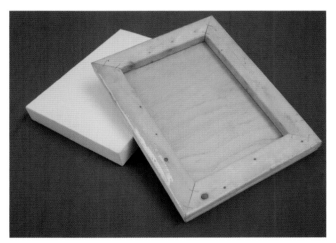

You can see the frame in this back view of a wooden panel. The purpose of this frame is to support the ½-in. (1.27-cm) panel so that it does not warp.

Stretching the Canvas on a Stretcher Frame

Materials:
— Unprimed linen canvas or unprimed cotton duck canvas
— Measuring tape
— Scissors
— Lightweight staple gun
— Mirror

Now that the stretcher is prepared, we will proceed to stretch the canvas. The finest canvas is unprimed linen canvas. The uneven weave of this canvas is considered by most artists to produce a far superior surface quality than the more even, machine-woven regularity of cotton duck canvas. Unfortunately, the cost is prohibitive, but more economical alternatives can be found; I recommend unprimed heavyweight cotton duck, which is relatively inexpensive and almost indistinguishable from the linen variety. Another practical advantage of unprimed cotton duck is that stretching pliers are not required.

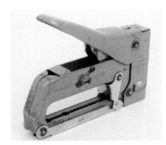

Staple gun: Make sure that you can squeeze with one hand. If you require two hands, you cannot hold the canvas to control the stretch.

Cotton duck canvas: Popular with students thanks to its low cost, compared with fine linen. Over the years, it has also become quite acceptable in professional painting situations.

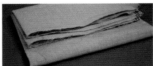

Fine linen canvas: Good quality but costly. It still requires preparation with gesso and sanding, but can be purchased already primed and will require the use of the canvas pliers due to the rigidity caused by the primer (see p. 67).

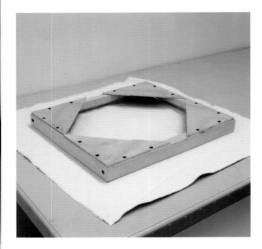

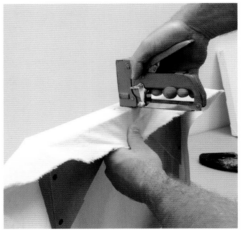

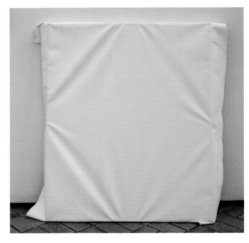

1 Measuring the canvas

Your canvas can be purchased cut to size or by the roll, which is much cheaper over the long run. The most important part in stretching is making sure you have enough canvas to cover the surface of the frame with some extra overhang for gripping. To achieve this, it is advisable to leave at least 5 in. (13 cm) overhang of material on every side of the stretcher. So if, for example, your stretcher size is 24 x 36 in. (60 x 90 cm), your piece of canvas would need to measure at least 29 x 41 in. (73 x 103 cm).

Once you have cut the canvas to size, lay the stretcher frame on the floor or a table. You will need to lay the canvas over the stretcher bars to make sure it is centreed, with an even amount of the canvas hanging over each side. Take hold of the stretcher bars and the top edge of the canvas and stand them up.

2 Starting to staple

Pull the canvas over the stretcher bars toward you, with the painting surface facing away from you. Using a staple gun, place one or two staples directly in the middle of the top side of the stretcher. It does not matter which side you start on. Then go directly to the opposite side from where you started on the stretcher and repeat the same procedure, pulling it a little tighter before you place the staple. Rotate the stretcher and repeat the process on the remaining two sides. Always pull the opposite side a little tighter.

3 Pulling the canvas taut

If you have pulled the canvas equally tight on all four sides, you will now have a slight diamond shape forming on the front of the canvas. Turn the canvas upright so that you can both pull and stretch the canvas with your hands. Working in a clockwise fashion around the four sides of the stretchers, place one or two staples on each the side of the canvas, next to the original staple, and keep pulling and stretching as you go.

As you stretch the canvas, the diamond shape will begin to lose its distinctive edges, becoming more oval as the canvas is pulled taut. As you continue the stretching process along each side of the stretcher, this shape will completely disappear.

Preparing a Painting Support

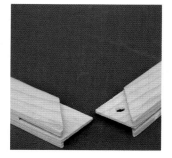 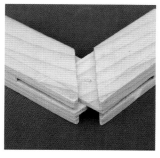 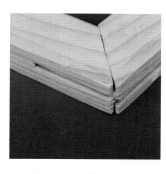 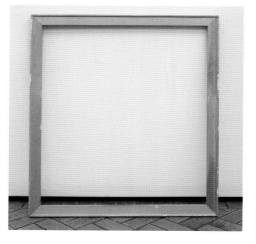

The description of this preparation may seem like dreary busywork, yet I find that this time provides space for reflection and imagination. I do most of my important planning while preparing a painting surface.

Stretcher bars may be purchased from an artists' supply store. They are wooden bars designed to be wedged tongue-and-groove into one another and will guarantee a tight fit. By wedging these bars together, you form either a square or a rectangle, depending on the dimensions chosen. A wooden mallet or hammer will be needed to force the four sides together. After you bring all four sides together, you will need to make sure the corners are at right angles.

You can do this by using a T-square or by leaning the stretcher bars against a corner of a room and seeing if all four sides are flush. This is important, because lopsided or uneven corners can cause warping of the wood once the canvas is stretched onto it.

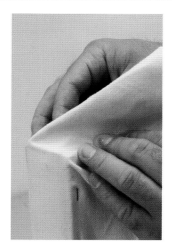 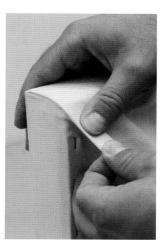 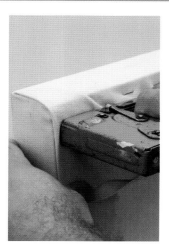 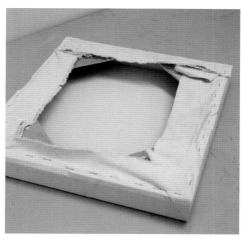

4 Folding and stapling the corners
It is now time to finish off the corners. This is a matter of folding over and stapling the edge, which is best done in a similar way to making up the corners of a bed. Whichever folding pattern you choose, your canvas will look better if the same method is used for all four corners. The best way to achieve a uniform look is to work in a clockwise direction until each corner is finished. This folding over of the edges takes care of excess canvas.

5 Finished stretched canvas
The finished stretched canvas viewed from behind. The larger the canvas, the more important it is that extra material be tacked out of the way.

Priming the Canvas

Materials:
— Gesso (1-gallon tub)
— Small roller or 4-in. (10-cm) house-painting brush
— Small block of wood or sandpaper block
— #1 sandpaper 100 grit dry

It is now time to prime the canvas by applying the gesso. When using oil-based paint, priming is absolutely necessary in order to protect the canvas from the corrosive effects of the oil paint and solvents. Priming is also necessary for acrylic painting, although it is not as crucial an issue as for oil. Acrylic paint will not harm unprepared canvas, but a lack of priming can result in the paint's seeping through and staining the canvas rather than remaining on the surface. Although many experienced artists find this staining quality attractive and have learned to work with it for their own creative needs, for our purposes we want the painting surface to be impermeable and so will use a primed surface.

I recommend that the gesso should be applied with the stretcher flat on a table or the floor. Any extra gesso will drip downward to the floor rather than sliding across the surface, as it would do if canvas were primed in an upright position, leaving lumps and drips.

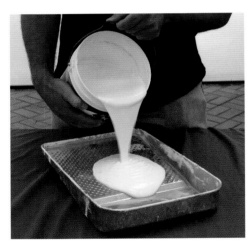

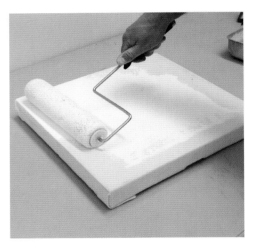

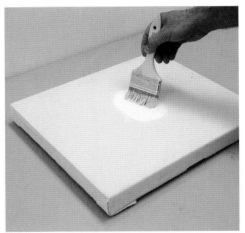

1 Before use, the gesso should be mixed or shaken in the can until smooth. This will aid in creating a flat surface texture on the canvas. If you can afford it, buying the gallon tub will save money in the long run. Keep the lid on securely so that it does not dry out. Here, the gesso is being poured into a tray in preparation for using the roller.

2 The advantage of using a paint roller (as opposed to a brush) is the speed and ease of application. The roller goes over very quickly, and the initial raised areas caused by the paint oozing at the edges of the roller quickly smooth out over the canvas.

3 When using the brush, it is best to start in the centre of the canvas, applying the gesso in a circular fashion and working it into the surface of the canvas.

When the gesso circle covers the centre of the canvas, draw gesso lines diagonally across to each corner with the width of the gesso brush, so that there is an X through the circle. After that, continue to apply the gesso in a circular motion until you reach the sides. The logic behind this is that the wet gesso in the circle and the X will dry evenly, preventing the canvas from warping.

Using Preprepared, Stretched and Primed Canvas

Stretchers can also be purchased with the canvas already stretched and primed (painted with gesso). However, it is still important to paint an additional two coats of gesso on the front and sides of the panel. This is because factory gesso is generally sprayed on and tends to sit on the surface. Adding another layer or two will push the gesso further into the surface of the canvas, adding a stronger layer of protection.

Alternatively, you can purchase primed linen or cotton duck and use this to stretch over stretcher bars. In this case, you will not need to prime the canvas, but you will require a pair of stretcher pliers to pull the material over the frame of the stretcher bars. This is because the factory priming makes the material inflexible and subject to cracking when stretched. Such cracking usually occurs right along the edges.

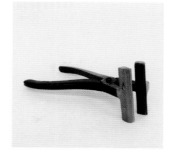 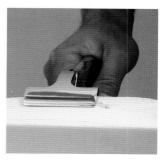

Stretcher pliers: These are necessary when using canvas that has been factory primed with gesso. Primed canvas is much less flexible than the unprimed variety, and you need a tighter grip to pull the canvas over the support.

This photograph illustrates what happens if you use canvas that has been precoated with gesso. Stretcher pliers are required because of the stiff, nonpliable nature of this kind of canvas, which makes stretching by hand to create a tight drumlike surface nearly impossible.

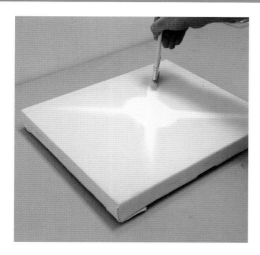 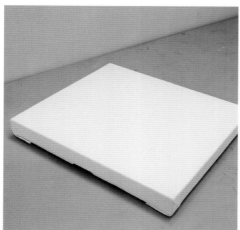 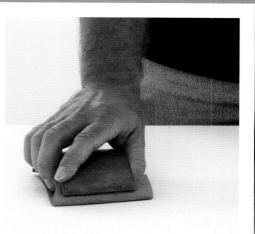

4 When you are finished with the front you will need to paint the sides of the canvas with gesso. This will allow the canvas to shrink more evenly as it dries. It is this shrinking, combined with the manual stretch, that gives the material its taut quality. You are aiming for a drumlike effect: something that is firm yet has flexibility.

5 Because the gesso that we are using is water-based, we have to take into consideration the drying time. The roller has the advantage of speed, allowing a first coat of gesso to be applied on multiple canvases one right after the other. This can also be done with the brush, but because the gesso dries quickly it could dry on to the brush in the process.

Regardless of how you apply the gesso, the canvas requires two to three coats. In between these coats the brush or roller should be washed and allowed to dry. If you start to gesso the canvas with a wet brush or roller, you will dilute the gesso.

6 You should sand each coat of gesso so that the final layers are uniformly smooth; sanding also provides the necessary tooth for subsequent coats to stick. A small block of wood or a sandpaper block will save your hands and allow for even sanding throughout. Allow each coat to dry thoroughly, overnight if possible.

Rigid Stretcher Construction

Tools and materials:
— 3 strips of ¾ x 4-in. (1.9 x 10-cm) stud, 8 ft. (2.44 m) in length
— Hand saw
— Measuring tape
— 2 strips of ½-in. (1.27-cm) round wood dowel, 8 ft (2.44 m) in length
— Wood glue
— Small brads (finishing nails)
— ¼-in. (0.6-cm) depth plywood
— Corner clamp
— Hand drill
— Screws
— Phillips-head bit
— Countersink bit
— Quick-grip clamp

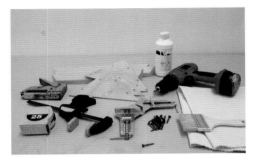

Tools and materials for building, stretching and priming a canvas. From the bottom left: measuring tape, wood clamp, stapler, bevelled wood with corner supports resting on them, metal angle clamps, screws, power drill, container of gesso, gesso brush, unprimed cotton duck canvas.

Bevelling strips for the stretcher frame

Bevelled wood means wood cut with a sloping edge. Using bevelled wood for a stretcher frame prevents the canvas from lying completely flat on the stretcher and forming an ugly indentation. The easiest way to bevel the strips without a power tool is to add a piece of wood dowel. Take two of your three ¾ x 4-in. (1.9 x 10-cm) wood strips, and glue each ½-in. (1.27-cm) round wood dowel along the narrowest side of both strips, nailing them down firmly with small brads or finishing nails.

Cutting the strips to size

You will then cut these two bevelled strips in half widthways to make up four strips for all four sides of the frame. Measure the strips according to the desired canvas size—the largest possible square canvas size when using these lengths of wood is approximately 48 x 48 in. (1.22 x 1.22 m). Mark the wood for the mitre cuts, i.e., cuts at a 45-degree angle, so that the strips will fit together at the corners of the frame. Using the hand saw, cut along these marks to make four strips with a 45-degree angle at each end.

Assembling the stretcher bars

Place two stretcher bars in the corner clamp to make a 90-degree angle. Note: If you are not making a perfectly square canvas, make sure that you place one long side and one short side into the corner clamp.

Drill a screw into the stretcher bars at the mitred cuts (to prevent splitting the wood, you may wish to drill pilot holes

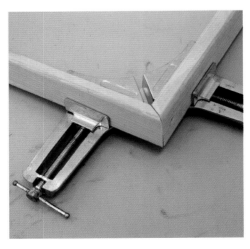

1 Fix your stretcher bars in a corner clamp, holding them steady for the screws.

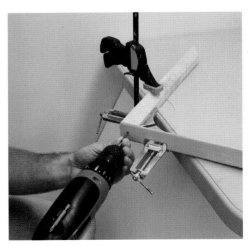

2 Drill screws into both sides of each of the mitred corners. (Making pilot holes before drilling the screws helps to prevent the wood from splitting.)

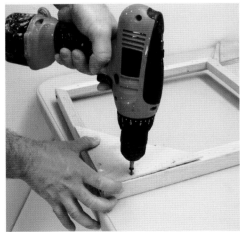

3 Make triangular supports and drill them on to the back of each corner of the stretcher.

Hand Drill: Health and Safety

— Make sure your hand drill is the proper size for your grip
— Keep your hands well away from the drill bit
— Only use a wood drill bit for drilling into wood
— A battery-operated drill gives you a wider range of movement than an electric drill

— If you choose to use an electric drill, do keep track of the cord, and make sure it is plugged into a three-pronged socket; if using an extension cord, make sure it is a heavy-duty one
— Keep the drill bit clean and free of wood chips so that there is complete visibility

before screwing the mitred corners together). I recommend using drywall screws, which are around 1 to 1 ½ in. (2.5 to 3.8 cm) in length, because their galvanised grooves hold a little better than regular wood screws. Repeat this process until you have all four 90-degree corners screwed together. Since a mitre cut is the weakest form of joinery, the screws only hold the stretcher bars together until the corner supports are added.

Cutting the corner supports

Now for the corner supports. Using ¼-in. (0.6-cm) depth plywood, measure and draw out two perfect squares. Make sure that the sides of your squares are less than half the size of the shortest sides of your stretcher bars.

Using a hand saw, cut out the squares in the plywood. Draw a diagonal line between two opposite corners of one of the squares. Cut the square along this line to make two triangles. Repeat this on the second square, so that you end up with four triangles.

Assembling the corner supports

Once all four sides of the stretcher bars have been assembled, flip the stretcher over so that the bevelled side is down. Place the plywood corner supports on all four corners and screw them down to the stretcher.

Support beams

Support beams are two perpendicular strips of wood that support the inside of the stretcher. To make these, you can use the

third ¾-in (1.9-cm) wood strip left over from making your stretcher. In order to measure them to the exact size of the inside of the stretcher, place the end of the wood strip flush with the inside of the stretcher and mark where it goes under the opposite side. Use a hand saw to cut two lengths, this time at 90-degree angles.

Place one beam inside the stretcher and mark it on the outside for the countersink holes. Drill screws through the side of the stretcher into the support beam.

To add the second support beam running perpendicular to the first, you will first need to cut a notch into this second beam so that the first can rest easily in it.

Now follow the instructions on pp. 64–65 to stretch your canvas over the bars, and pp. 66–67 to apply gesso.

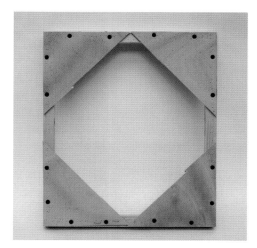

4 Back view of the finished stretcher, showing all four corner supports in place.

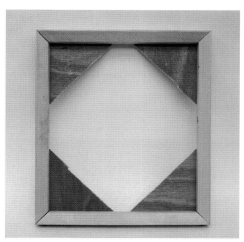

5 Front view of the finished stretcher, on which you are now ready to stretch your canvas.

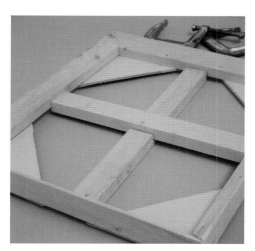

6 Back view of a frame with added support beams.

In this section you will:
— **select your subject matter;**
— **use a viewfinder to order the composition;**
— **make a sketch using a pastel pencil;**
— **consider the composition by using a focal point or by using natural or indoor lighting;**
— **learn to recognise the use of chiaroscuro shading and reflected colour.**

Beginning Your Painting

Materials
— Rectangular canvas or wood panel, primed, roughly 11 x 14 in. (28 x 35 cm)
— Viewfinder
— Light-coloured pastel pencil

Now that you have your first painting support primed with gesso, you are ready to begin the painting. For your first painting, I suggest you try a still life of fruits and vegetables. Fruits and vegetables offer bright primary and secondary colours, which will enable you to pick out the colours easily in the composition. We will begin by arranging the still life and then making a preliminary sketch.

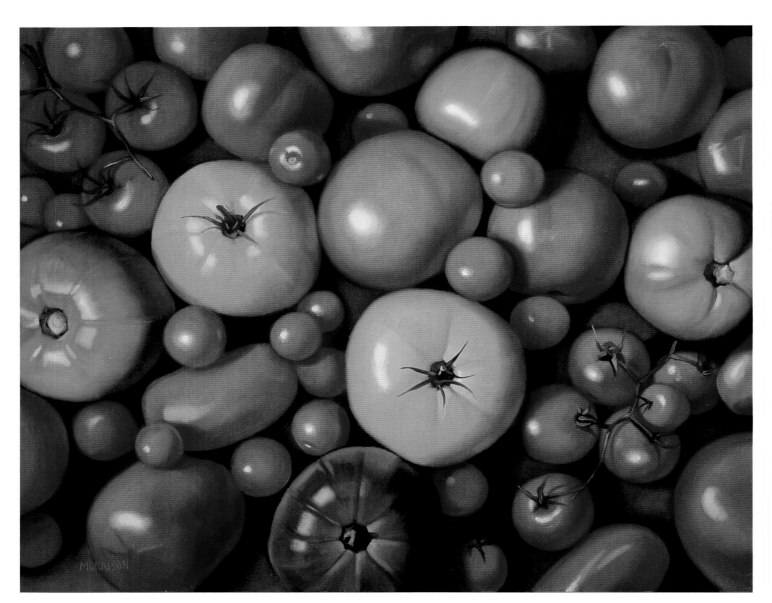

Margaret Morrison
Tomatoes
2005
Oil on canvas
24 x 30 in. (60.9 x 76.2 cm)
Courtesy of the artist and the
Woodward Gallery, New York

Margaret Morrison's illustration of tomatoes in all their variety is deceptively simple in composition, yet extremely elegant in design. By using different variations of one still life object, she creates a colourful checkerboard effect.

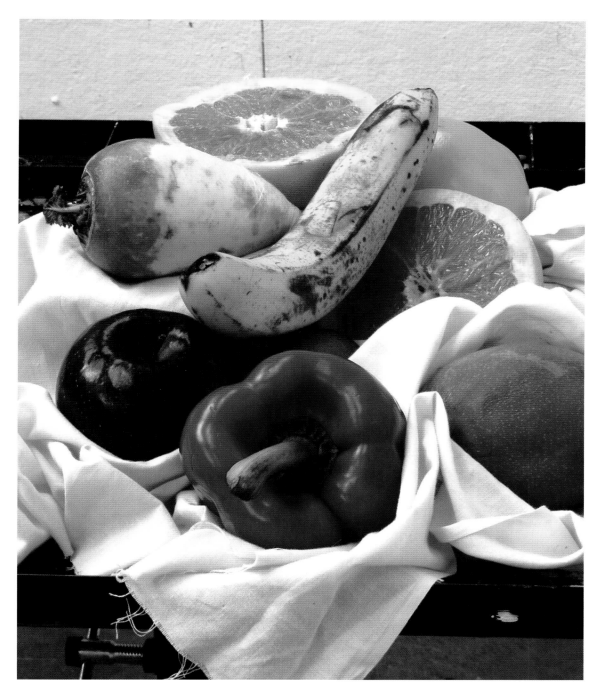

Photograph of still life
An assemblage of different shapes, sizes and textures of fruit is here arranged on a neutral-coloured cloth. This will be the subject matter for the still life painting shown on the following pages. An arrangement like this allows for the overlap of the fruit and vegetables and some space between, thus creating positive/negative space integration.

Selection of Subject Matter

Fruits and vegetables have very distinctive colours and shapes, which will help you identify patterns and values in your first sketch. Try to have a selection that includes both shiny and dull surfaces, both large and small forms, some tactile texture and, most importantly, fruits and vegetables that are very colourful. Place these on a flat surface, which could be a neutral colour or a piece of printed material. Striped material, for example, will be reflected in the objects, adding another compositional ploy. Refer back to the colour and design principles in Chapter 1 when arranging your still life (see pp. 25–27) and think of design as an organizational chart guiding your composition.

Composition: Using a Viewfinder

After arranging your still life, a handy tool in composition is the viewfinder. As in photography, a viewfinder helps in editing a composition by putting a border around the chosen subject matter. This border represents the outside edges of the painting surface. A viewfinder can be constructed out of paper or cardboard. By cutting out the centre of a piece of paper in roughly the same dimensions as your painting surface, you will have a handheld viewfinder. I find that when a still life includes multiple items, holding up the viewfinder crops out extraneous visual information by allowing me to zoom in on a section of the composition that catches my attention.

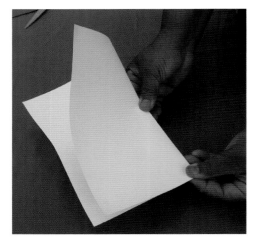

1 Fold a white piece of paper or card in half.

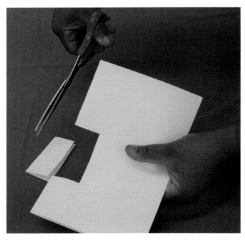

2 Cut out a shape in the crease. The size of this shape should be half the dimensions of your painting surface.

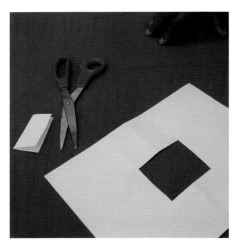

3 You now have a very basic viewfinder. Be sure to give yourself enough outside "frame" so that you are able to hold it with a steady grip, and use cardboard if you want to prevent it from flapping about.

Using the frame of a photograph as a viewfinder, student Eleanor Simmons created a useful tool with which to compose her fruit and vegetable still life. You can see how she has held her viewfinder to frame her work, and her painting reflects these decisions.

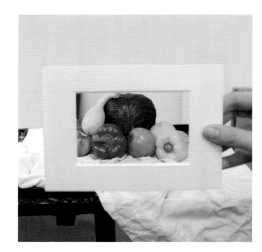

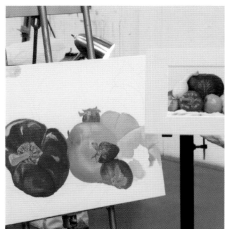

Making a Preparatory Sketch

Make your preparatory sketch, arranging your composition and observing the value patterns (see below). As you begin this sketch, use the still life as a guide, but feel free to change the placement of the objects based on compositional effects. For example, if an apple is in the foreground of the painting and a banana is behind it, have the apple overlap rather than just placing it next to the banana: Overlapping objects illustrate spatial relationships. Cropping some of the fruits and vegetables off the painting surface will make the painting feel fuller and more open. You may want to avoid the trap of a composition with nothing at the top, the objects in the middle, and the surface on which they are sitting at the bottom. Make your choices based on how the colours of the fruits and vegetables work best.

Begin by carefully drawing your still life using a light-coloured pastel pencil. The advantage of using pastel pencils to draw these lines is that they will dissolve into the paint as you apply it. If you use graphite pencil, you will find that it almost always leaves a greyish tone that requires more paint applications to cover it up. As an example, if you are painting with the colour yellow, which has the least hide (covering ability), you will need to apply many layers of paint to cover the grey tone of the pencil beneath.

In the activity of drawing, the outside line of an object is the contour line, but in this preparatory sketch try to imagine the line you are drawing as a string being pulled around and over the items in your still life. As you draw these items, show how different objects may overlap each other. This will show the spatial relationship, help you to illustrate the volume of a form, and create the illusion of a three-dimensional collection of objects on a flat surface.

Another technique you can use to create a three-dimensional drawing is to draw the value patterns. Value patterns describe the shape of patches of colour on the surfaces of the subject matter. Generally, when we observe colour, we are not inclined to notice that every tone and shadow forms a shape. For the purpose of creating a painting, this is exactly what you should look for. Lines are formed where different patches of colour meet and individual colour shapes become clear. It is the lines formed where these colour shapes meet that you should include in your preparatory sketch. As you draw the shapes you will see that these patches of colour follow the contour of the object, and so including them in your sketch will help you to create the illusion of three dimensions. Observing these patterns will also help you to choose the composition of your painting by choosing an area of interesting shapes. You will also be looking at colour combinations and will be able to choose an area with interesting colours.

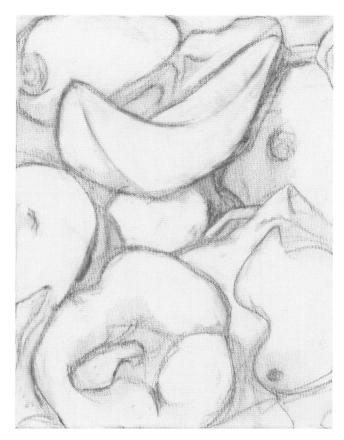

Above
Student Brittany Gabey's preparatory sketch for her fruit and vegetable painting was composed using a viewfinder to help edit and make decisions about her subject matter. She used the method of cropping to bring the viewer even closer to the middle of the painting.

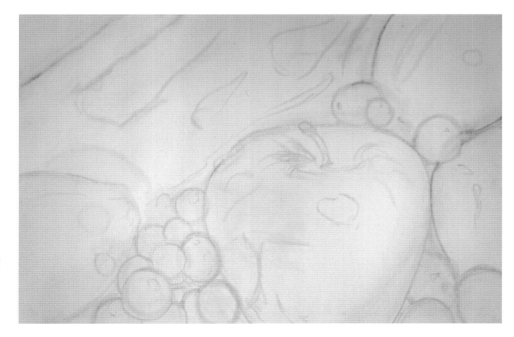

Right
Student Jasmin Kern's preparatory sketch is another example of the creative use of a viewfinder to organise pictorial space. Her sketch has a sense of a bigger picture continuing beyond the frame of the canvas and its abstract arrangement makes it a very personal viewpoint.

Drawing in this way, following the shape of the colours as well as the outline of the object, is much like a puzzle requiring visual trust. I describe the term "visual trust" as accepting what you see, without question. By this I mean that sometimes the first thing you see without question is most likely to be correct. This is not scientific, but I have observed it in students and in myself over the years. We tend to spend time unconsciously naming things in front of us, in a sort of intellectual interference. We tend to disregard what we actually see and instead self-correct—but not always rightly. So much of observation relies on trusting what you see, not what you think you see or expect to see. We know a pencil is straight and we unconsciously expect it to stay that way no matter the circumstances. But just look at a pencil reflected in a shiny sphere and you will get the point. So, as you continue drawing you will find that painting from observation demands a willingness to believe the unbelievable. What this actually means is that you are seeing a different point of view, one that you cannot easily imagine. Try the upside-down drawing experiment: If you place a photograph upside down and draw the image as you see it, you will find that your accuracy is greater than if the photograph were the right way up.

This preparatory painting sketch can look similar to a paint-by-numbers kit. Most of these shapes individually can appear to be very abstract or nonrepresentational. In describing value patterns, the term motif is also used, usually to describe shapes that are created by the repetition of forms within a design.

When you start to apply your paint colours on the painting surface, you will gradually find that your composition begins to lose this initial pixelated look, becoming clearer as you delineate the objects and the space around the objects and/or the surface on which they lie. Do not worry, this sketch is not an exacting blueprint: You can and will change these patterns as you progress.

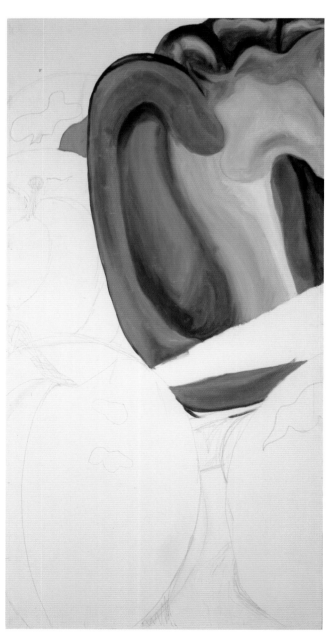

This preparatory sketch and the beginning of a painting by student Miriam Rowe is an example of what is meant by figure/ground ambiguity. The ground is considered the negative space in terms of understanding this phenomenon. Clearly, there is no true negative space, but rather the difference between the objects and the surface on which the objects are sitting.

Miriam Rowe
Oil on canvas

Here is the finished fruit and vegetable painting by Miriam Rowe, as sketched opposite. The issues of negative space are now muted by her use of chiaroscuro shading and cast shadows in particular. Spatial relationships in representational painting rely on shape, form and overlap. This is what separates the objects from the surface on which they are placed.

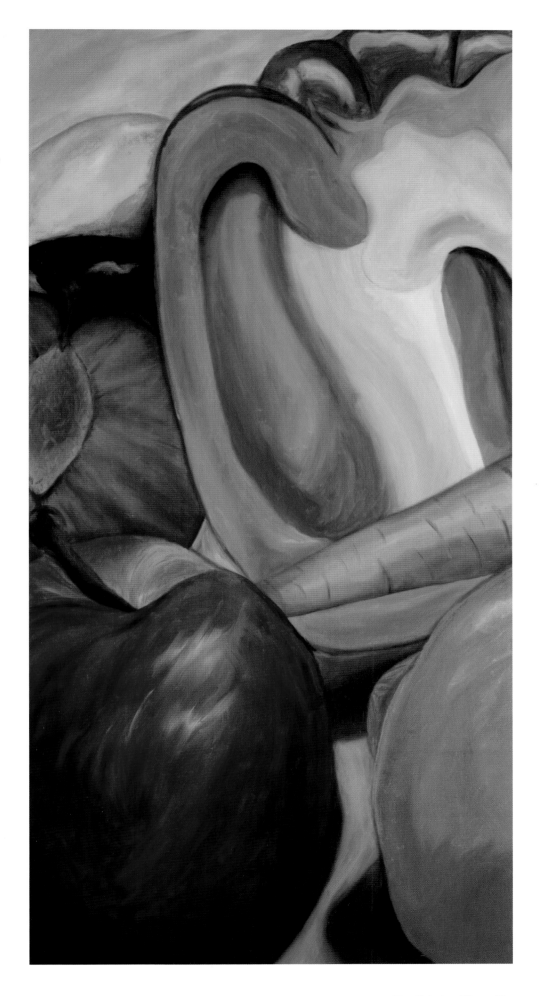

Negative Space

As you continue drawing, pay close attention to the shape of the canvas, with emphasis given to the four corners. It is important that the four corners be activated visually, either with objects or with interesting negative space shapes. Negative space is the space created around an object or arrangement of objects, creating a visual shape or pattern. This is a neutral term to describe a particular phenomenon: For example, if you draw the inside shapes of a metal fence, you end up with the solid fence itself as well.

There will be a tendency to direct most of your energy and attention to the centre of the canvas, but a well-composed drawing is an open composition, a term I use to describe an arrangement that visually extends beyond the literal borders of the painting support. It alludes to continuation. The four corners of your painting support represent a frame that surrounds your imagery. Imagine the view outside from behind a window and observe how the outline of the window encloses what you see.

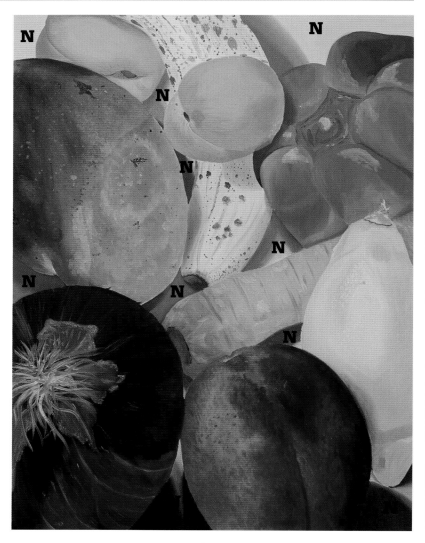

This fruit and vegetable painting by student Christin McMurray is a clear example of how considering negative space as much as positive space can produce great results. The negative space and cast shadows help to bring the fruit and vegetables into full focus. The colours on the objects are also made more brilliant by the cool and subdued colour of the surface on which they are placed.

Choosing a Focal Point for Composition

Having arranged your still life, you have one of many compositional choices to make during this drawing stage. You may find that only one small area of the still life interests you. As we have seen, pattern or colour combinations can determine this area. This is not a problem; you simply change the scale of the drawing and enlarge a section, making it the focal point of your composition. Objects that are drawn larger are naturally more detailed and will draw the viewer in. As you draw, you can continue to rearrange the objects to isolate areas of interest or, finally, if the painting surface is canvas, you can physically crop the painting after completion. Cropping or cutting the canvas is a way of focusing on a particular part of the painting.

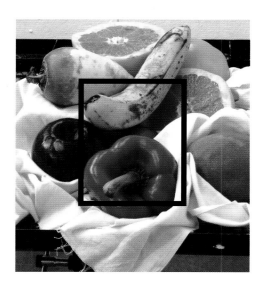

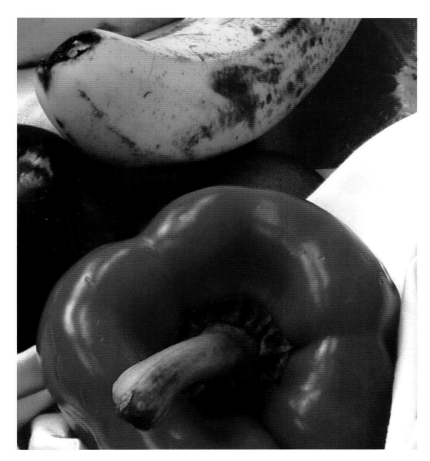

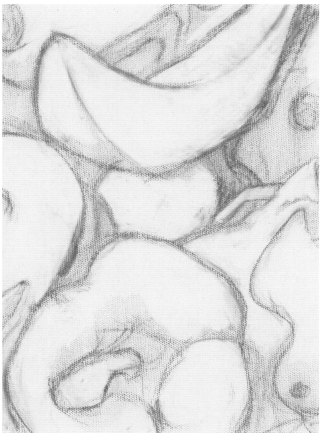

Close-up (left) of the area in the still life arrangement that was chosen using the viewfinder. See the crop on the whole photograph (top). Then note how Brittany Gabey has matched her preparatory sketch to this detail (above).

Using Light: Chiaroscuro Shading

Chiaroscuro is a traditional painting or drawing method that employs the full-range value of lights and darks, resulting in a stronger overall sense of volume and an illusion of deep and shallow space. Notable historical examples can be found from the Renaissance. This technique places the emphasis on the dramatic play of light and dark across forms.

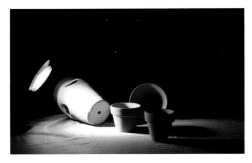

This collection of pots shows clearly all five stages of the chiaroscuro shading. See if you can identify the lightest light, the shadow, the core of the shadow, the reflected light and the cast shadow.

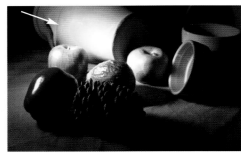

The arrow shows the direction of the light source. When other objects are added to the still life, note the difference in the light as it strikes the varying textures and colours of these objects.

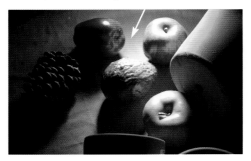

The light in this picture is coming from the right, and is at a steeper angle than in the previous image. This is most evident when you look at the apples, as the stalks are now producing shadows of their own.

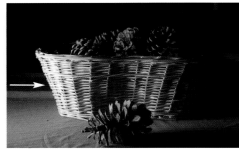

Their multifaceted forms make pine cones interesting objects on which to observe light and shadow. Here, the light is coming in from middle left.

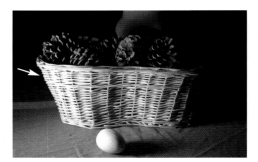

See how an egg creates a cleaner cast shadow than the pine cone. The light is coming from slightly higher up on the left here.

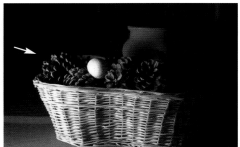

When the egg is moved to the basket, its cast shadow is considerably darker due to the surrounding pine cones reducing the reflected light.

There are five stages to consider when using chiaroscuro shading:

1. the lightest light (source);
2. the shadow;
3. the core, or darkest part, of the shadow;
4. the reflected light (light that bounces off nearby objects or the surface they are sitting on);
5. the cast shadow (which in itself has at least four different tones as well).

This way of shading and blending, coupled with careful attention to value patterns, is the most basic building block in realistic and figurative painting.

Using a perfectly round ball as an example, start by mixing and laying down the colour that best represents the lightest area. The colour for the shadow will be a darker shade of the first colour. After you have placed this colour down, blend the edges to create a soft transition. Continue in this fashion with the core of the shadow, which is the darkest part of the shadow. Then lay down the reflected colour, which is based on colour from nearby objects or the surface that the ball sits on. The cast shadow follows the shape of the ball somewhat and is usually much darker than the object itself. The shape is also dependent on how close the light source is to the ball. As you mix the colours above, remember to consider how the many colours and tones of the ball are all affected by reflected colour.

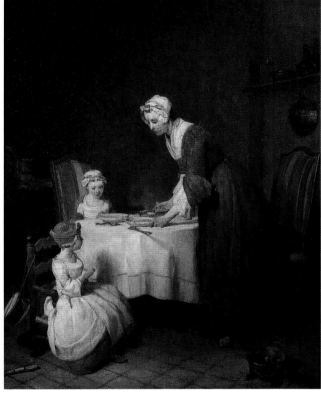

Jean-Baptiste Chardin
Saying Grace
c. 1740
Oil on canvas
19 x 15 ¼ in. (49.5 x 38.5 cm)
Musée du Louvre, Paris

The natural light source in this scene is pointing upward from the lower left-hand corner of the canvas. This creates a directional light upward, which joins the subject matter and the environment.

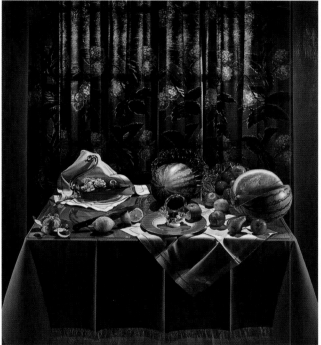

James Valerio
Still Life with Melons
1997–99
Oil on canvas
96 x 84 in. (243.8 x 213.4 cm)
Courtesy of George Adams Gallery, New York

Valerio's still life is literally and figuratively a production. The curtains serve as a backdrop and a continuation of the lush display of fruit. The whole scene is lit from above with artificial light.

Reflected Colour

Reflected colour is colour reflected from one object to another, in the process changing the colour of the second object. This is especially noticeable in landscape painting, where a sunset, for example, will produce a very different colour effect from the morning sun.

Claude Monet
Rouen Cathedral in Morning Sun
1894
Oil on canvas
41 ¾ x 29 in. (106.1 x 73.9 cm)
Museum of Fine Arts, Boston

It was not unusual for Monet to paint subject matter at different times of the day, and this painting and the one to its right are prime examples of how the colour and light of the day reflect on the subject matter. As this is reflected light, it is atmospheric, creating a kind of haze produced by particles in the air as well.

Claude Monet
Rouen Cathedral at Sunset
1892
Oil on canvas
39 ⅓ x 25 ⅜ in. (100 x 65 cm)
Musée Marmottan, Paris

In this painting of Rouen Cathedral, one of many of Monet's sunset variations, the cool colour of the sunset reflecting on the stone creates a blue-grey tonality, whereas the warmth of the morning light with a hint of the evening colour creates the lighter tones.

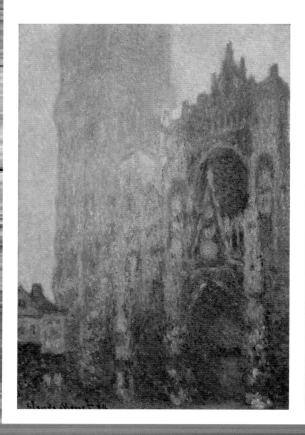 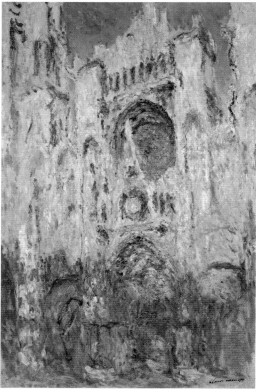

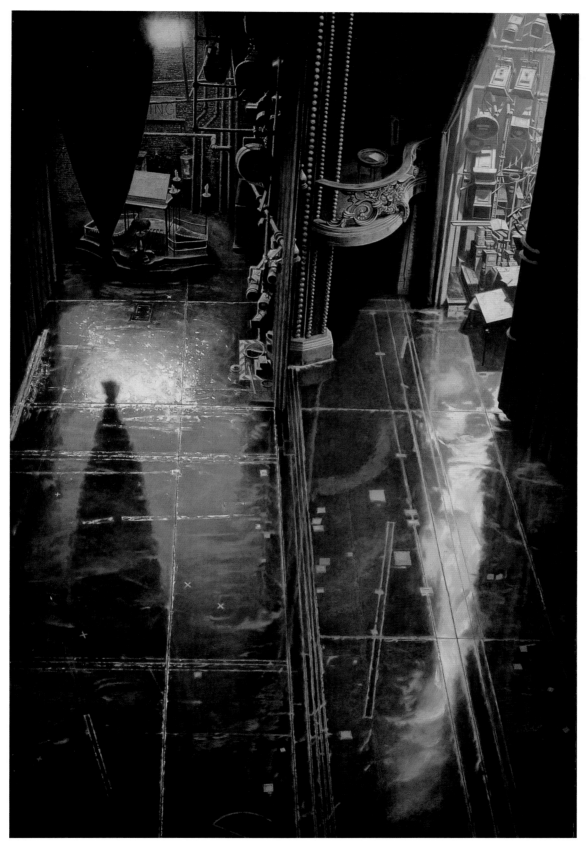

Craig McPherson
Empty Stage (Fly Rail)
2001–4
Oil on linen
72 x 48 in. (182.8 x 122 cm)
© Craig McPherson, courtesy
of Forum Gallery, New York

In Craig McPherson's *Empty Stage (Fly Rail)*, the use of reflected colours and cast shadows produces a sense of deep and shallow space using simple abstract shapes. The almost monochromatic colour schemes emphasise this dichotomy of light and dark.

Preparing Your Palette

Now that you have arranged your still life and completed the preliminary sketch, you are ready to prepare the palette. Lay out your paints so that you have easy access to them: If they are readily available, you will use them. I suggest that you start with the palette of colours shown below in either the full-range or the limited palette.

When applying paint from the tube to the palette it is helpful to study the subject matter in front of you at the same time. You should also make sure you have both the colour wheel and the chromatic chart to hand. You will find it helpful to refer to these as you search for a colour match—and they will remind you of what you are capable of in terms of colour mixing.

The method you will use for this first painting will be the alla prima, wet on wet, or direct painting technique, in which the whole painting or sections of the painting are completed in one sitting, working wet paint into wet paint. With this method you will also be able to employ a style of glazing that I call "blending as you go", laying one wet paint colour atop another with enough firmness to mix the two together on the surface. As the paints remain wet, you are not confined to mixing just two colours together, and so the colours you mix on your palette to start need not be the only colours that you use. You can continue to mix these with other colours as you complete the painting. However, it is best to start by mixing about thirty colours on your palette before you begin, as described below.

Materials
— **Paints**
— **Paint mediums**
— **Palette knives**
— **Palette**
— **Paint tube squeezer**
  (or rolling pin or similar object)
— **Plastic plant spray**
  (acrylic paints only)

— **Use the paint mediums and**
  ingredients listed on p. 42 in
  Chapter 2.

Paint colours (acrylic or oil) for a beginning full-range palette. Those marked with an asterisk (*) are recommended for a limited palette. It is advisable to purchase professional-grade paints whenever possible—they perform better than the student grade, and therefore you will know which mistakes in colour mixing are the result of an incorrect colour choice rather than an inferior product.

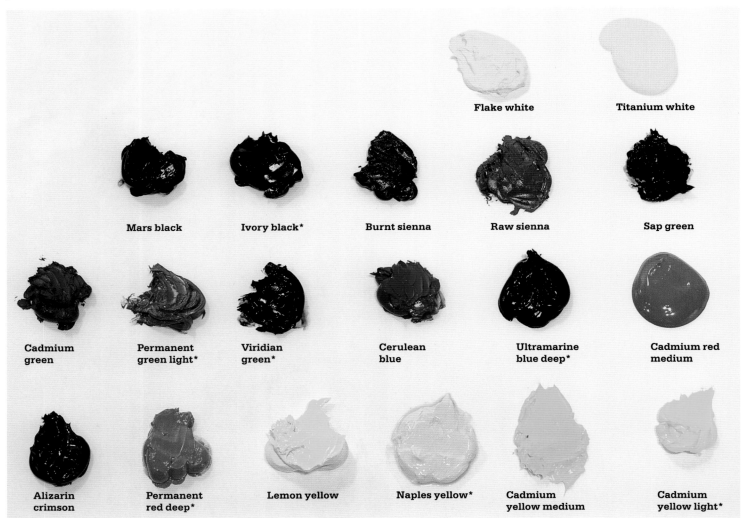

Flake white   Titanium white

Mars black   Ivory black*   Burnt sienna   Raw sienna   Sap green

Cadmium green   Permanent green light*   Viridian green*   Cerulean blue   Ultramarine blue deep*   Cadmium red medium

Alizarin crimson   Permanent red deep*   Lemon yellow   Naples yellow*   Cadmium yellow medium   Cadmium yellow light*

Place your painting mediums in containers near your palette. (Acrylic paint will also require a plastic plant spray.)

With your choice of either oil or acrylic paints (see p. 40), lay out all of your yellows in a row along the edge of the palette. Follow the same pattern with all of your oranges, reds, blues and greens. Your palette should be lined with your colours. Lay out small amounts of white for the yellow section, the blue section, the red section and the green section. The amount of paint you need will be determined by the size of your canvas. The amount you squeeze from the tube will pretty much turn out to be an estimate.

Start by observing the most visually obvious reflected colours in your still life and mix these colours first on your palette using your palette knife (see pp. 48–49). As you look at your still life, you will begin to see that, technically speaking, every colour is a form of reflected colour, not an object in isolation.

Then look closely for other colours that remain to be mixed. While each object has its own colour, each will affect, and be affected by, the colour of nearby objects. The first thing you discover is that the fruits and vegetables contain much more variety in colour than you might have seen at first glance. For example, that lemon may contain much more of the red from the apple directly next to it.

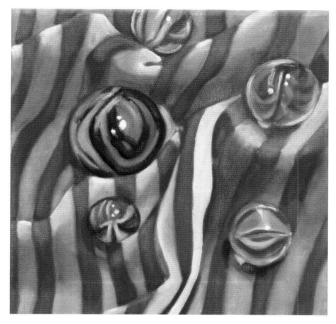

Kari Ann Gertz
Oil on canvas

This painting by student Kari Ann Gertz is a strong example of reflected colour and highlights. The red and white stripes provide counterpoints to the round shapes of the marbles.

Jasmin Kern
Oil on canvas

In this painting by student Jasmin Kern, marbles are revealed to be perfect examples of reflected light on spheres. She has used the Venetian technique of painting in layers with glazes, which is discussed in the next chapter.

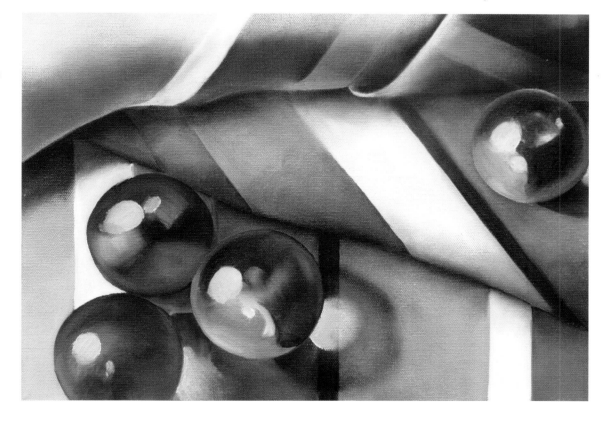

If you have trouble distinguishing a colour, create a peephole viewfinder. This is a variation on the viewfinder (see p. 72). To make a peephole viewfinder, take a sheet of white paper and using scissors or a notebook hole-punch, make a small ½-in. (1.27-cm) hole in the centre. Look through it while placing it close to the area in question, using it to isolate that colour area. Colour accuracy is important, but so is experimentation and interpretation.

Using about ten of the full-palette colours, mix three or more colours. You will have roughly thirty different colours. When the palette colours are thoroughly mixed, add a small amount of your oil painting medium to each patch of colour. For acrylic paint, you can use acrylic medium gloss (for a shiny surface) or acrylic medium matt (for a flat surface).

Mix all the paints to an equal consistency—this will ensure a uniform drying time in each layer. When painting wet on wet, I mix my paint to the consistency of smooth yogurt.

Just before you start applying the paint, place a drop of Liquin (oil paint only) in each mixed colour. Try not to add too much Liquin, which can cause the paint surface to become brittle after drying.

Use acrylic medium and acrylic retarder to slow down the drying time of your acrylic colours.

Peephole Viewfinder

The construction of a peephole viewfinder is quite simple. Fold a piece of paper in half and tear out as small a piece as you can. The peephole viewfinder is used to isolate colour when colours are so close in tone it is hard to recognise what colour is needed for the mixing. The viewfinder is also a way of understanding the relative nature of colour; to simply say something is red ignores the context in which it is found. In the following examples, the colours red, blue and yellow are being isolated with the peephole viewfinder. As you can see, the red surrounded by the white of the paper appears to be of a different shade than the overall red of the background. This is precisely what is happening. Try this yourself as an experiment. The blue colour, when isolated, is quite different than the blue object itself in the other examples. The same is true of the yellow, which appears to be quite dark surrounded by the white of the paper.

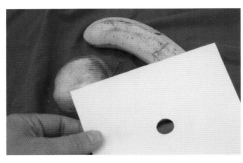

Peephole viewfinder isolating a red area.

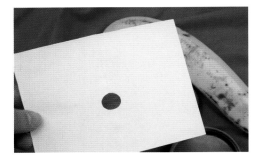

Peephole viewfinder isolating a blue colour.

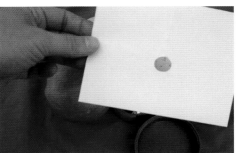

Peephole viewfinder isolating a yellow colour.

Using Black and White

As mentioned in Chapter 2 (p. 36), there is certainly a place for black and white when mixing colour, but try not to rely exclusively on the shortcut of using white to lighten and black to darken. This will lead to monochromatic colouring. Remember that by adding white to a colour, you lighten it—but you will also create a chalky colour that has less chroma (brilliance of colour) than before. Consider choosing a pale yellow that has a lot of white in it to lighten a colour. If the colour becomes too highly tinted (lightened), add some more of the original colour to make it less chalky.

Black will not only make things darker, it will make the colour duller; a very dark blue or brown is preferable in most cases. The best way to darken a colour without dulling it is to use a combination of chromatic greys as well as black and white, as you learned in Chapter 2 (pp. 50–53). You have the complete colour wheel to guide you, along with your chromatic charts.

When observing your subject, it is important to understand that white objects are just as prone to reflected colour and the effects of light as any other. The white you see in front of you does in fact have colour and tone when observed in the environment. It is a mistake to assume that the white straight from the paint tube will be enough to depict this. The same is true of black, in that there is always some colour bias. A shiny black object, for example, reflects all of the surrounding colours. Study the colours carefully as you lay out your paints.

José Bedia
…Lo que hace falta (Things I Could Use)
2000
Acrylic on canvas
72 x 132 in. (182.8 x 338.3 cm)
Courtesy of George Adams Gallery, New York

Bedia's *Things I Could Use* is a compelling image in which the monochromatic colours are rich and dramatic, combining chromatic neutrals and black and white to create the looming movement of the ship as it plows front and slightly off centre toward the viewer.

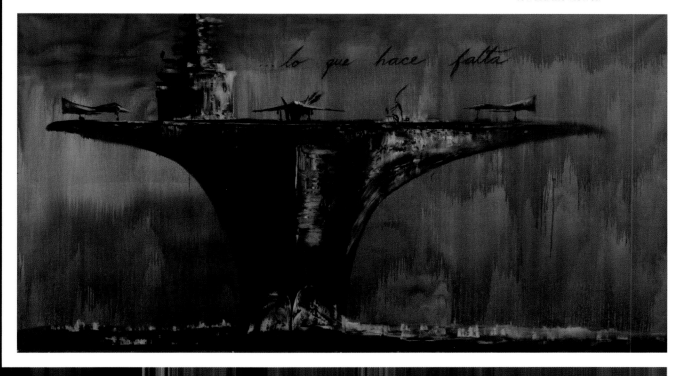

Choosing Brushes

In painting as in any other field, one should have a working knowledge of the tools required. Our most basic tool is the brush. There is a wide variety of brushes available that can be used for both oil and acrylic painting, and the differences between the two are subtle. It is best to keep one set of brushes solely for oil painting and one for acrylic, and to avoid mixing the two.

A basic brush consists of three main sections:

— **the handle**, which may be constructed out of wood or plastic;
— **the ferrule**, which is generally metal and holds the hairs in place;
— **the tip**, which consists of the brush hairs.

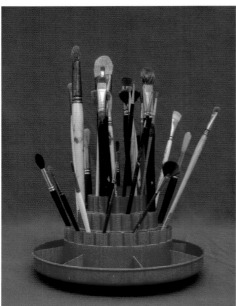

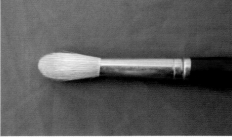

Round:
This brush has long hairs tapered to a point. The ferrule is round.

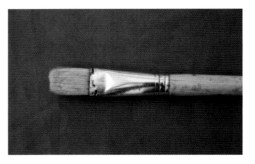

Flat:
This brush is flat with long hairs.

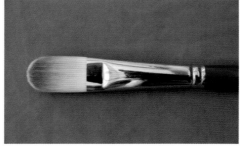

Filbert:
This brush is flat, oval-shaped and fairly thick.

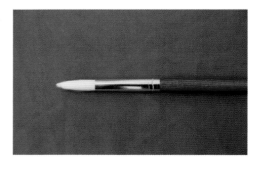

Bright:
This brush is flat with short hairs.

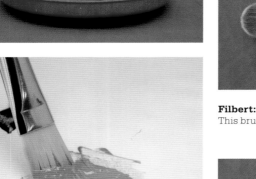

Dip the brush into the paint you have mixed on your palette, taking care to load up only the tip and no further than halfway down. You do not want to push paint into the ferrule of the brush. If you do, the paint will not come off easily and it will clog the hairs, which will eventually stiffen and ruin a brush.

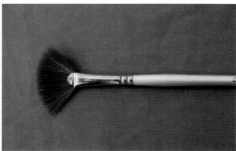

Fan:
This brush is fan-shaped. It can be flat or thick and fluffy and comes in a variety of hairs. It is generally used for shading.

To start I recommend using as large a brush as you can comfortably handle. Try to hold your brush at the far end with your arm extended, allowing as full a range of motion as possible, so that you stay loose. Holding a brush like a pencil will enable only the short range of motion of your wrist, and you will end up trying to "draw with the paint". Drawing with the paint is something that a beginning painter will often try to do, rather than pushing the paint around as a liquid on the canvas. To practice doing the latter will help you learn the properties of paint. This loose stance also makes it easier to see your painting and the still life as well.

The handle of the brush is tapered, with the fullest part at the top. The length of the handle will determine how far you can step away from your painting.

Traditionally the main brushes used by professional artists were made of sable or bristle hairs. Today, there is a great variety of hairs available on the market. Sable, a natural animal hair, is very soft and pliable, leaving a smooth surface finish. Bristle comes from hogs (though these brushes may now be made from nylon) and, being stiffer than sable, is a good choice for the technique of scumbling.

Many artists prefer to draw their preliminary sketch on the painting surface using a stiff-bristled brush, because the stiffness of bristle lends itself quite well to drawing with the paint, giving a line that is closer to one that can be drawn with a

pencil point than can be achieved with a soft brush. The advanced painter develops a preference for different brushes through trial and error. Most of my paintings are created with a sable brush, and I use the bristle variety only for scumbling or for drawing with paint.

Over the years, imitation sable and bristle brushes, which are much less costly, have become available and offer the beginning student a chance to learn without spending a lot of money. I have sampled some of the new synthetics and have found that they hold and spread the paint quite well. However, although it is possible to buy good-quality synthetic brushes, I would recommend that you also

acquire some top-of-the-range sable and bristle brushes. As a beginner, it is better to use as high-quality a tool as you can: You do not need to suffer from the self-doubt that arises from a poor-quality painting caused by using poor-quality tools.

I find that the filbert brush is one of the best all-around brushes for painting. The flat brush design, with its rounded edges, makes the placement of paint more manageable, and it does not leave a raised edge on either side of the brush mark. This brush can also be purchased in a "fatter" version.

When brushes are newly purchased, check for loose hairs and remove them before using.

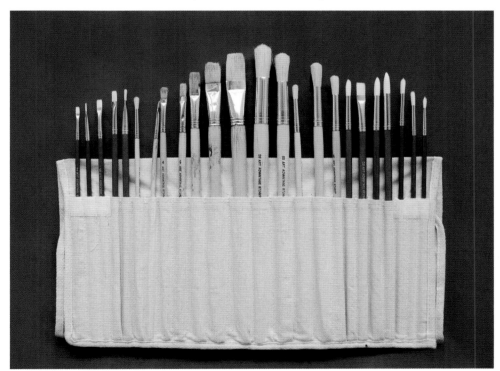

Brush apron

Painting Using the Wet on Wet Method

As we have noted, a painting using the wet on wet method is often completed in a day. However, it is not assumed that you, as a beginner, will finish your first painting in one sitting. In fact, even with wet on wet you can easily take a week to complete your painting by working on individual areas in turn. Drying time for paint is never completely predictable, but on the whole, the lighter colours tend to take more time to dry than the darker ones if you are not using a painting medium—and since painting mediums contain driers, they can change the equation.

In general, when painting wet on wet, you should plan which areas you can more or less complete in a given session, because if you resume painting a whole day later, the areas you have already painted will have begun to dry to the touch or become tacky, meaning that you cannot work wet on wet on those sections. As areas begin to dry more fully you can employ some scumbling of paint (see next chapter).

For this, your first painting, therefore, you should aim to complete either the whole painting in one session or work on specific individual areas each day.

Your preparatory sketch allowed you to observe the colour patterns, and the mixing of your palette was built upon this observation. Now, while painting, you will continue to observe the colour, and the way in which you handle the paint in the wet on wet method will allow you to continue refining and mixing those colours.

The decision of where on the painting surface actually to start is affected by an artist's years of experience and preference. For the beginner, I suggest you start painting in the areas in which you are able to recognise the colour combinations the best. This may be a dark area or a light area. (I still work in this fashion.)

Start by looking for and painting the patterns, just as you did in your preparatory sketch. Painting the value patterns will help you represent space and volume. However, do not worry about staying in the original lines of your sketch; you can always refine your painting later. (In wet on wet painting, applying colours right next to each other will always give you an opportunity to correct.) Here we are concentrating more upon representing colour.

It is helpful when mixing your colours to think of colour as transparent as opposed to solid in all of your colour observation. Try to imagine the colour process in photography or the coloured gels used to change the colour of lights in movie-making—adding another colour on top of the one you have already laid down will change the first colour. Use a very bright and colourful palette for the first layers of painting with wet on wet technique. This will build a strong foundation for adding colours while the paint is still wet, as these bright colours will still be visible through any more subdued colours on top. When you place wet paint onto wet paint, the trick is to apply just enough pressure to mix the two colours together without disturbing the layers too much. The wet on dry technique (discussed in the following chapter) allows much greater control over the transparencies of the colours than wet on wet.

Hieronymus Bosch
The Ship of Fools
1490–1500
Oil on wood
22 ⅞ x 12 ⅞ in. (58 x 32.5 cm)
Musée du Louvre, Paris

The Ship of Fools is an allegory for a group of listless individuals going everywhere and nowhere. Bosch's use of one-point perspective adds to the visual sense of stagnation and the obvious inattentive behavior of the shipmates.

Using Contrast

Greater contrast between the lights and darks in the earlier stages of the painting will make it easier to observe the actual shapes. As you continue with the painting, the contrast may be less intense as you begin to blend the edges of one colour onto another in your painting.

A very bright area in your painting will seem much lighter if you have darker tones next to it. Contrast in painting is relative from the darkest to the lightest colours. Reflected colour is the colour that bounces off one object to the next. By the time you finish painting the reflected colours, what remains is a small amount of the imagined colour of something. For instance, an object that is metallic and shiny is not grey but a combination of the other colourful objects casting reflections. A lemon will be yellow in the metal object but changed in colour by the metal surface itself. See box on Using Light: Chiaroscuro Shading (pp. 78–79) or p. 80 for a discussion of reflected colour in objects.

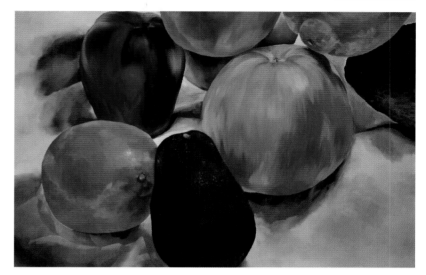

Elizabeth Baek
Oil on canvas

Student Elizabeth Baek's fruit and vegetable painting uses colour contrast to dramatic effect. Ordinarily, the warm colours tend to come forward visually, while the cold colours recede into the background. This phenomenon is dependent on the tone of the colours being used. Here, the dark cool green of the avocado more than holds its own thanks to its placement —the orange behind it creates a contrast and focal point. This is repeated with the other avocado in the background.

Remember, the chromatic charts show colours that you will be using for most of your paintings. Even objects that are simply primary colours are affected by lights and darks and will require light and dark tones.

As you lay down your colours, observe how each colour reacts with the one next to it, both in the still life and on your canvas. For example, if you look at an apple next to an orange in your still life, you will see that both fruits will be reflected onto the surface of the other. Therefore, some of the colours you will need to mix for the apple can also be used to paint the reflections in the orange. While the paint is still wet, you will easily be able to adjust these colours, but they will be variations on the first colour you mixed on your palette. You can do this by blending as you go, mixing the paints directly on your canvas, because you will always have a wet edge of paint onto which you can mix and add fresh paint. This soft blending has a more three-dimensional effect than a hard, "cut out" edge.

Wet on Wet Technique

Load up the brush with paint and lightly apply it to the painting support with just enough pressure to push it onto the surface. When applying your next colour, overlap the first and allow the edges to blend. For example, if you apply red and overlap it with yellow, the overlapped area becomes orange. As much as possible, hold the brush closer to the end. Your painting strokes will work best when you are attempting to follow the shape you are painting. The stroke will vary depending on these shapes. Sometimes it will be a short stroke, usually for a small object. The control that you have learned from drawing will serve you well. As with any technique, it will require practice to control the brush.

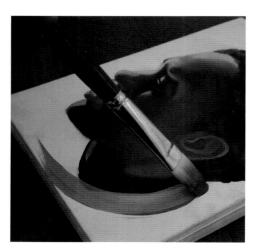

1 A pink-orange colour is being laid around the collar of the figure.

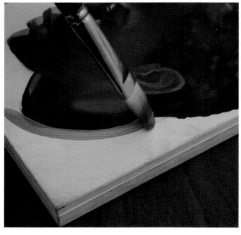

2 While this is still wet, a darker version of this colour is placed right next to the first one, slightly overlapping.

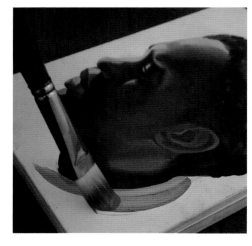

3 The two colours are blended while still wet.

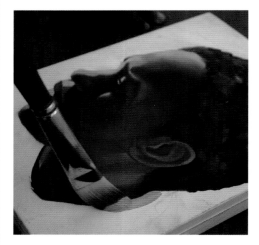

4 A cerulean blue colour is placed next to and slightly overlapping the orange and pink colour, placed earlier..

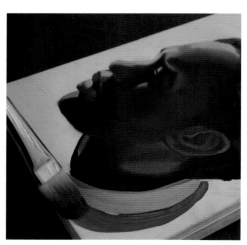

5 The blue colour is completed around the collar.

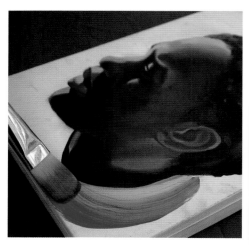

6 The colours are blended together, with firm but light pressure of the brush.

As you continue to apply the paints to the canvas and lose the white of the original canvas, the colours will appear different from when they were surrounded by white. This is because all colour is relative and dependent on the colours adjacent to it. For this reason, it is recommended that you paint a little all over the painting surface, rather than completely finishing one section, thereby moving toward completion with all the areas together. I call this "rendering as you go". The juxtaposition of colours optically creates new colours according to their placement. (An example would be to group dots of the colour blue and dots of the colour red in close proximity and observe how they optically become the colour purple.) To a lesser degree, large patches of adjacent colours will also have an optical effect on how each colour is perceived. This means that you need to take this into account when you are mixing your colours. Again, you can make adjustments by mixing the colours on the canvas. Remember to continue to observe your still life as you paint. New painters will often spend so much time concentrating on the application of paint that they forget to *look at what they are painting*. Try not to think about sections of the painting as individual units, but rather see the whole picture.

As you paint, you can use the technique of chiaroscuro shading (see pp. 78–79). This means that you look for the lightest light, the shadow, the core (or darkest part) of the shadow, the reflected light and the cast shadow, painting each in turn and looking at how the colours from each area affect each other. In chiaroscuro shading, the steps are as large or as small as the object and the shape being painted.

Brittany Gabey has nearly finished her painting (below) based on the still life arrangement of fruit and vegetables (below left) that we saw at the beginning of this chapter.

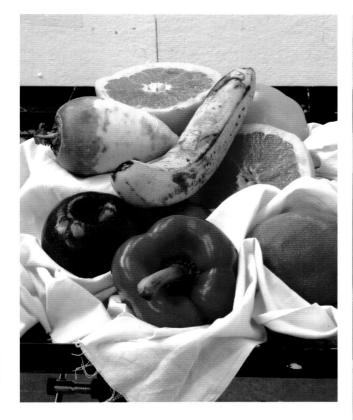

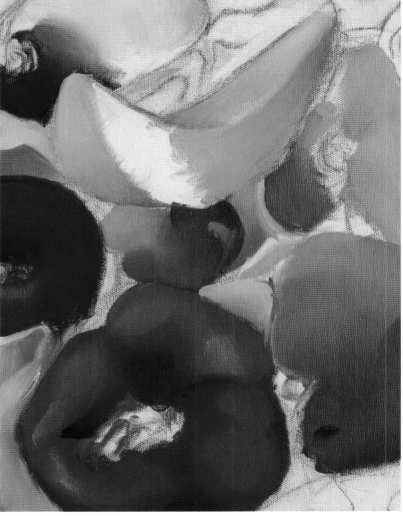

When to Stop

We have already discussed where to start a painting, so the next big question is how to finish it. How to know when it is finished is the most common question. It is not a question that is necessarily solved by time and experience. For these early paintings, there are some things you can look for in deciding whether you have completed your painting:

— Given that the style of this painting is representational, or "realistic", is your subject matter mostly recognizable? I say "mostly" since a decision to do some cropping may render some objects not clearly identifiable. As I often instruct my students, I am more interested in the sense of colour, volume and composition in a painting.
— Is the space in the painting understandable in terms of where objects sit from front to back and the negative space surrounding them?
— Do the reflected colours follow the shape of the objects onto which they are reflected?
— Do you have unpainted areas left on the painting surface?
— Are the colours blended carefully without streaks?
— Finally: Do you like it?

It is better to have your painting slightly unfinished than to overwork it. Every painting builds on the last one, so be patient.

There are also practical considerations in knowing when to stop. In wet on wet painting, you usually attempt to complete the whole painting or a section of a painting in one session, working with wet paint blending into wet paint as much as possible. (One note of warning: excessive mixing on both the palette and the canvas without careful observation can lead to muddy colours.) When using oils, once the paint becomes tacky to the touch on the painting surface, it is best to stop on that section.

At the end of each day you should clean up your palette and wash your brushes (see pp. 56–57).

Brittany Gabey
Oil on canvas

The finished fruit and vegetable painting created by student Brittany Gabey. She uses contrast in her colour choices to create tension and a colourful still life. The reflected colour from the fruits and vegetables is more than evident in the colour of the cast shadows that they sit on. Her interpretations are indicative of the kind of freedom you can have in thinking about the context of colour placement.

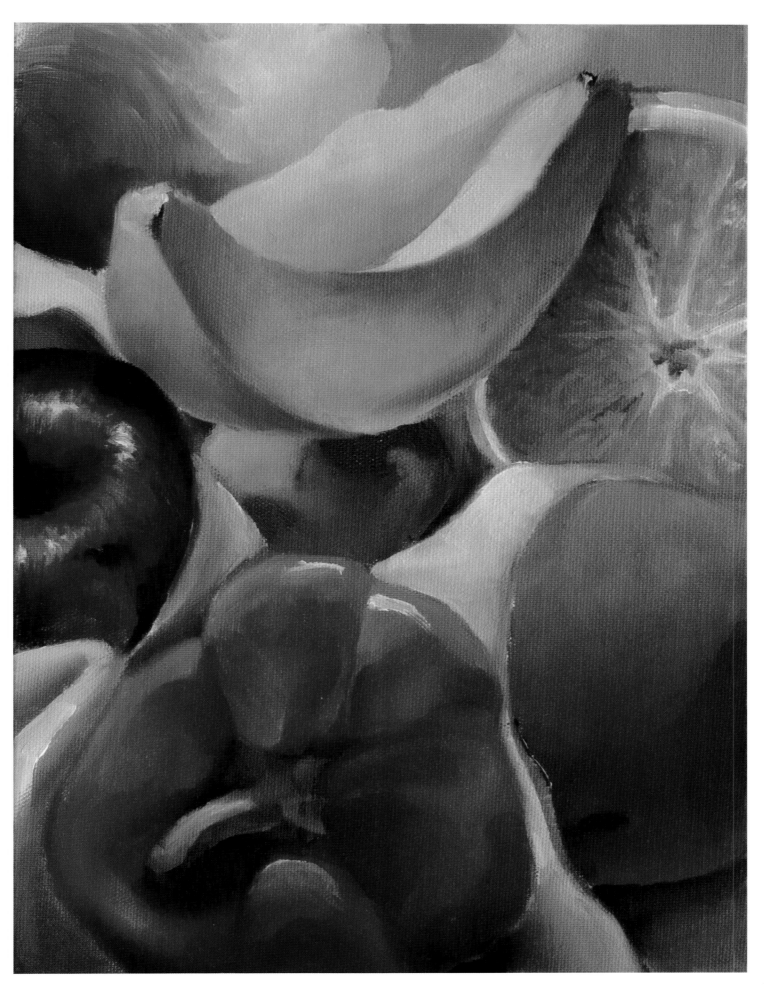

Chapter 4:
Second Painting:
Wet on Dry
and Scumbling

In this chapter, you will create your second painting using the technique of scumbling, which allows you to apply very light layers of paint over fairly dry older layers. A stiff bristle or old dried-out sable brush will give the best results for this technique. After mixing your colours, you take a very small amount of paint on the tip of the brush and spread it on the canvas, leaving trace amounts of colour over the previously painted areas. This is a form of glazing that can be done quickly, without the worry of disturbing older coats of paint. Wet on dry simply means you are adding wet paint to a section of your painting that is dry at least to the touch. Scumbling is a technique that will help you accomplish this.

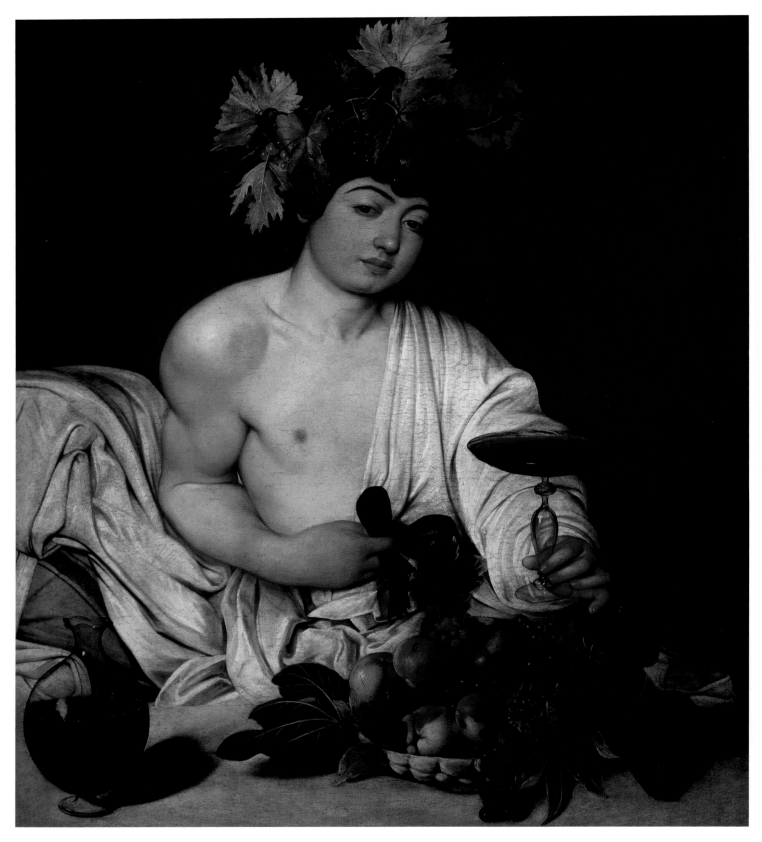

Michelangelo Merisi da Caravaggio
Bacchus
1595–96
Oil on canvas
37 x 33 in. (94 x 83.9 cm)
Uffizi Gallery, Florence

Caravaggio sets the figure of Bacchus (the Roman god of wine) within a still life environment of wine and fruit. This lush bounty combined with laurel leaves portrays a satisfied and relaxed figure.

Claudio Coello
Sagrada Forma
1685–90
Oil on canvas
c. 9 ft. 10 in. x 16 ft. 4 in. (3 x 5 m)
Sacristy, The Escorial

Sagrada Forma is a strong example of Renaissance linear perspective, where the viewer enters the painting from a rectangular entrance with two- and three-point perspective. The receding figures add to the illusion of deep space, and the light from the windows onto the figures in the foreground gives this scene a focal point.

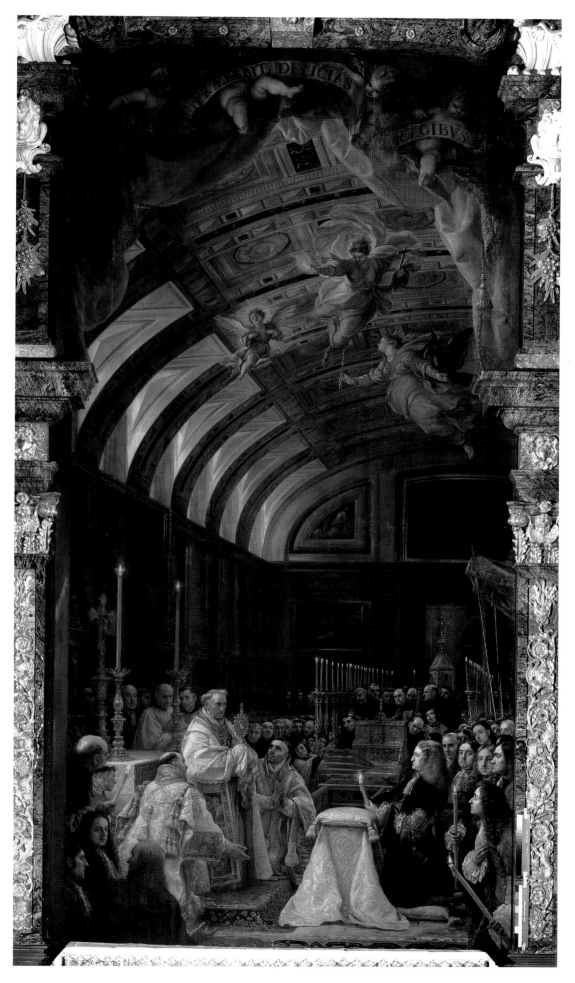

In this section you will:
— arrange your still life;
— set up your lighting;
— use a pastel (chalk) coloured pencil
  to draw your subject matter;
— prepare your palette while
  observing your still life and
  preliminary sketch, keeping your
  colour charts handy;
— start your painting using the wet
  on dry and wet on wet techniques;
— clean up and prepare for the next
  day's painting.

Our first painting, using fruits and vegetables, allowed you to experience the brilliant play of reflective surfaces and their overall effect on colour. At the same time, you were able to enjoy and discover colour in a relaxed manner. By contrast, the next painting will involve a more nuanced and somber image—earthenware pots that have non reflective surfaces, contrasted with coloured glass marbles. The earthenware pots will also allow you to accentuate chiaroscuro shading (see pp. 78–79). The dry, dull finish of an earthenware pot sharply brings into focus the play of shadows as they move across the form of the pots. Variety in the sizes and shapes of the pots will make it easier to compose your still life.

In our first painting, the primary technique was wet on wet painting. In this next painting, we will combine wet on wet and wet on dry, which is laying down fresh paint over and next to dried paint, working into the unfinished or blank areas, gradually matching the new colours with the old, and employing a technique known as scumbling. Many paintings are completed over a period of time, and so in most cases when work needs to be executed on a day-by-day basis, the working of new paint onto old becomes the habitual method.

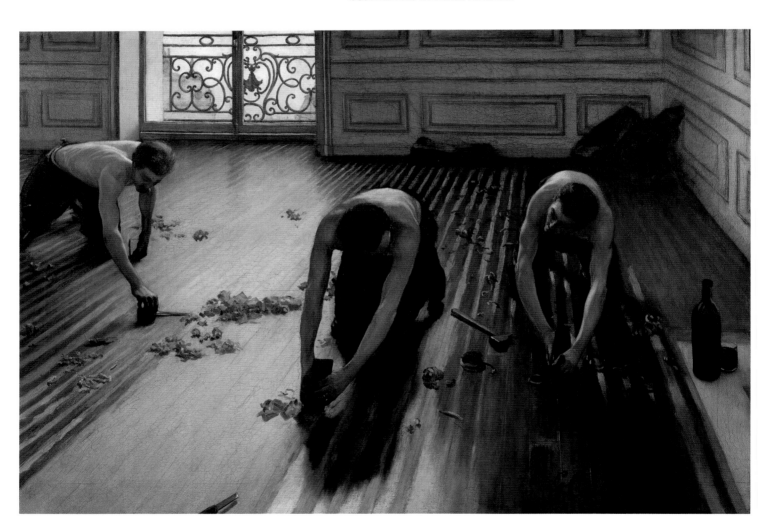

Gustave Caillebotte
The Floor Scrapers
1875
Oil on canvas
39 x 57 in. (100 x 145 cm)
Musée d'Orsay, Paris

The Floor Scrapers is an homage to physical labour painted with passion and observation. The figure in the upper left next to the light source is balanced by the two figures that are in shadow. The workers seem to be creating the composition by their labours within the composition.

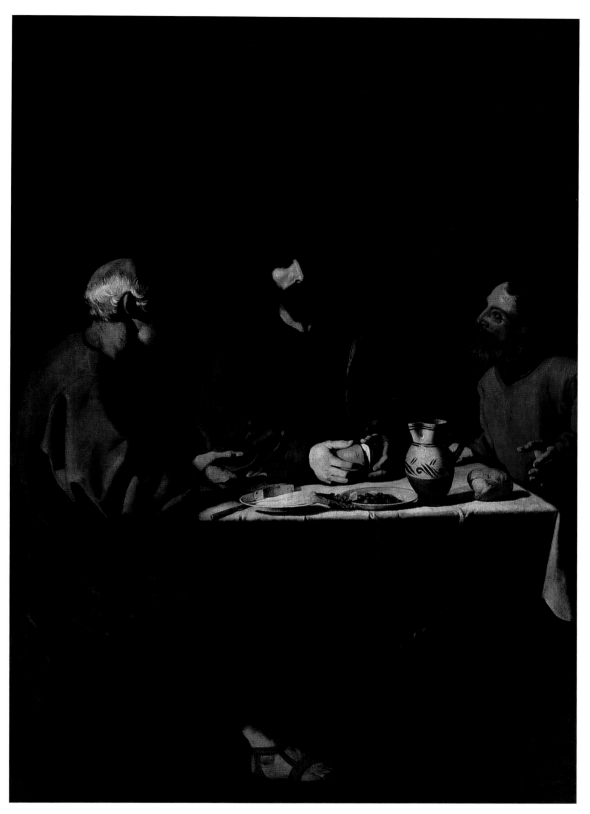

Francisco de Zurbaran
Supper at Emmaus
1639
Oil on canvas
7 ft. 5 ⅜ in. x 5 ft. ⅜ in.
(2.28 x 1.54 m)
Museo National de San Carlos,
Mexico City

Supper at Emmaus is an excellent example of the chiaroscuro technique of strong lights and darks. This is especially true in the rendering of the fabric and the three figures highlighted from a dark background.

Selecting and Arranging Your Still Life

Using your viewfinder (see p. 72), start arranging several pots in groups, some upright and some overturned. Some should face the viewer, while others should be turned slightly away, showing their elliptical shape. The elliptical shape of a circle in perspective is a very commonly found shape, which is sometimes very difficult both to see and to draw. I have found that the exercise of learning to draw this shape is something of a confidence builder. Arrange the pots using bright, direct lighting. Try to use a light source coming from one direction, such as a spotlight, to make it simple. If most of the ambient light in the room is toned down, the still life will become more dramatic, showing strong lights and darks and a variety of dramatic cast shadows that will allow you to use chiaroscuro shading to great effect. The way in which cast shadows are arranged can create wonderful patterns in the overall composition.

Because the fired-clay pots are dry and nonreflective, include some shiny colourful objects in your still life for reflections and colour contrast. Coloured glass, such as marbles, will serve this purpose well. Since glass is transparent, you can place it in front of and around some of the pots. Colour reflected onto the pots will help you distinguish the surface characteristics. Light will also diffuse through the glass and spread colour in the cast shadow.

Your painting, if you choose, can take on quite an abstract point of view; the more interesting compositions are often those that are more abstract in nature. Just as with the fruits and vegetables, you will find that, by zooming into a section of the still life, what you focus on may have an abstract appearance.

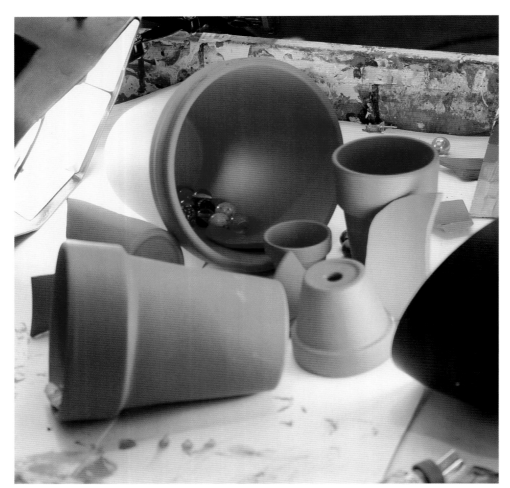

Photograph for still life
The composition for a still life painting begins at the moment the subject matter is chosen, the next step being the physical arrangement of the various objects. The lighting is the final touch prior to preparatory sketches, in order to decide which viewpoint works best. Take note of the proximity of the light source from the right-hand side in this example, and the dramatic shadows and tones that are produced as a result.

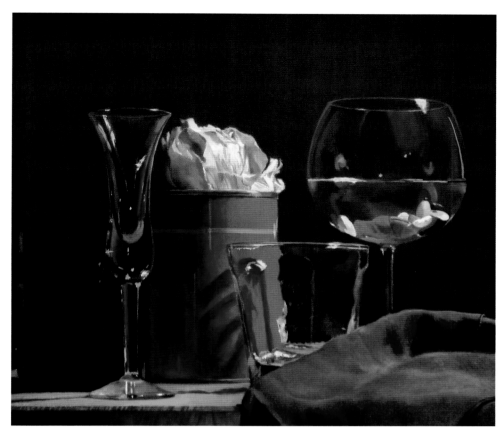

Robert Durham
Into the Wee Hours
2001
Oil on panel
13 x 15 in. (33 x 38 cm)
Courtesy of the artist and the
Cumberland Gallery, Nashville

Robert Durham's *Into the Wee
Hours* combines wet on wet
as well as wet on dry to create
a lush canvas of rich colours
reflecting from glass to metal
to wood. The strong light from
the right produces drama and
emphasis.

Making a Preparatory Sketch

Using your viewfinder and following the same procedure as you did in
your first painting, begin to draw the still life (see pp. 73–74). With this still
life, you will find the colours and values much more nuanced, but, as in the
first painting, look for value patterns on your pots and, especially, in the
cast shadows. You should also pay close attention to the negative space
shapes that are created between objects (see p. 76). This negative space
can help you to organise your composition.

In this painting you will have to search a little harder to see the variety
of patterns. This requires a different emphasis and sensibility, and the
viewfinder will come in handy. In the first painting, we started off with
bright colour; now you will be taking bright colour and toning it down.
Some of the bright colours you used in your painting of fruits and
vegetables will also appear within these pots, but now we are looking at
how best to illustrate the more subdued colours that we will find in the
tones of the pots.

Keep a light touch with the pastel pencil while maintaining flexibility
in your drawing. In this painting, the circular and elliptical shapes must
always stay round, never coming to a point no matter how much they
appear to do so. When drawing these shapes it will be helpful to remember
the fact that a perfect circle will fit into a perfect square and, by the same
token, an elliptical shape will fit into a rectangle. If you were to put a
straight line through the horizontal length of an elliptical shape you would
discover that the shape of the top and bottom halves was the same. The
two halves effectively reflect each other. Viewfinders and rulers help you
to see this phenomenon by showing you the contrast between their
straight lines and the curvilinear shape of the pots.

As in the first painting, if you are drawing the value patterns
throughout, the sketch will take on a paint-by-numbers appearance.
This effect does not last long and can serve as a type of blueprint for the
paint to follow, disappearing once the paint is applied.

Mixing Your Palette

This wet on dry painting assumes an ongoing daily painting schedule that will allow time for a larger-scale painting. You should try to plan your palette mixing with a sense of how much time you can devote in a given day.

Lay out your choice of either oil or acrylic paints on your palette (see p. 40) and begin to mix them using your palette knife (see pp. 48–49). For this painting, you will need to mix your paints with the rule of "fat over lean" in mind (see box opposite). As you begin to mix specific colours, remember to refer to your chromatic chart, as you will find there many of the colours that you will be using for this painting. Knowing that you have already learned to mix these colours will make you more confident as you continue. Pay special attention to the colours within the cast shadows and value patterns as you mix. You will see that the shadows are made up of several different colour patterns and values. The colour of the shadow bears some relationship to the colour of the object it represents. This is another example of reflected colour. Beginning students tend to see shadows as only dark tones, or more often black, rather than their actual colours. If an object is solid green there is a reasonable expectation that some green tones will appear in its cast shadows. The farther away the light source, the lighter the shape will be. Cast shadows have at least five separate tones and colours created by how near the light source is placed.

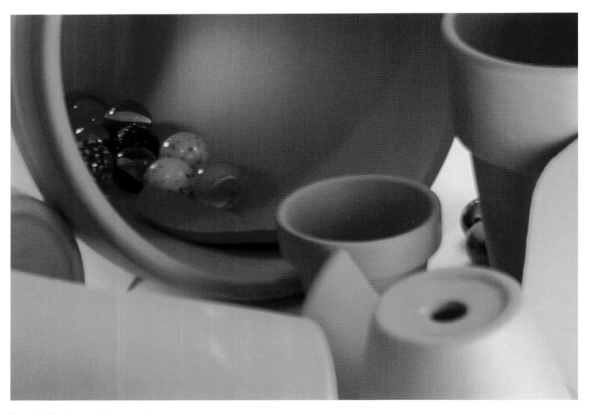

Detail of the larger photograph on p.100. The light is coming from two directions and you can see the difference in reflected light in the marbles and on the pots themselves.

Keep the First Layers Thin

One important rule to keep to when using oil paint is the principle of fat over lean (or thick over thin), particularly on occasions where the drying time is crucial, as it is in the wet on dry technique. "Fat" paint is paint that contains more oil (such as paint straight out of the tube), while "lean" paint has a lower oil content (such as paint mixed with turpentine). If your last layer of paint dries more quickly than your first layer, this will lead to problems such as cracking in the finished painting. Fat over lean means that earlier layers of paint should be leaner, so that the first coats dry faster. When using a painting medium that speeds up the drying time, a good rule is to add a drop or two less for each layer. Each subsequent layer should be thicker and fatter than the one before it.

Fat over lean becomes especially important when using glazing, a technique in which you lay down very transparent colours over a dry underpainting. You can layer many glazes to create particular effects, but each layer must be allowed to dry fully before the next application. In glazing, a very thin consistency of paint is used, as the painting is built up in layers. When using layers, the rule of thick over thin applies for acrylics as well as for oils: Owing to the quick drying time of acrylics, ignoring this principle may result in uneven areas across the painting surface.

Mix your colours as soon as you observe them. Each tone will be a slightly different shape based on how the light falls on the objects. Within the same shadow, you may observe several variations of colour; you will want to also include this observation. The shiny glass objects will have a shadow that is darker but with light tones caused by the light coming through. These pieces of glass will also reflect colour onto the pots, which will be subtle in tone but bright nonetheless.

Since this painting assumes a daily work habit, mixing new colour from day to day by its very nature results in variety. This tends to prevent you from making exactly the same colour combinations over and over again, when the reality is that there are many permutations of colour. For example, if you are mixing red and it seems to work in one part of a painting section, that is no guarantee that it should be used again in that same section. Try to observe how many varieties of red there are in that area first. Matching wet colours on dry is trickier than wet on wet, since wet colours pick up light very differently than dry colours. With the variety of colour within any still life, matching the colours exactly need not be a concern.

Applying the First Layer of Paint

All painting will, of course, start out wet on dry, as you are applying liquid to a dry painting surface. As you apply your paint, you will need to bear in mind the principle of fat over lean (see p.103), in which earlier layers of paint need to be leaner (contain less oil) than later ones. Unless you paint incredibly fast or work in miniature, you will find that, as is common with most painters, you will usually continue your painting at a later time.

On your first day of working on this painting of pots, you should apply some colour all over the painting surface, following the patterns you have set up in your sketch. Load up your brush and lay down colour with a left-to-right motion, making sure the paint is gently pushed onto the surface. It is worth mentioning that it is much more difficult to mix and place small amounts of colour on to the colour wheel and chromatic charts that you created than it will be to mix and place colours on this painting, where you do not have to worry about staying strictly within the lines. Here, your lines will be created where one colour pattern meets a different one. Do not draw with the brush, but make your strokes follow a pattern that blends the colours together.

You will find that a round brush with its tapered point will be most helpful in blending two colours together where their wet edges meet. The filbert brush with its flat, rounded shape will cover much more ground

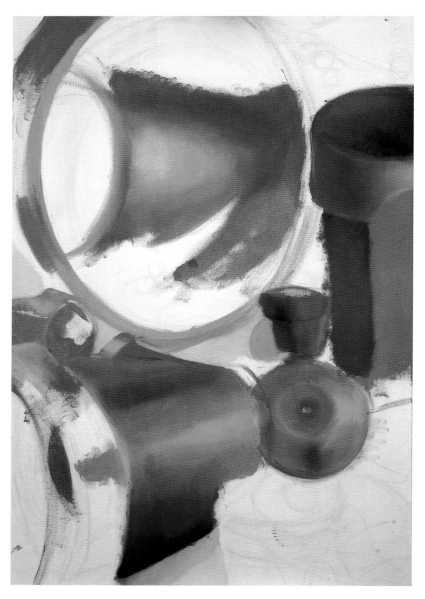

Student Brittany Gabey begins her pot painting by placing colour throughout the canvas. She carefully starts to delineate value patterns with colour. Even at the beginning stages, one senses the strong organization of space.

when painting larger areas, while the flats and brights will hold a larger load of paint to spread around. You should get used to all of your brushes so that you can begin to understand how each one behaves. If I had to choose only one brush, it would be a very large filbert, which I consider to be one of the most versatile of my collection. (See pp. 86–87 different brush types.)

The visual difference in this painting from your painting of fruits and vegetables, in terms of the value patterns, will be the more uniform shapes made by the pots themselves. In the fruit and vegetable painting, you could be more creative in the patterns and still have a believable painting. With the pots, however, the application and the blending of paint must continually follow the round shape to accentuate the smooth surface. You will discover while painting the pots that there will be no straight lines. When pots are leaning against each other there may be the illusion of a straight line. But, like the elliptical shape that the pots take on in perspective, in a frontal view they continue to be round, never coming to a point. Viewfinders are helpful in this regard because they have right angles against which to compare the curvilinear shapes of the pots.

When you have covered most of the surface of the canvas with paint, it is time to finish for the day. Clean up your brushes using the procedure discussed earlier (see pp. 56–57). The next day, you will continue to add more wet paint onto dry surface, but this time you will try to blend in the paint optically or physically with yesterday's rather than painting onto a blank canvas.

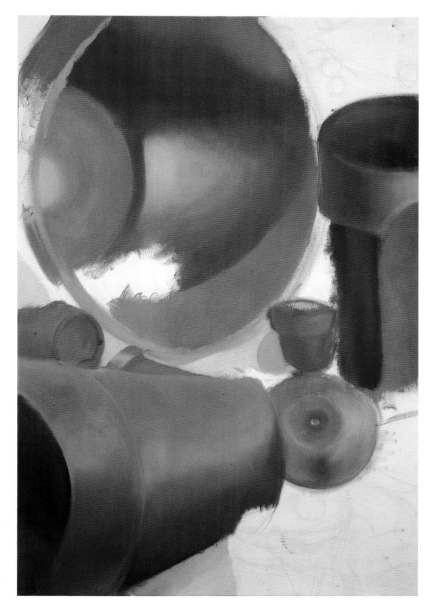

Brittany continues to build up the surface of her painting, starting to use scumbling on dried paint from earlier painting sessions. As more of the white of the canvas begins to disappear, the colours become richer and change in appearance. Colour is relative, and the white of the canvas makes any colour appear darker than it actually is.

Scumbling

Starting fresh the next day is an opportunity to create new colours that have a slightly different hue and tone. Do not worry if the new colours are not exactly the same as those mixed the previous day—it is likely that colour variety will exist within the still life anyway.

Scumbling comes into play when you are applying fresh paint and need to combine it with previous layers that have dried to the touch. Paint colour applied most recently will usually look richer and brighter because it is still wet; with scumbling, however, the trace amounts applied are visually closer in appearance to the older layer.

Scumbling relies on the texture, or tooth, of the painting surface. The tooth creates a drag on the brush so that you do not saturate the area you are glazing. The trace amounts of paint are still wet, but not as juicy as paint you would use for wet on wet. As you scumble across the surface of paint that has dried from the previous painting session, you are laying thin layers of paint with the idea that the original colour will still show through. With this technique, you can be as vigorous or as soft as you like with your brush because you will not be disturbing the dry layer. Naturally, you want to make sure that the paint is indeed more than dry to the touch. Traditionally, scumbling has been used to create a lighter tone over a darker colour, although it can also be used to add a darker tone. Unlike with other forms of glazing, you may use opaque or transparent colours. Remember, the rule of thick over thin still applies when scumbling.

In this section you will:
— **continue your painting using the scumbling technique;**
— **decide when to stop;**
— **clean up;**
— **varnish your painting.**

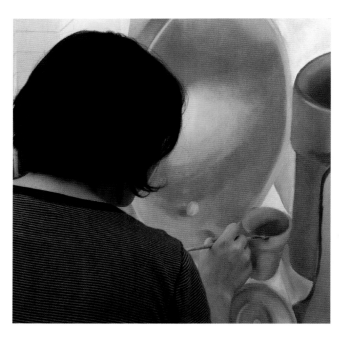

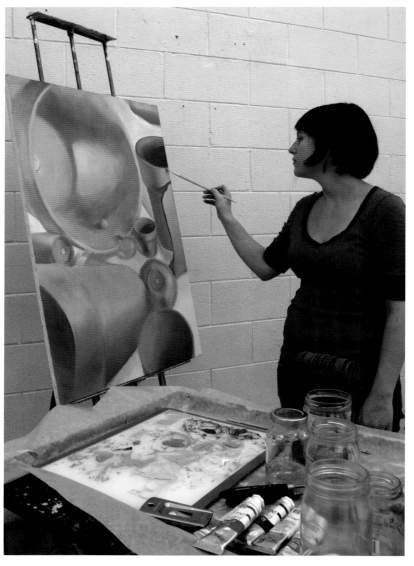

Above and **right**
Brittany Gabey scumbling her painting. She brushes fresh paint over the already dried colours, adding a slightly lighter tone to the rims of the pots.

Opposite
Brittany Gabey
Oil on canvas

The completed painting by Brittany shows exactly what the colours look like once the background colour and shadows are put in. With the white of the canvas completely eliminated, the warmth of the colours and the strength of the composition are revealed.

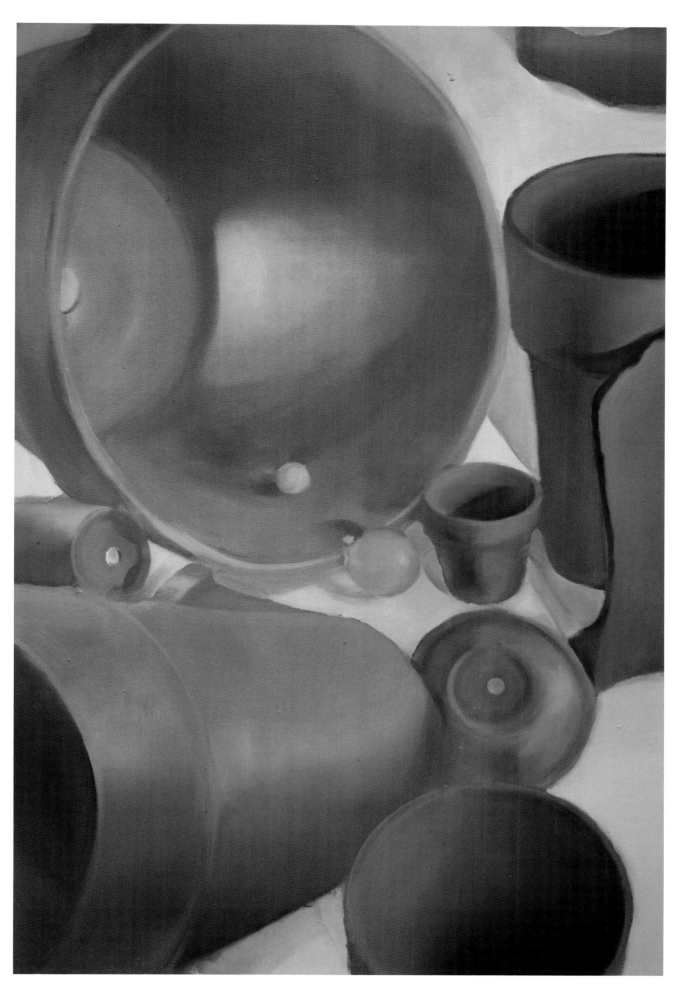

Scumbling Technique

Scumbling is a glazing technique, but rather than adding a juicy wet layer of paint, trace amounts of wet colour are spread over the dried paint film, leaving a thin layer of colour that changes the appearance of the older paint. Scumbling allows the artist to add some finishing touches to a paint surface that is already dry without having to repaint whole areas.

This is especially useful in creating highlights, though you can also use scumbling to add darker tones. Many artists prefer to add a bit of painting medium before they start to scumble an area; I tend to keep the paint more on the dry side and work it into and on top of the older paint. What you decide to do will be determined by how wet the old paint is—you do not want to disturb the original paint layers. After

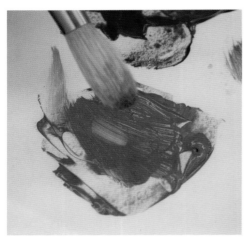

1 Using a stiff bristle or old dried-out sable brush, load up a very small amount of acrylic paint on to the tip.

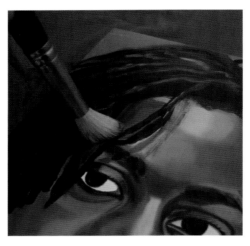

2 Place a thin coat of paint on the side of the head of the figure (or wherever it needs to be highlighted).

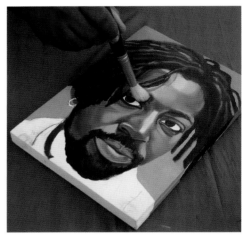

3 Apply just enough pressure to push the paint around the surface of the painting.

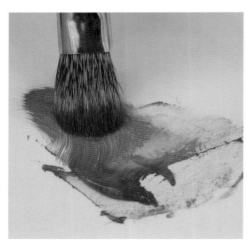

1 If using oil paint, the technique is very similar, but you don't need to worry so much about drying time. Pick up small amounts of paint with a stiff brush.

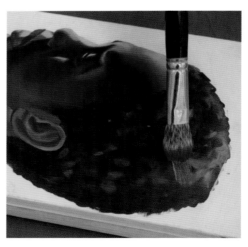

2 Apply pressure to move the colour across the surface of the painting.

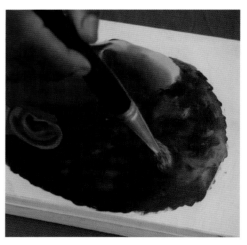

3 Blend in the colour.

scumbling, you may want to varnish it
to give all the layers a uniform sheen.
Note that the quicker drying time of
acrylic paint allows you to scumble
over a surface many more times
than oil paint over the course of a
day's painting.

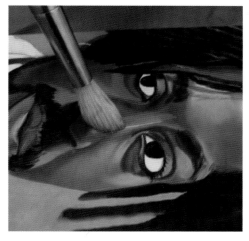

4 Add more pressure on the brush as you continue scumbling.

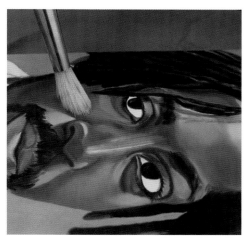

5 Pull the brush with colour along the surface of the painting.

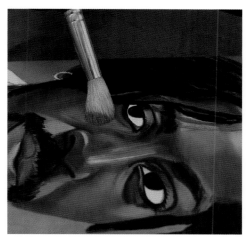

6 Blend the scumbled area in so that the colour is less harsh against the dried paint colour.

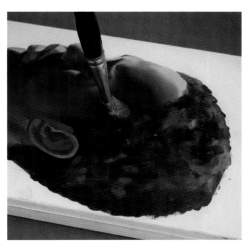

4 Add colour to a different area of the painting.

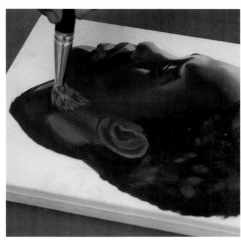

5 Blend in around the ear and neck.

Completing Your Painting

As you continue with your daily painting schedule, you will get the hang of how much paint you will need, how much you can paint over the course of the day and especially how to save old paint. If you have leftover paint that has been kept covered and in good shape (see p. 56), use that as well as mixing new paint for the next day's painting.

You can continue to add successive layers of paint over a period of time using this technique. Always follow the cleanup procedure at the end of each day. To know when to finish the painting, consider some of the questions raised at the end of the previous chapter as you completed your painting in the wet on wet method (see p. 92).

Varnishing

Many artists may choose to varnish their finished paintings after letting them dry for six months to a year. Varnishing is a form of glazing that helps liven up colours that have receded somewhat into the painting surface, something to which the darker colours can be especially prone. It also gives the painting surface a uniform overall shine. This is the key to the difference between a glaze and a varnish. A varnish can only sit on top of the surface and hold the paint underneath, and can be removed without harming the painting. A glaze becomes part of the permanent painting film and cannot be removed without disturbing the paint.

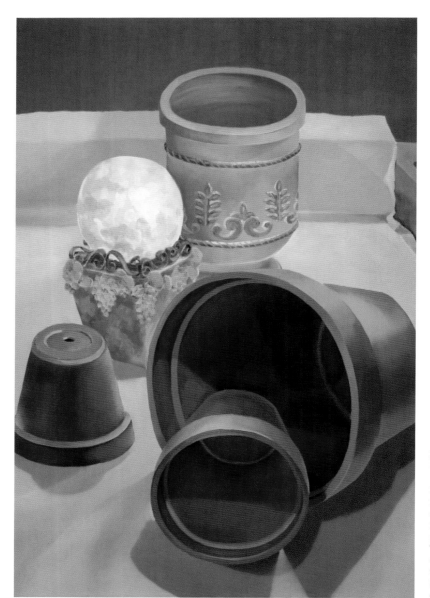

Elizabeth Baek
Oil on canvas

Elizabeth Baek's still life of pots illustrates the illusion of space in the insides of the pots in the foreground. This is instructive in its dramatic use of chiaroscuro: The cast shadows of the pots are examples of wet on wet painting to create this layered effect. Scumbling is later used to create volume.

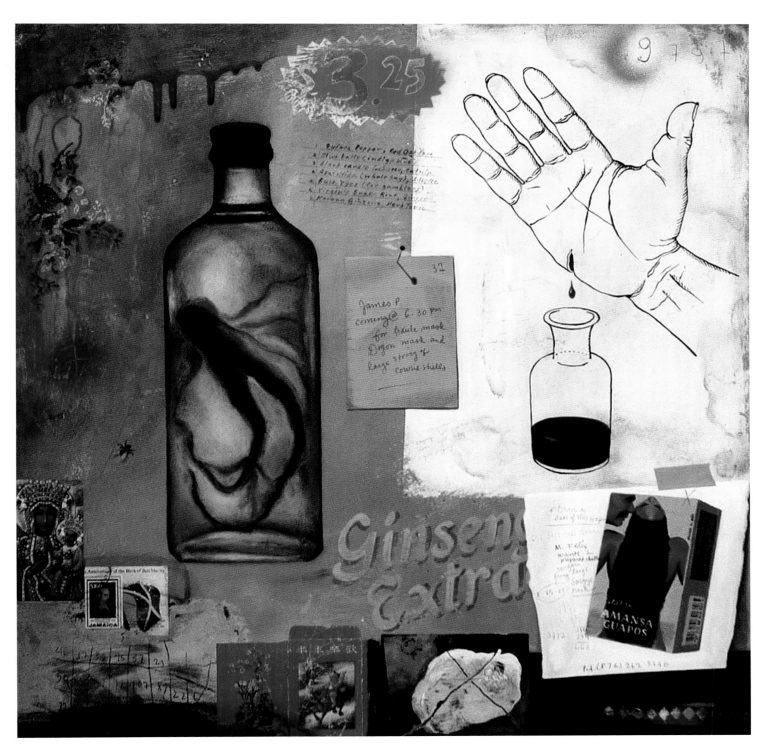

Renée Stout
Ginseng Extract
2005
Acrylic, oil, collage and mixed
media on wood
24 x 24 in. (61 x 61 cm)
Courtesy of the artist

The imagery in Renée Stout's *Ginseng Extract* is deeply influenced by African-American culture. This picture represents Africa and the belief in the intrinsic power of roots, herbs and charms—a belief also found in many other cultures. The motif is based on the design of a poster, with a nod to African-American dichotomies of self-image.

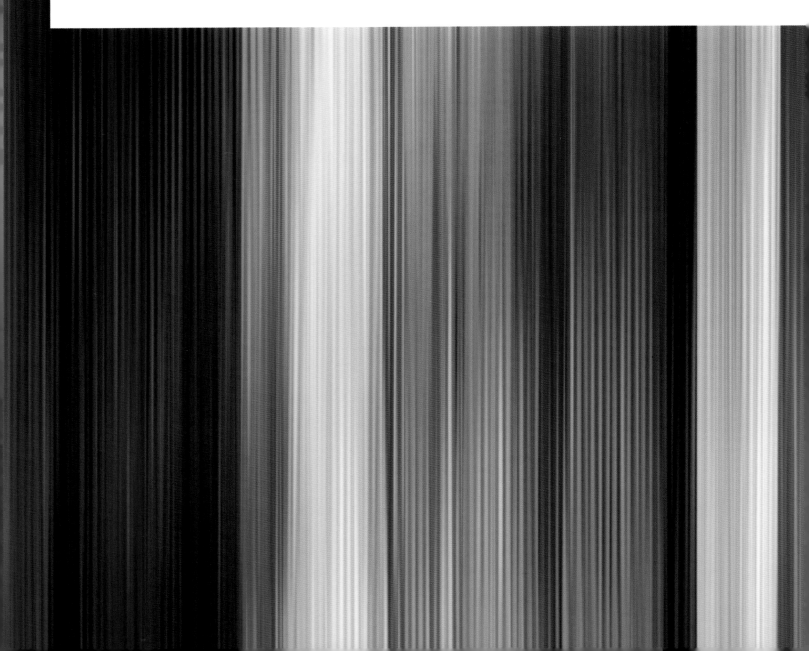

Chapter 5:
Third Painting:
Venetian Painting
Technique

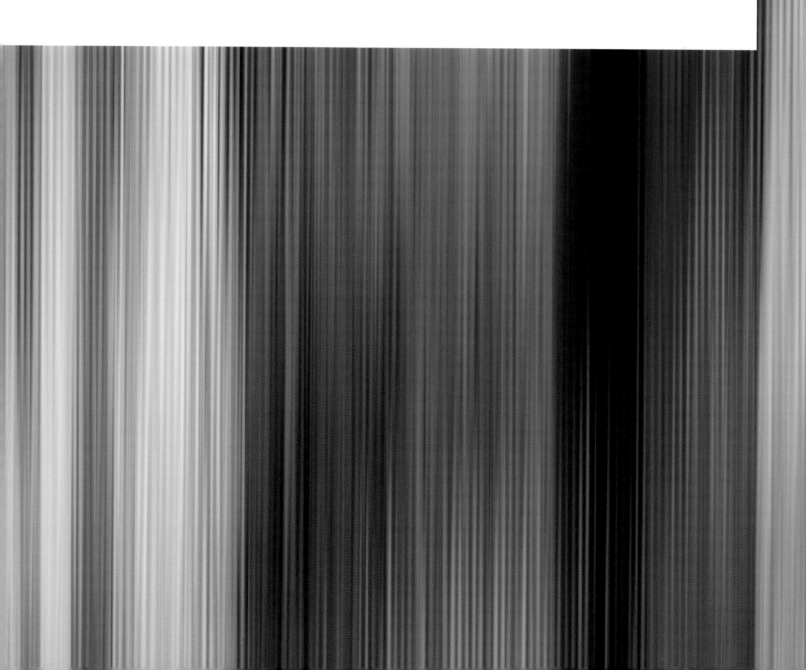

The Venetian style of painting, which takes its name from its origins in Venice, became most prominent in the Renaissance between the fourteenth and sixteenth centuries. It uses a method of glazing that involves a number of fixed steps and depends on the colour Venetian red both for toning the painting surface and the underpainting itself. First the painting surface is toned with a light covering of Venetian red, which serves as a middle tone. After making a preparatory sketch using a light pastel pencil, you will begin a monochromatic painting using Venetian red, flake white, and ivory black, and some transparent colours used in glazing.

The Venetian technique is closely associated with drawing. It relies solely on a monochromatic underpainting over which, when dry, transparent glazes are applied, allowing it to show through. Treat this underpainting as if it were a charcoal drawing going from dark to light using chiaroscuro shading—you want to put in as many dramatic lights and darks as possible. The colours that are then glazed over the top have the advantage of this value showing through each layer, just like colours over a black and white drawing. One way to achieve this is to apply Venetian red for darker tones and, with the paint still wet, use a clean cotton cloth to pull out some of the darker tones, thus exposing lighter areas. This is a reductive painting technique—it is important to allow the layers to dry before new colours are added in glazes. This style of painting is usually completed in several stages, with small amounts of colour applied at a time. Of the three painting techniques covered here, the Venetian is the only one that should be used on its own, owing to drying time.

This is a different route to achieving full-range colour, allowing you to build up your tones and colours gradually through multiple layers. In many ways, this style of painting is more akin to drawing, in that you are dealing with values first rather than colours.

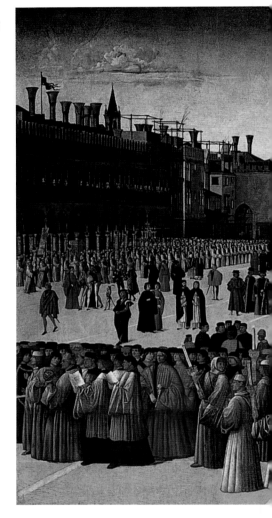

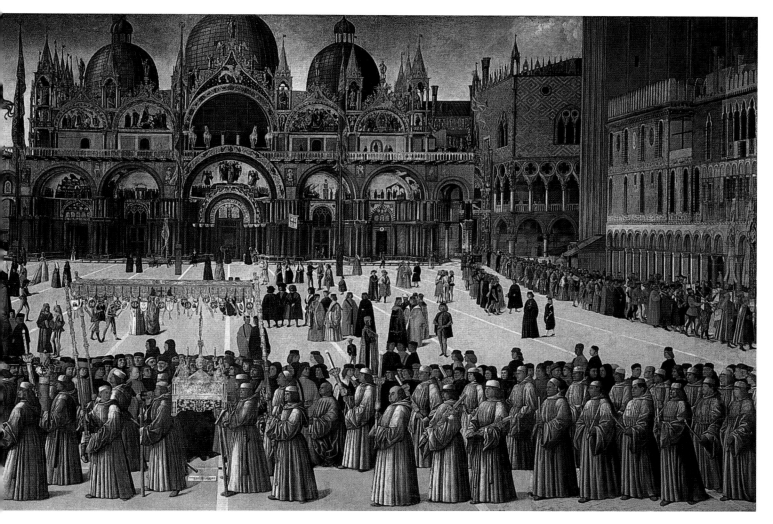

Gentile Bellini
Procession in the Piazza
San Marco
1496
Tempera on canvas
12 ft. x 24 ft. 5 ¼ in. (3.7 x 7.5 m)
Gallerie dell' Accademia, Venice

This painting gives both a flavour of the type of
Venetian paintings produced in the fifteenth
century and the beauty of Venice itself. Bellini paid
as much attention to portraying the buildings as
he did in painting the dignitaries themselves.

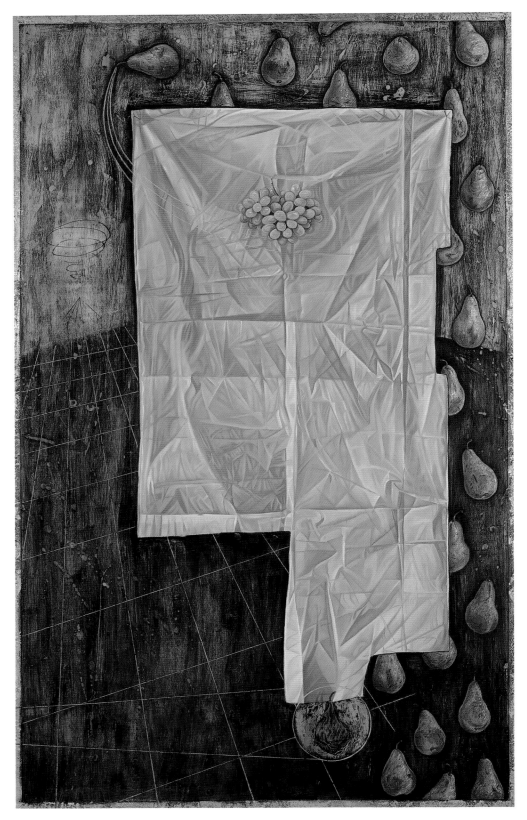

Kristy Deetz
Transmigrations
2000
Encaustic and oil paint on
wood panel
66 x 40 x 2 in.
(167.6 x 101.6 x 5 cm)
Courtesy of the artist

Kristy Deetz's *Transmigrations* combines the abstract with the real
using a variety of techniques. Deetz combines encaustic painting
(the mixing of heated beeswax and pigment) with oil paint on wood
to produce both an illusion and a tactile surface.

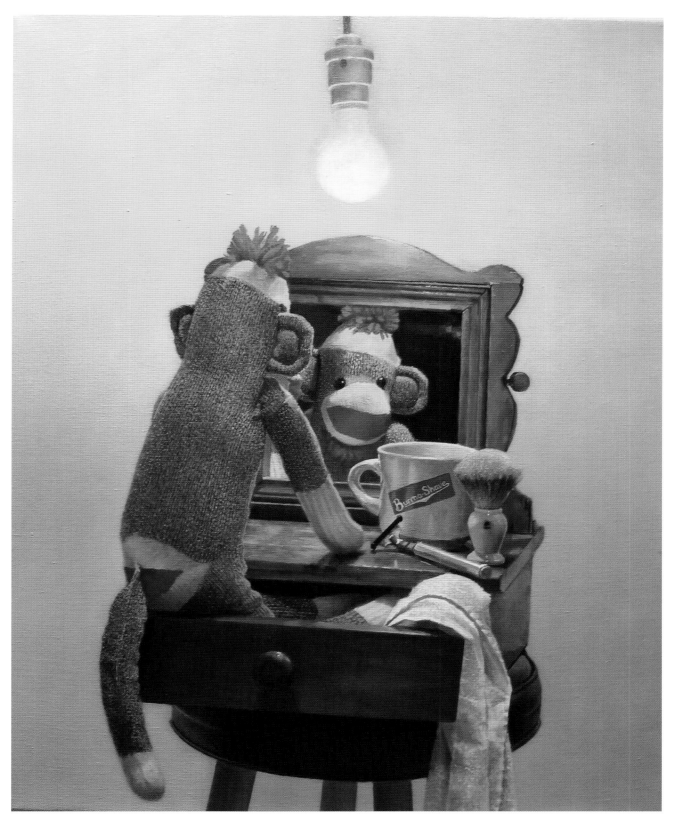

Robert Durham
The Well-groomed Male
2006
Oil on linen
32 x 24 in. (81 x 60.9 cm)
Courtesy of the artist and the
Cumberland Gallery, Nashville

The Well-groomed Male is part of a series of tongue-in-cheek paintings poking fun at conventional thinking. The vanity of a stuffed animal and the reference to older popular culture, in the nod to Burma-Shave, give a historical slant as well. Though Durham has not used Venetian red here, the luminosity of his glazing is certainly reminiscent of the Venetian technique.

In this chapter you will:
— **arrange your still life;**
— **prepare your painting surface with gesso;**
— **tone your painting surface with a wash of Venetian red oil paint thinned with turpentine and trace amounts of the glazing medium;**
— **use a chalk pastel pencil to draw your subject matter;**
— **use Venetian red and your glazing medium to paint in all the dark tones;**
— **use flake white to paint your highlights;**
— **add the final transparent layers using coloured paint.**

Selecting and Arranging Your Still Life

For this still life painting, I suggest you use a combination of marbles and drapery. Choose a variety of coloured marbles and find a piece of material with a striped pattern.

Using your viewfinder (see p. 72) arrange your still life so that the striped fabric is draped loosely, creating a pattern in its folds. Then add some glass marbles, looking at how the striped fabric is reflected in the glass. A very strong and focused light source will produce multiple combinations of reflections for this painting, to dramatic effect.

Preparing with Gesso and Toning the Ground

Start either by using preprepared stretcher bars (see pp. 64–65), or construct your frame before stretching the canvas (see pp. 68–69). Then prepare your painting surface with gesso in the normal way (see pp. 66–67).

The next stage in the Venetian painting method is to apply a toned ground, or surface. Traditionally, Venetian red oil paint has been used for this layer (but you can also use acrylic), thinned down with turpentine so that it has a loose and watery consistency. Apply this with a brush to the gessoed ground, which should be thoroughly dried beforehand, and then wipe off the excess with a cotton cloth.

Allow a day for the ground to dry and then sand to a smooth surface texture.

Photograph of the marble still life arrangement that is to be painted in stages throughout this chapter.

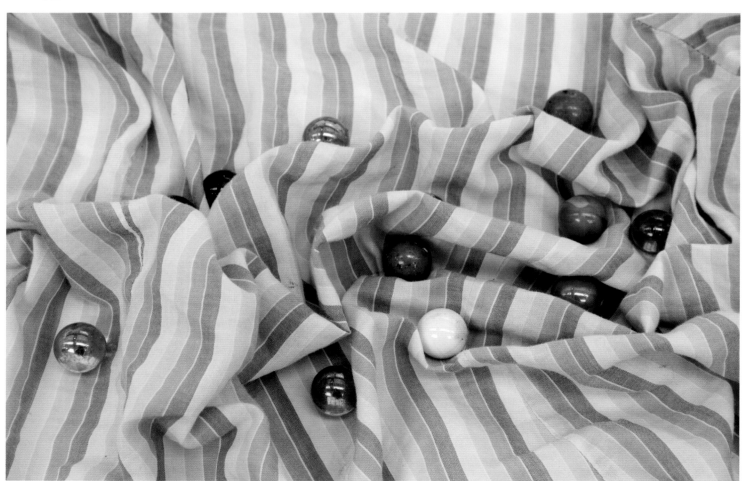

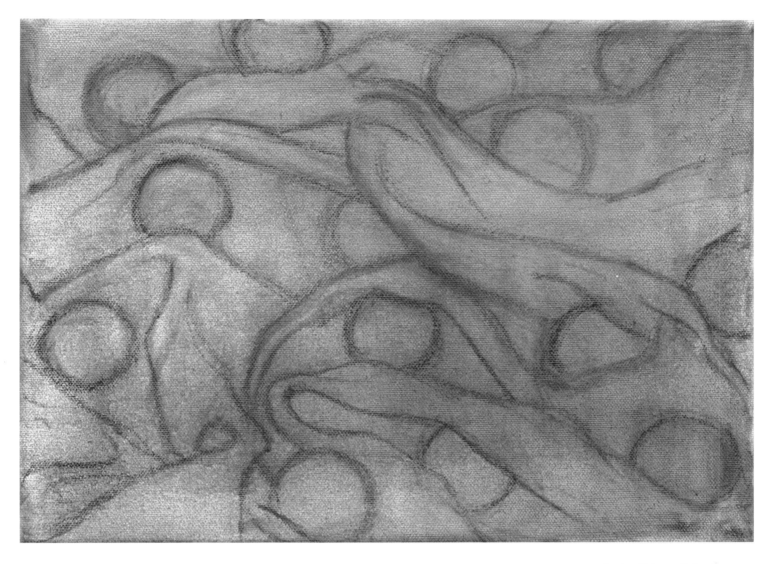

Making a Preparatory Sketch

Make your preparatory sketch on the dry surface using a light-coloured chalk pastel pencil (using a pastel rather than a graphite pencil means that the lines of your drawing will dissolve when you apply wet paint). As you begin your sketch, you need to pay close attention to the patterns of the material and how they may distort when seen through the marbles. You will see that the shadows the marbles make on the material contain reflections and may behave quite differently from the shadows of solid objects, in many instances appearing lighter than the marbles themselves. Try a number of arrangements: You can move the marbles around during the course of the painting to achieve the effect you want. Once you begin to understand how the marbles and the material behave visually, you can become more inventive. The marbles and material will appear slightly different from one day to another according to the light. Allowing your light source to be aimed directly at some of the marbles will create shadows that have a sheen as well as a darker tone.

Do not forget to use your viewfinder to help organise your composition, and remember that painting from observation in many ways involves as much creative license as actual observation.

Student Brittany Gabey has toned her canvas with a wash of Venetian red and has placed her preliminary sketch on top of this using a pastel pencil. This initial sketch was done with the aid of a viewfinder to help her edit the original arrangement (opposite).

First Layer: Monochromatic Underpainting: Creating Dark Values

Once the sketch is complete, you are ready to start the next process. For this first layer, you will be using only Venetian red paint with a premixed glazing medium (see box below), applied in thin, dark layers, to put in the dark values. Just as with a charcoal drawing, you are concerned with seeing the values and the shapes that they form in your still life.

Apply the Venetian red to all the dark tones you see in your still life. Your first layer of paint should be the thinnest (leanest)—about the consistency of creamy peanut butter, with only a drop or two of the medium used—and relatively quick-drying so that the top layers do not dry before the bottom ones and lead to cracking. Successive layers should gradually become thicker (fatter) as you add more medium. Avoid excessive amounts of medium, however, as the paint surface will become too smooth for the next layer to adhere properly; layers of paint attach much more securely to a surface with some tooth. There will be variations in the dark tones of your still life setup, with some being lighter than others, and you should keep this in mind so as to avoid a cutout feel. You can always wipe some of the paint off with a cotton rag to create lighter dark tones.

Continue this process as if you were doing a black-and-white drawing, placing all the different values of the dark tones. In this underpainting, you will be creating combinations of tone. Remember that small amounts of paint spread over an area accomplish much more than one thick layer. In many ways this is very similar to a drawing using chiaroscuro for your lights and darks (see pp. 78–79).

Clean up for the next day's painting (see pp. 56–57) and let the canvas dry overnight.

Glazing Medium

You can control the thickness or viscosity of your paint by the use of your painting or glazing medium: the more medium, the thicker the paint. For the Venetian style of glazing, I recommend you use the following proportions to make your formula. Once this has been mixed, it should be kept in a separate container with a top.

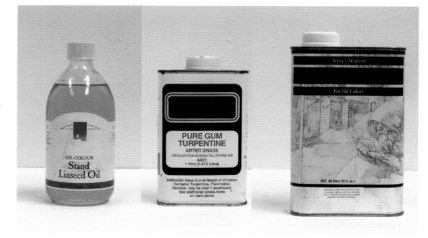

1 fl. oz. (30 ml) damar varnish
1 fl. oz. (30 ml) stand oil
5 fl. oz. (150 ml) pure gum turpentine
(or water if using acrylics)

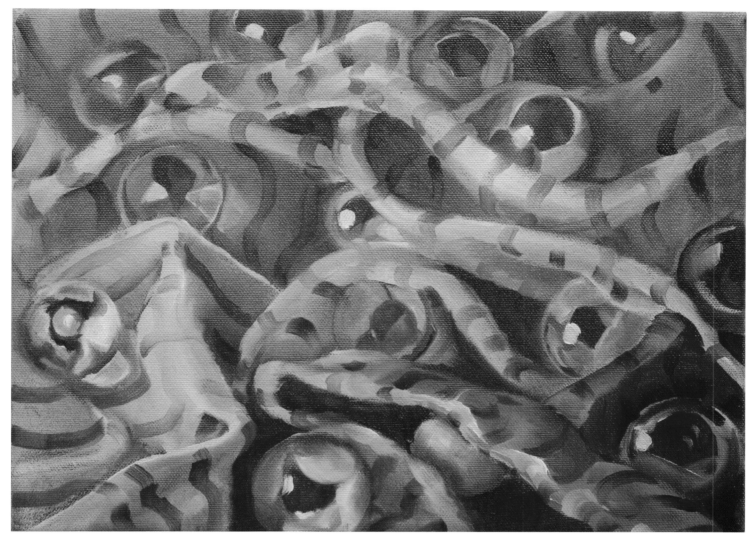

In this detail of the second layer, you will notice that the dark tones are beginning to be emphasised, and white tones have been highlighted.

Second Layer: Adding Highlights

Now that you have your dark tones and shadows, you will begin to paint the highlights in your still life. For this stage, use your flake white, noted for its transparency, which will still allow some of your original sketch to show through. (Use gloves because of the lead content of this particular paint.) Paint in all the light areas you see. As with the darker tones, there will be a variety of light tones for you to observe. If need be, you can go back and work on the darks and the lights at the same time by mixing the Venetian red with the flake white. If you are using the two colours in this way, keep the thickness (fatness) of the paints as equal as possible. You will need to wait until these areas are dry before starting to paint the next day. Clean up at the end of underpainting, which is now ready for the final stages.

Final Coloured Transparent Layers

The final stages of the painting are worked with a series of transparent glazes, using your full range of colours instead of just the Venetian red and flake white. This is where you need to be disciplined. You have been held back from using all that bright and juicy colour, but now you must try not to race to the finish; let the painting unfold slowly. The paint should be applied thinly and allowed to dry between each layer.

In this form of glazing, you will use particular paint colours that are noted for their transparency. A sense of luminosity is the goal for this painting. The colours that I recommended to you for your full-range colour palette (see p. 82) will also work with the Venetian technique. Some of the colours are more transparent than others. For those from the full-range colour palette that are transparent, see box below.

Mix your transparent colours on your palette with a palette knife (see pp. 48–49) and then add a drop of your glazing formula (see p. 120).

Once you have mixed your colours, start to apply them carefully to the lights and darks. You are not trying to cover up the underpainting; on the contrary, you want only to glaze colour over the top. As you add layers, you can wipe or dab paint away to create the effect that you want to achieve. As you gradually add colours, the image slowly evolves into richer tones. Because the darks and lights were applied first, the colour on top will be dependent on the shades underneath.

Transparent Colours from the Full-range Colour Palette

If there is no clue on the packaging as to whether your colours are transparent, you can check by drawing a series of dark lines in indelible ink on paper, taking a dab of your colour and spreading it over these lines with a palette knife. Those paints that go over the dark lines and cover them well are obviously not transparent. Although you may think that some of these colours (right) seem rather dark, their transparent nature is in their hide, or covering power, and is thus not immediately apparent.

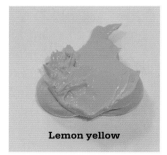
Lemon yellow

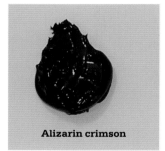
Alizarin crimson

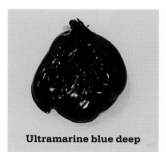
Ultramarine blue deep

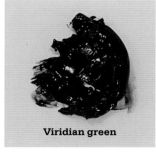
Viridian green

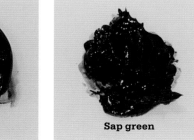
Sap green

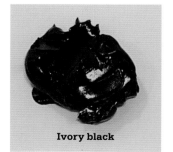
Ivory black

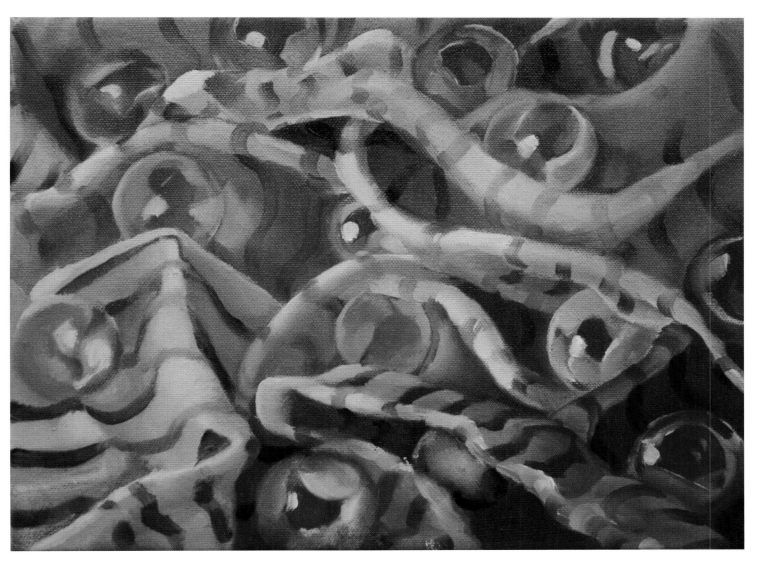

Having placed early layers using Venetian red and flake white, the green layers of colour are then added on top, allowing the darks and lights to come through. This is how transparency in layers is produced.

There are many ways to create and mix your colours. You can work over the entire painting in one day or concentrate on particular sections. Once the layer of glaze has dried, another layer of colour may be applied. Each layer should be a little thicker (fatter) than the previous one. Remember to clean up between each layer.

This form of glazing does not necessarily result in a reddish tone unless the subject matter happens to contain some reds. This underpainting is a middle tone between the darkest and lightest values within a painting. Just as a greyscale value chart is usually drawn or painted in nine to eleven steps, with black at the bottom and then equal stages of tone proceeding to the white of the paper, so this underpainting is the middle grey. As you add coloured layers on top, plan your mixing according to the effects you want to create: For example, if the material in your still life is green, placing yellow on top of the green in your painting will lighten it. You will still mix new colours on your palette, but you must allow for the mixing that occurs by way of glazing. As mentioned earlier, the shadows formed from the marbles are transparent in nature and, depending on the light source, will have highlights comparable to the lightest light of the marble itself. The lighter areas in your painting will have darker tones around them, as you have learned with chiaroscuro shading.

What makes this technique so interesting for the beginner is that you really have time for trial and error and you can observe the subtlety of the changing colour schemes. With this extra time, you can plan what areas to concentrate on as you move toward completion.

When you have finished (see p. 92 on tips on when to stop), clean up both your palette and your brushes.

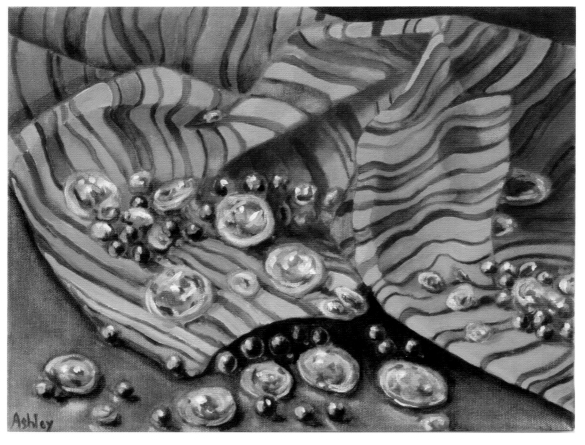

Ashley Long
Oil on canvas

Ashley Long's painting of glass beads on striped cloth is an example of reflective light on colourful material, also highlighting the transparency of the beads themselves.

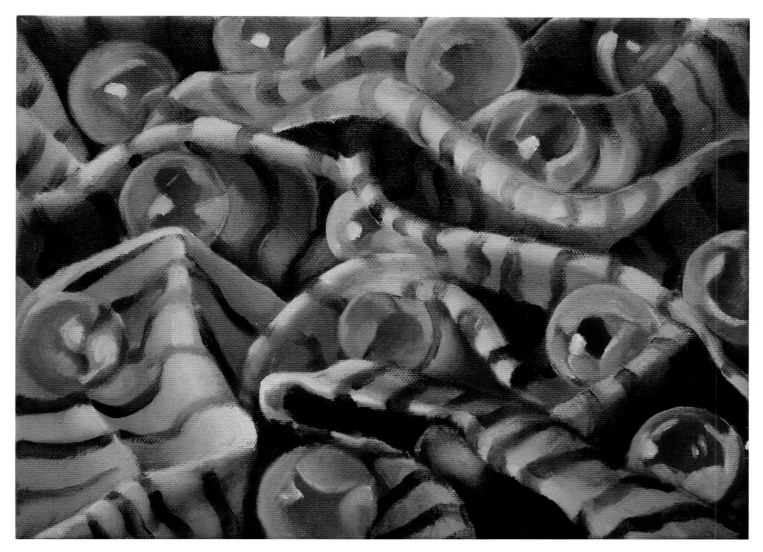

Brittany Gabey
Oil on canvas

In continuing the glazing, a fuller integration of the green tones of the still life becomes apparent. If you refer back to the preparatory sketch of the still life (p. 119), you can clearly see the evolution that has taken place.

This painting project is designed to take a week or more. The more layers you make, the more luminous the paint surface will be. The method is meant to be exacting yet still adventurous. In your very first painting, you were layering the colours while they were wet, deliberately disturbing the first layer. This style is just about the opposite of that. Yet, as with the other paintings, there is that moment of truth in terms of when the painting is finished. For this assessment, if you have kept your layers thin, you should be able to tell if your lights and darks are coming through properly. The highlights tend to be the last part of these early paintings. As you look over the surface of your painting, do some of your highlights look like pure white from the tube? If so, make sure it is dry and apply colour to it. Similarly, the darker tones should not look as though you have spread out black from the tube to represent your deeper dark areas. The pace of this painting gives you time to consider such questions without the spectre of not being able to change the painting later. Even though this technique is quite prescribed, what you have already learned from previous paintings will guide your hand, especially with colour usage.

Chapter 6:
Subject Matter and Content

In this chapter, we will look at portrait and landscape painting and end with a selection of contemporary abstract paintings. So far in this book, you will have spent time acquiring the skills of observational painting, but of course, this is not the only style open to you. While some painters do choose to paint in this style, trusting that their audience will see more in their paintings than simply a realistic drawing, others might paint in a more abstract manner.

As a beginner, it is important that you take the time to look at contemporary work to allow you to expand your awareness of other styles of painting. You also now need to question what you have learned and consider whether you want to break the rules. It is up to you to develop your own style, and you will only be successful in this if you feel a compelling reason to paint in a particular way. In my advanced painting courses, I leave the definition of what a painting is for my students to decide and judge the quality of the results.

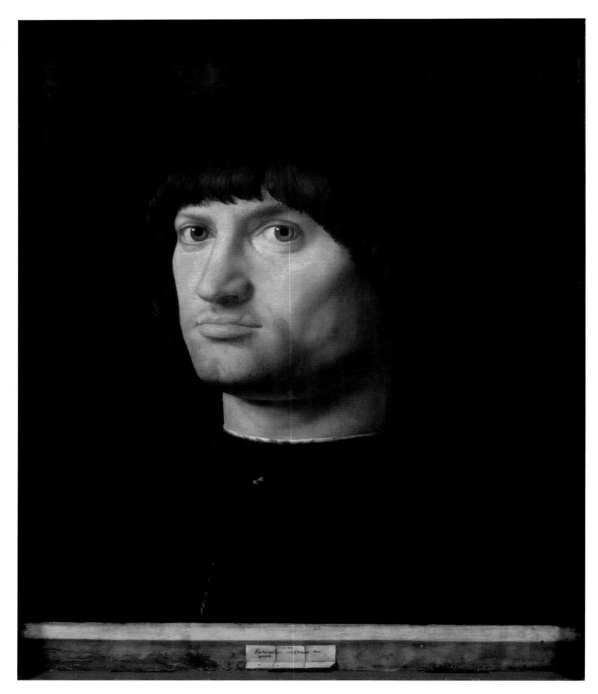

Antonello da Messina
Portrait of a Man
1475
Oil on panel
14 ¼ x 11 ¾ in. (36.2 x 30 cm)
Musée du Louvre, Paris

Messina's *Portrait of a Man* is treated in much the
same way that traditional portraits were conceived
during this period, with many contemporary
portraits adhering to this style. There is the strong
use of chiaroscuro shading where the figure
emerges from a darkened background. This
portrait is powerful and direct, with a gaze that
stares back at the viewer.

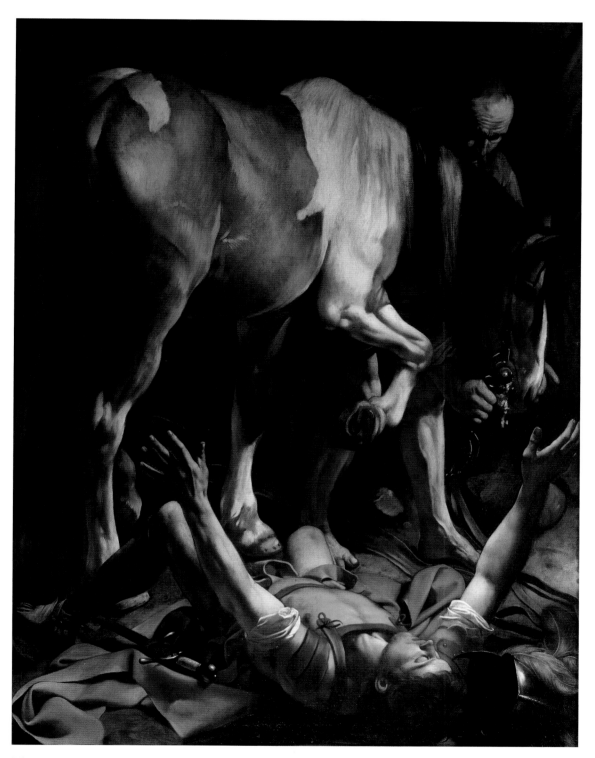

Michelangelo Merisi da Caravaggio
Conversion of St. Paul
c. 1601
Oil on canvas
90 ½ x 68 ⅞ in. (230 x 175 cm)
Santa Maria del Popolo, Rome

Caravaggio's *Conversion of St. Paul* presents a grand example of the chiaroscuro shading for which the artist was noted. Drawn in by the angular and curvilinear shapes, the viewer is enclosed within this setting. The greatness of Caravaggio is evident in his evocation of the cramped interior; its fearful and claustrophobic atmosphere is the key to its compositional power. As a new painter, you should take note of the way in which simple overlapping shapes are used to create this environment. The horse and the outlines of the figure overlap, creating a motif that visually unites both.

Now that you have gained an understanding of basic painting techniques, it is time to think about a new emphasis on subject matter and content. There is a subtle difference between subject matter and content: The subject matter you choose is a result of many decisions such as preference, ease and interest; the content of your subject matter is best described as the meaning you imbue in your painting. A concern for content transcends the act of painting well, because you can always end by doing something interesting with the results. As we progress, you will find that how and what you decide to paint is affected by your own personal point of view and interpretation of subject matter. The way in which viewers react to your work is often dependent on their own ideas of what art should be. You do not want to fall into the trap of painting to please or becoming too self-conscious. All subject matter is open to experimentation. Each style, medium and subject matter is as new as you make it.

Our first paintings were of a traditional subject matter and were based on realistic and figurative techniques. This style of painting from observation is useful for beginning students, who benefit from working from familiar, observable subject matter. A superficial description of the fruit and vegetable painting could simply be that it is beautiful. Yet I contend that an image can be visually enhanced by your intent: How you decide to compose such a painting can produce a personal point of view that invites the viewer to see something in a totally different manner. This is not to say that you can simply proclaim your intent and end up with a great painting, but that how and what you think and feel will come through the simplest of images if you put your passion into it.

Our next two paintings will be landscape and portraiture, and we will now try working with a combination of the painting techniques you have learned. Although we will continue to assume the possibility of an ongoing daily painting schedule, you may choose to work wet on wet, using a small canvas, so that you can make a single painting per day. Combining all the techniques is not only feasible but also common. It will take time to figure out what style best suits you.

Krista Franks
Oil on canvas

Student Krista Franks neatly sidesteps a realistic interpretation of fish in the sea by having the fish swimming in a black void (although some could argue that this is in fact realistic). The black enhances the rich and warm tones used on the fish.

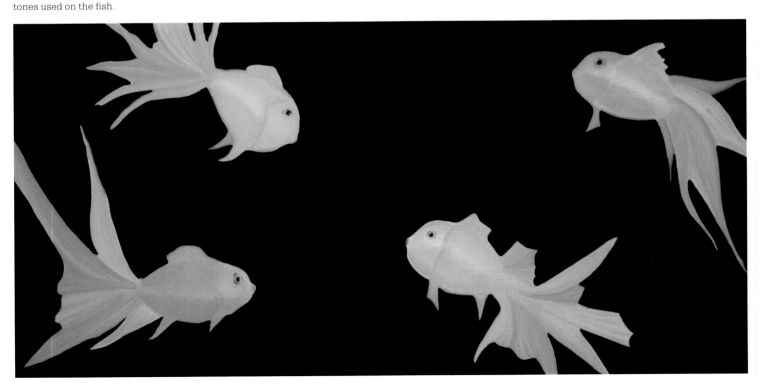

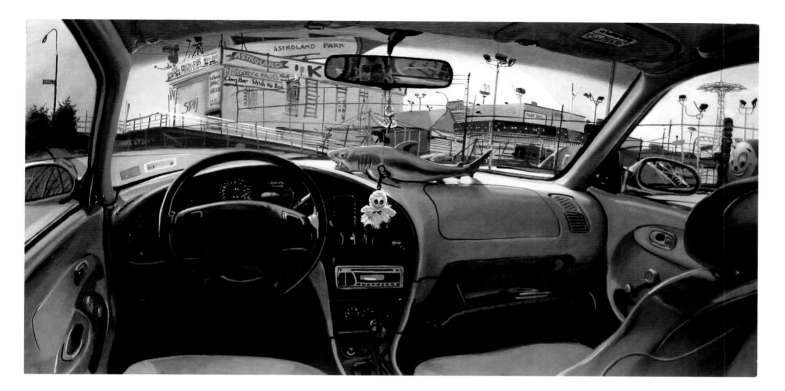

It is never too early to think philosophically of what you, as a new painter, hope to gain from this journey. Taste in art can be cyclical, predicated on changing mores and generational shifts in what is perceived to be of value. I personally find a sense of freedom in the notion that what was old is, or can be, new again. It is your stamp of individuality that creates newness. It is true, however, that you may not always find common ground with your audience, and I believe that it is more difficult to do so if your main aim is to please. Have the confidence to put your newfound skills *and* your passion into your work; then, when *you* are satisfied, present your work with the anticipation that others may appreciate and understand what you have done.

Thinking about these issues may seem unduly weighty and premature, but I would argue that it is an integral part of becoming a painter, along with honing your skills and gaining a knowledge of what has come before.

Andrew Lenaghan
Coney Self-portrait
2006
Oil on panel
12 x 24 in. (30.4 x 60.8 cm)
Courtesy of George Adams
Gallery, New York

Coney Self-portrait is an impressive example of on-site landscape painting from direct observation. Lenaghan literally puts the viewer in the driver's seat. It is a lively romp in what appears to be a fast-moving car, with a nod to "I see you looking" in the self-portrait in the rearview mirror. Most artists who work in this tradition take creative liberties to interpret what they see and feel, and pull you in. This painting—part still life, part portrait and part landscape—combines many of the simple painting elements that you have learned, taking them to a very sophisticated level.

In this section you will:
— **prepare your painting surface with gesso in advance;**
— **choose your painting site and bring along a sketchbook and/or a camera;**
— **using a viewfinder, make a few preliminary drawings in your sketchbook;**
— **prepare your palette while observing your subject matter;**
— **use a chalk pastel colour pencil to sketch out your subject matter, referring to your early sketches as well as working from observation;**
— **start your painting.**

Opposite
Ken McLeskey
The Narrows, S.W. Utah
2004
Oil on linen
40 x 58 in. (101.6 x 147 cm)
Courtesy of the artist

McLeskey's landscape presents the viewer with an open composition, which means his cropping decisions allude to a continuation of the imagery beyond the borders of the canvas. Strong visual drama is borne of careful use of scale and contrast. Additionally, the compositional ploys used here are the severe angles, close cropped spaces and organization of the negative space. Nature has its own sense of design, and it is the artist who decides how to order the given elements within a painting. The simple design principle of overlapping, with objects appearing smaller as they move farther from view, is in some ways thrown on its head here. In this image, we are invited to walk in and sit at the bottom of the space looking up. By not having a traditional horizon, the viewer can look up and down and feel the size of the area.

Landscape

Landscape painting is best done from life and, therefore, outdoors. Working from life helps you to understand colour, because you will see how light changes the colours in front of you over the course of the day. For the beginner, the landscape may seem quite overwhelming at first, but like all paintings, landscape is always your interpretation. The artist Claude Monet was known to leave friends and dash away to paint if a certain time of day produced the desired match of colour for him to complete a landscape painting.

If you do not want to paint outdoors, there are alternatives. You could arrange an indoor still life to include a mirror facing outside, which serves to bring the outdoors into the composition. You could start to paint outdoors and then continue indoors, using a photograph taken of your chosen view. However, you should be aware that a photograph does not always show all the possibilities that you would see in the landscape if you were actually sitting outside looking at it. The camera freeze-frames a moment via the lens and can flatten, darken and exaggerate different parts of the image without necessarily showing the subtlety of tonal changes. When shown a snapshot, most observers will look for specific information, not necessarily the intricate details about light and dark. The photograph gives the appearance of complete accuracy, and most viewers do not challenge this point. Nonetheless, working from a photograph in combination with painting from life is often done and can be quite useful. The challenge is to learn how best to use the photograph, rather than merely making a copy. As you study a photograph, use it to give you ideas about the natural world. After all, you make the decisions about what to include in your landscape.

Painting on site requires a travelling kit. You can purchase what is called a French easel, which is a combination of a seat and easel plus drawers for your art supplies. It folds into a suitcase for ease of travel. As an alternative to such expensive equipment, you could use a fish-and-tackle supply box to hold your paints and brushes, which also doubles as a surface against which to lean your painting. Your travel supplies are not very different to what you would use in the studio: paint mediums, canvas, brushes, palette and an umbrella to ward off the elements and protect your painting surface from dust and insects. Remember to bring your colour wheel and chromatic colour chart as well. Many artists choose to make small, very detailed painted studies and photographs to reproduce later on a larger scale in the studio. Whatever you decide, remember that paint tends to dry faster outside, so plan with that in mind.

What you learned from the first three paintings regarding colour relationships, patterns, reflections, lighting, chiaroscuro shading and composition will serve you well in this landscape painting. Painting the landscape or cityscape is a study in making sense out of vastness using a combination of inclusion and exclusion. We generally notice only what we need to as we move through our environments, giving attention only to what is relevant. For example, while climbing up stairs you might notice

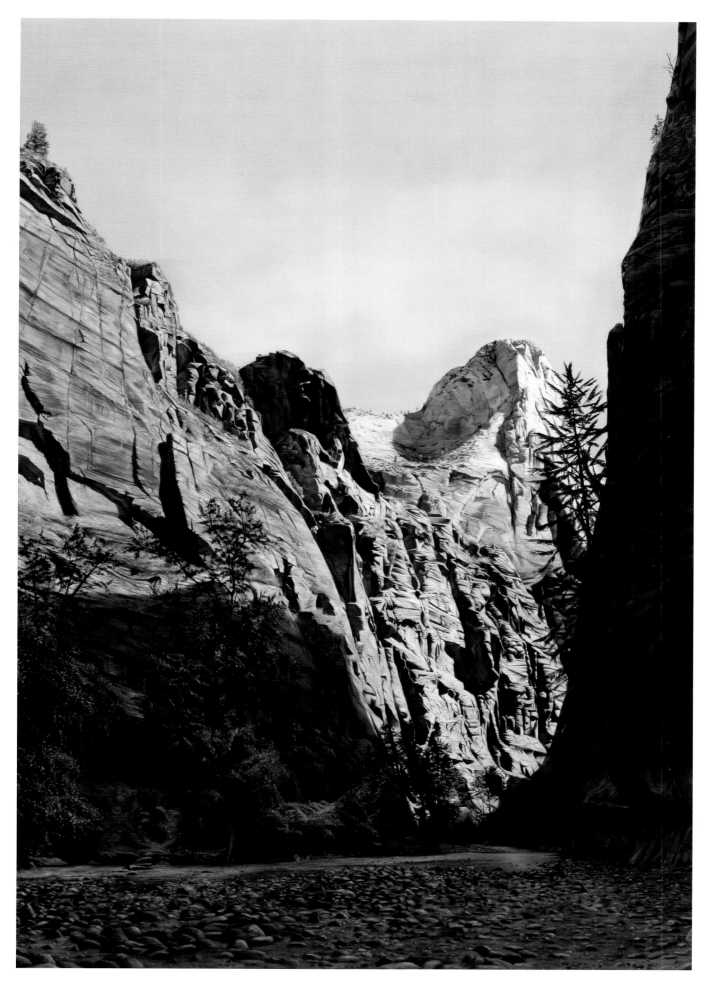

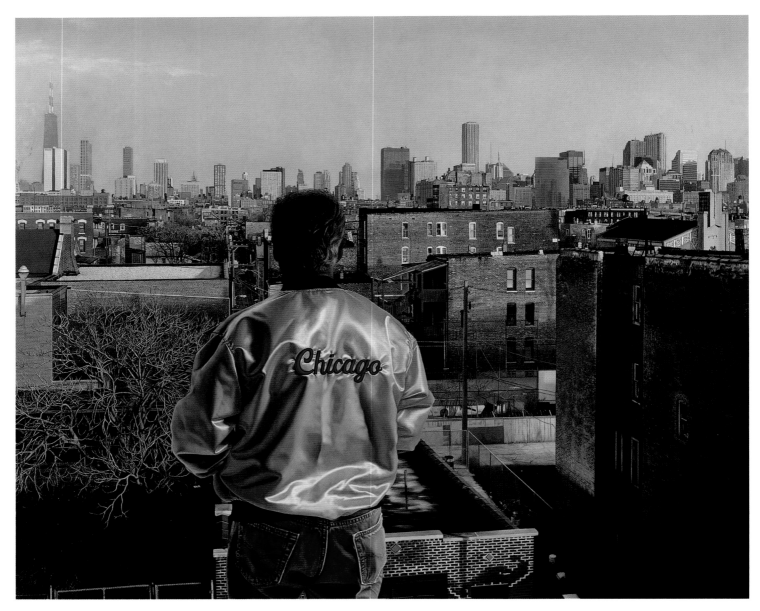

James Valerio
Chicago
2002
Oil on canvas
60 x 72 in. (152.4 x 182.8 cm)
Private collection.
Image courtesy of George
Adams Gallery, New York

James Valerio places his back to the viewer while he is engaged in a private moment. The image offers the viewer an invitation to look over his shoulder and share in his love of place, time and contemplation. The experience of viewing the painting then becomes a private moment for the viewer as well. The observer is witness to a naturally occurring cityscape, which is an individual interpretation of the artist's viewpoint.

the step, but not the colour or shade. Conversely, as you begin to observe with an eye to detail, you can get caught up in the naming and understanding of what is around you. You now see the step and the colour, but not in the most natural way.

My theory is that you should paint things as you see them, as opposed to trying to include every single detail. However, as you start to really observe colour, you will automatically see things in a new way. In the same way that you learned to understand how a piece of striped cloth behaves with a shiny object placed on top, you should learn to look at and understand the outside environment as well.

After choosing and preparing your painting surface with gesso, make your preparatory sketch in the same fashion as all of the previously mentioned painting methods. The major difference in painting outdoors, however, is the greater role that your viewfinder will play in organising your composition. You can make a variety of choices of what to include as you begin this sketch, and you would still look for the kinds of value patterns that appear in nature. For example, you may decide to rearrange the landscape in your sketch, ending up with a composite representation.

Most of all, choose for your interpretation what interests you in the landscape. As you did in the early paintings, use your pastel pencil to draw the many abstract shapes that are found in nature.

Try to notice the basic shapes and colours as they interact with each other. You will see that the landscape can have a rather abstract appearance as you continue to look in this way. Use your viewfinder to see the interaction of positive and negative space and start to create designs, which can be incorporated into your painting. In many ways, there will be more of a sense of inventiveness and risk-taking. Your point of view is the lens through which you visually interpret your world. No two artists will see the same place in the same way, so even though you may be influenced by others, you will put your individual stamp on the image.

Once you have completed your sketch, palette preparation is next. Your colour wheel and chromatic colour chart should be available for reference.

So far you have learned wet on wet, wet on dry with scumbling and Venetian glazing painting techniques. Depending on the size of your canvas and how much time you can give for a painting session, a variety of techniques could be used over the course of the painting. If you decide to work with Venetian glazing, it would be best to keep the canvas small.

— Place your painting mediums in containers near your palette (acrylic paint will also require a plastic plant spray).

— With your choice of either oil or acrylic paints (see p. 40), lay out all of your yellows in a row along the edge of the palette. Follow the same pattern with all of your oranges, reds, blues and greens. Lay out small amounts of white for the yellow section, the blue section, the red section and the green section. The amount of paint you need will be determined by the size of your canvas, so the amount you squeeze from the tube can only be an estimate. As you observe your landscape, start off by mixing at least ten colours. See Chapter 2 if you need to refresh your memory about mixing and mediums.

— Choose an area of your landscape to paint.

Make every effort to trust the first few strokes of colour that you make, because the painting is going to go through many changes before you decide that it is complete. Remember the principle of fat over lean (see p. 103). If you are working over several hours, the colour of the sky will change, and depicting this in your painting presents challenges. As a beginning painter, experiment and see what happens. Some artists choose to paint outdoors at times when the conditions are as close as possible to those when they started the painting. Some choose to average out the changes in colour that can be seen any time between sunrise and sunset. Clearly, if you are after a sunset, you will want to time your outings accordingly. If you are making a series of paintings, perhaps making small paintings daily will help you find the right pace.

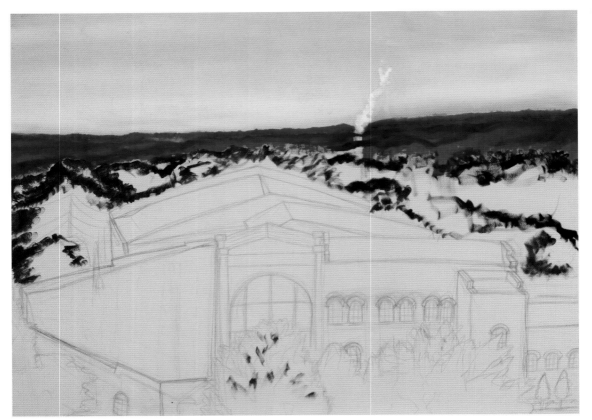

These two preliminary sketches are examples of open drawings. Open drawings allude to a continuation of the image beyond the boundaries of the canvas. This sense of the open drawing has to do with cropping in ways that suggest that the image continues beyond the borders of the painting surface. When you aim a camera, the rectangle of the viewfinder creates a window around a part of the view. Many times students will start in the middle of the canvas and have their subject matter floating. This would describe a somewhat closed composition.

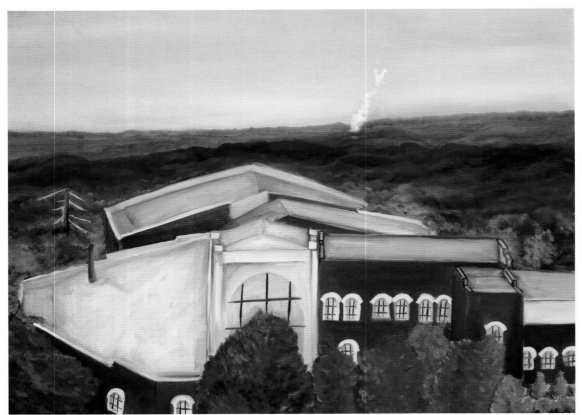

Above top
John Lutz landscape in progress.

Above
John Lutz completed landscape painting.

These two finished examples of student landscape paintings show the same view from different angles and viewpoints. (See also another example on p. 7 by Laurin Ramsey.) What is evident in each is the panoramic sense of space defined by atmospheric perspective. Atmospheric perspective is the effect that you see in a faraway landscape on a day when the clarity is affected by particles in the air, which cause a subtle change in the colours and, to some extent, the shapes in the view. These students chose to include some buildings and trees that were closer to them, thereby also giving the viewer a sense of scale, with the mountains in the background creating a sense of distance. Their use of softer and lighter colours for the background adds to the spatial qualities as well. Each student has depicted his or her own interpretation of a similar scene from varying focal points.

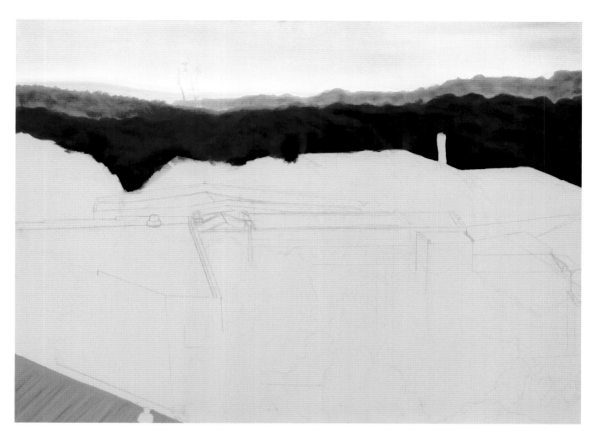

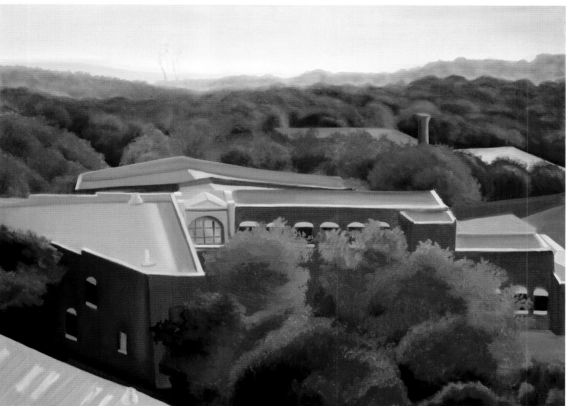

Top
Amanda Henke landscape painting in progress.

Above
Amanda Henke completed landscape painting.

Portraiture

In this section you will:
— prepare your painting surface with gesso in advance;
— choose yourself, or a friend, and bring along a sketchbook and/or a camera;
— use a mirror and/or a viewfinder to make a few preliminary drawings in your sketchbook;
— draw the face, carefully observing the bone structure and the shape of the value patterns;
— prepare your palette while observing your subject matter;
— use a chalk pastel colour pencil to sketch out your subject matter, referring to your early sketches as well as working from observation;
— start your painting.

Portraiture and the self-portrait have rich historical and cultural traditions that range from the straight depiction of likeness to other more psychological and allegorical premises. For the beginner, painting a person often seems to awaken built-in fears. I find that students are more affected by success or failure in making a self-portrait than in other forms of painting. The beginner's assumption, I believe, is that we ought to know what we or others look like. Instead, I encourage my students to think of portraiture as a series of impressions. What you feel about your subject and what he or she is willing to let you see are key components in making a likeness, which is much more personal than a quick snapshot. When I paint a portrait, it is usually someone I either know well or want to know well. I engage in conversation and encourage the sitter to look at the work in progress, so that he or she starts to feel involved. In my studio I often ask the sitter whether the image feels familiar—not "Does it look like you"?

The best way for the beginner to learn portraiture is to start with the self-portrait. Who else, after all, will be so committed for the long haul? A mirror and a series of photographs from multiple viewpoints is more than enough to begin. As an aid to really seeing colour in skin tones it is recommended that you choose black-and-white photographs so that your colour choices will come from what you see in the mirror rather than being an attempt to imitate photographic colour. New painters are often quite shy about the revelation a self-portrait may convey. Remember, this painting is also an interpretation and you should allow yourself to take creative liberties. I have made many self-portraits over the years and no two look alike, but they all reveal aspects of who I am and how I was feeling at that point in time.

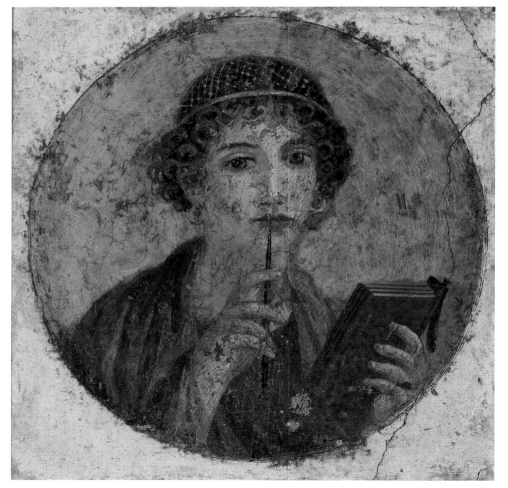

Anonymous
Portrait of a Young Woman Wearing a Hairnet
1st century AD
Wall painting
11 ⅜ in. (28 cm) diameter
Museo Nazionale Archeologico, Naples

This example of a fresco portrait of a young woman has a rather contemporary gaze that is somewhat inward in nature. That it was discovered in the city of Pompeii covered in volcanic ash makes it even more poignant and timeless.

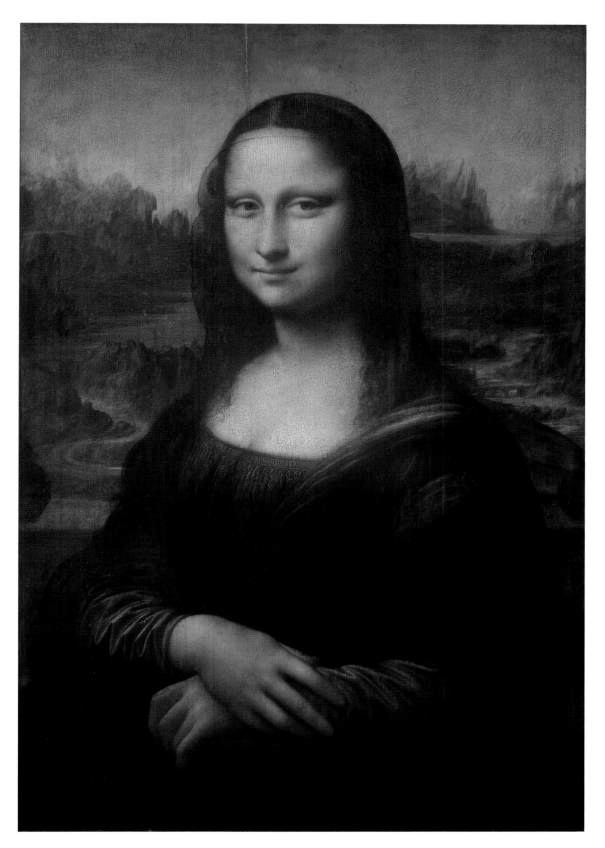

Leonardo da Vinci
Mona Lisa
c. 1503
Oil on panel
38 ½ x 21 in. (97.8 x 53.3 cm)
Musée du Louvre, Paris

Leonardo's *Mona Lisa* is famous for the subject's visual placement and enigmatic half-smile. For students of portrait painting, it is important to understand the crafting of this work. The atmospheric perspective of the background emphasises the closeness of the figure on the picture plane.

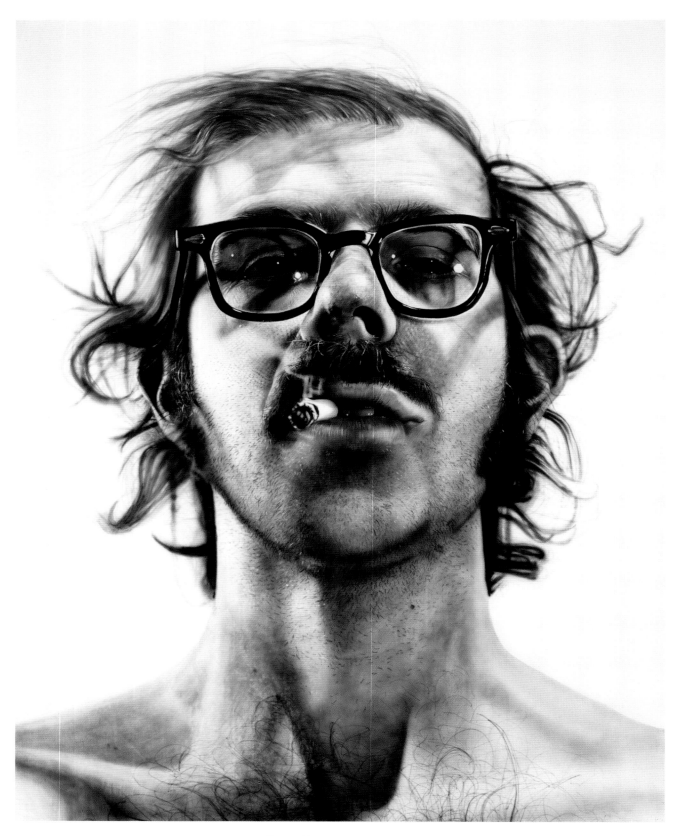

Chuck Close
Big Self-portrait
1967–68
Acrylic on canvas
107 ½ x 83 ½ x 2 in.
(273 x 212 x 5 cm)
Collection Walker Art Center,
Minneapolis

In Close's *Big Self-portrait*, his portrayal is one of self-assurance: What you see is what you get. The shape and direction of the shadows across his face form a focal point, which keeps his gaze on the viewer. The use of greyscale rather than colour allows no distraction from this engagement with his persona. Despite the cyclical nature of art conventions, Chuck Close presents the portrait as a dialogue that must be taken on the terms of the artist.

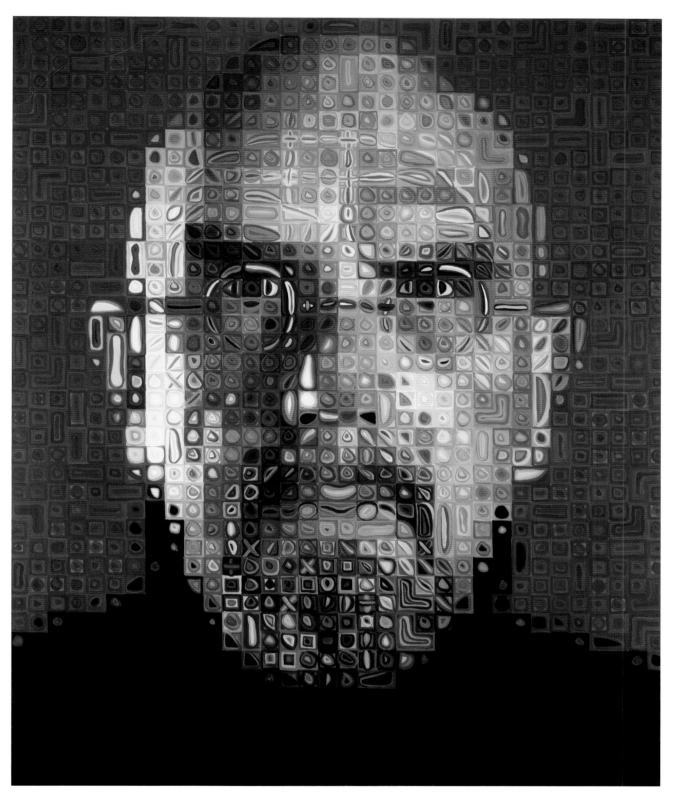

Chuck Close
Self-portrait
2004–5
Oil on canvas
8 ft. 6 in. x 7 ft. ½ in.
(259.1 x 214.6 cm)
Courtesy Pace Wildenstein,
New York

The thirty-seven years separating the *Big Self-portrait* (oppposite) from *Self-portrait* have not changed the visual impact and gaze. Close's more recent work in colour has centered on a painting style using a series of abstracted shapes and marks, which, through the juxtaposition of individual colour patterns, results in full chiaroscuro shading. If anything, the gaze has become more penetrating and poignant since his earlier self-portrait.

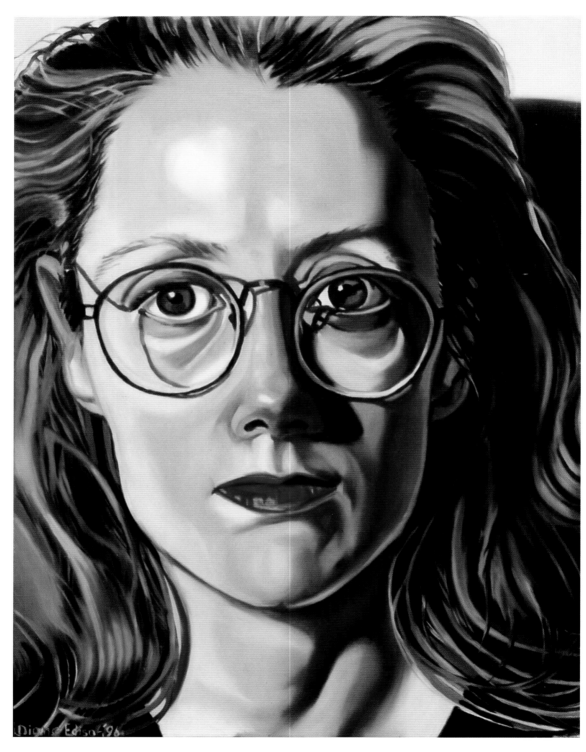

Diane Edison
Portrait of Lesley Dill
1996
Oil on panel
9 x 12 in. (22.8 x 30.4 cm)
Private collection

As a realist, I am concerned with accuracy in depicting the anatomical structure of a face; at the same time, in my portrait of Lesley, the power and gaze of the sitter is most important. In this portrait, I used a chromatic grey for the background to highlight and bring her face into the forefront. This choice was made after the principal part of the painting was completed. The painting was executed in wet on wet style over a long day, working from both photographs and life.

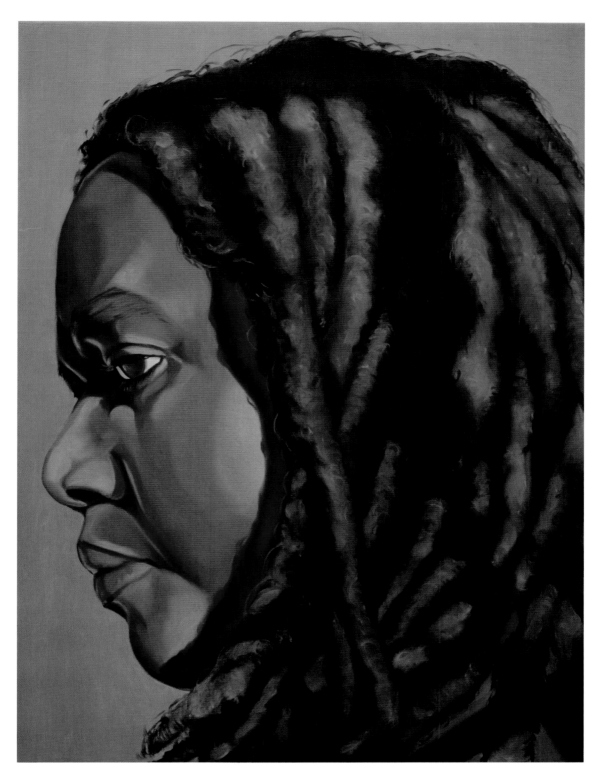

Diane Edison
Self-portrait, Side View
1996
Oil on panel
9 x 11 in. (22.8 x 27.9 cm)
Private collection

I created my self-portrait using three mirrors to capture the side view, together with a photograph. By moving completely away from the viewer's gaze, my image is private and inward. The style of this painting is wet on wet.

Before you begin any portrait, you first have to decide how much of the subject you want to include. There is no right way, only the way that you think works—you may choose a full-frontal, three-quarter, or side view, or the whole body. Be prepared to break the rules the moment you understand them: They are guideposts and parameters that you may break free from if you choose. Also, do not underestimate the creative possibilities of a so-called mistake—your painting and which point of view you decide to show will usually be well-planned, but there will almost always be some accidental, unplanned element to it, which you can turn to creative advantage. I would suggest that you start by working small and completing a painting in a day, as this gives you more time to experiment.

It is useful to note that although the term "portrait painting" may, to some, connote a commercial aspect, you are free to improvise as you wish. Defining what constitutes a portrait should be left open to the artist and the viewer. When I am working on a portrait, the emotion and power of the interaction between the sitter and myself is quite evident. I choose to work in the traditional chiaroscuro technique to add to the complexity of the subject. The portrait might loosely be defined as simple point of view, as in a camera angle; you might just as well state that what you choose to include is a portrait of a viewpoint. The real issue is not to let yourself be hedged in by what you think your viewers might like to see. As new painters, take care that you do not become so bogged down in the mastery of technique that you forget about why you want to do this. Painting is first and foremost about self-expression.

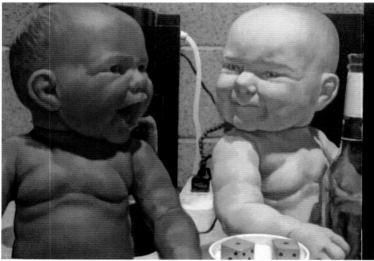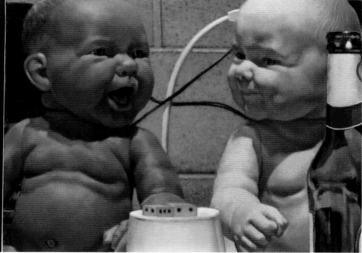

Robert Durham
*What You Never Knew
About Daycare*
2006
Oil on canvas, diptych
Each panel 12 x 16 in.
(30.4 x 40.6 cm)
Courtesy of the artist and the
Cumberland Gallery, Nashville

Robert Durham's painting of the secret lives of babies is at once arresting and funny. He depicts the physicality of infant bodies with a sly nod and a wink to eventual grown-up behavior. Through keen observation, Durham has captured the wonderful richness in the individual colour distinction in each child, especially the way in which colour and light reflects onto and over the surface of brown skin tones, while lighter skin tones are more absorbent of light.

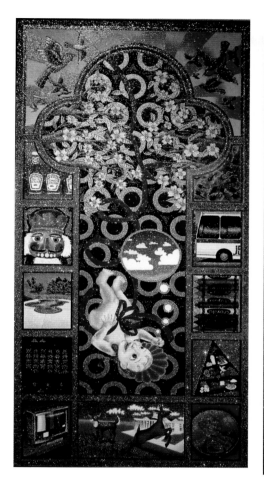
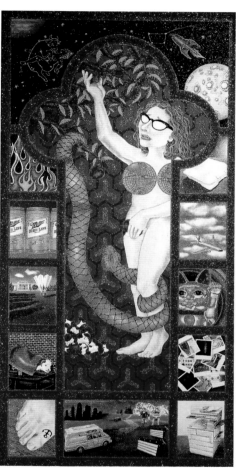
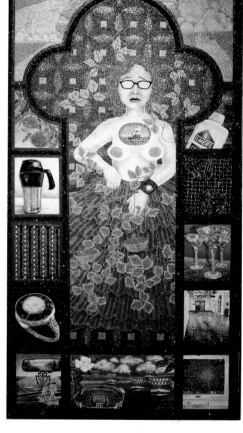

Claire Joyce
*A Quarter-life Crisis in
Three Parts*
2005–6
Elmer's glue and glitter on panel
Each panel 8 x 4 ft.
(244 x 122 cm)
Courtesy of the artist

Claire Joyce's three-panelled self-portrait using
coloured glitter on wood panels exemplifies a
playful trickster's point of view, with the
nontraditional media serving as a counterpoint
to the serious nature of the unfolding narrative,
which is about journey, growth, doubt and
fulfilment.

Portrait in Progress

Step-by-step portrait of Rebekah by student David Zoellick.
David Zoellick began this step-by-step painting with good preparation,
combining a photograph with sitting with his subject Rebekah, also a student.

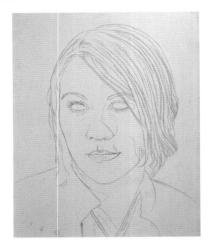

1 Preliminary sketch of the subject for this portrait using pastel pencil on the painting surface.

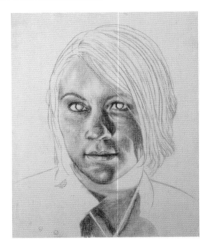

2 Using pastel to shade in some lights and darks.

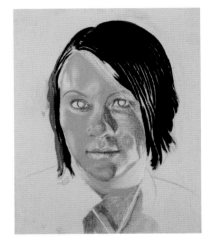

3 Starting to paint light and dark areas on the painting surface, bringing in dramatic lights and darks using chiaroscuro shading.

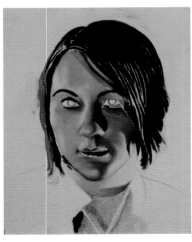

4 Contining to paint in a variety of values and shapes throughout the painting.

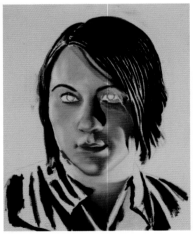

5 Painting light and dark shapes through the figure.

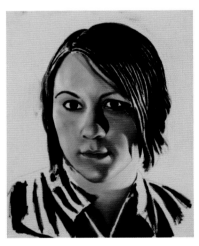

6 Fully blended dramatic lights and darks.

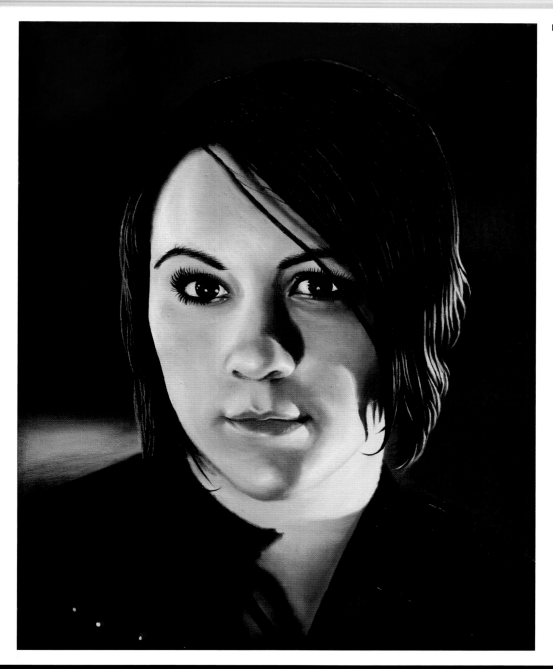

7 **David Zoellick**
Oil on canvas

David's completed portrait of Rebekah clearly shows the effect that the lighting has on the contours of her face. The cast shadows, reflected colour and contrast of dark against light create a dramatic composition that exemplifies chiaroscuro shading. Taking photographs of each stage of the painting enabled David to spend time making good decisions based on previous developments.

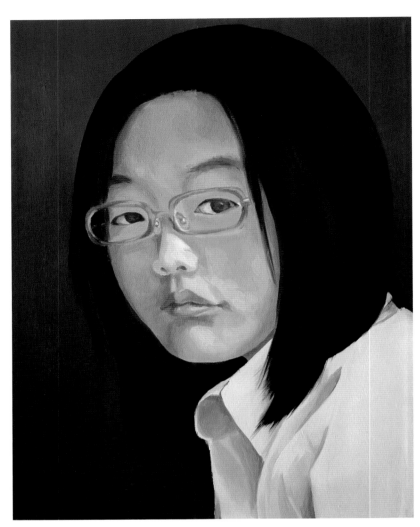

Left
Elizabeth Baek
Oil on canvas

The self-portrait of Elizabeth Baek is created in a three-quarter view. This angle has her face turning slightly away from the viewer. It has been painted with a combination of the wet on wet and wet on dry technique using a combination of a photograph and a mirror for reference.

Right
Tyler Brantley
Oil on canvas

This self-portrait of Tyler Brantley is direct in its gaze and full-frontal. The point of contact in this painting is his eyes, which are level with the viewer. The background colours and patterns direct you to his face in an almost halo-like way.

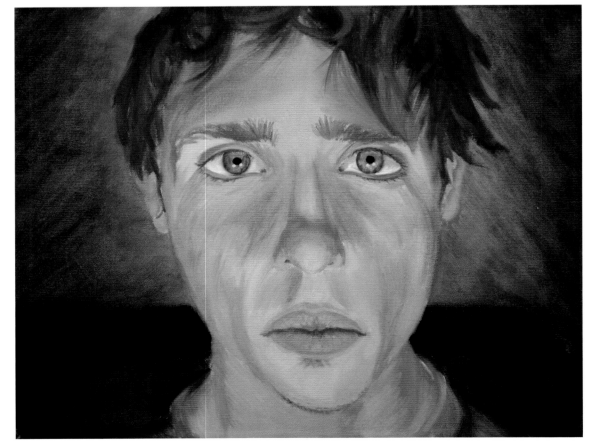

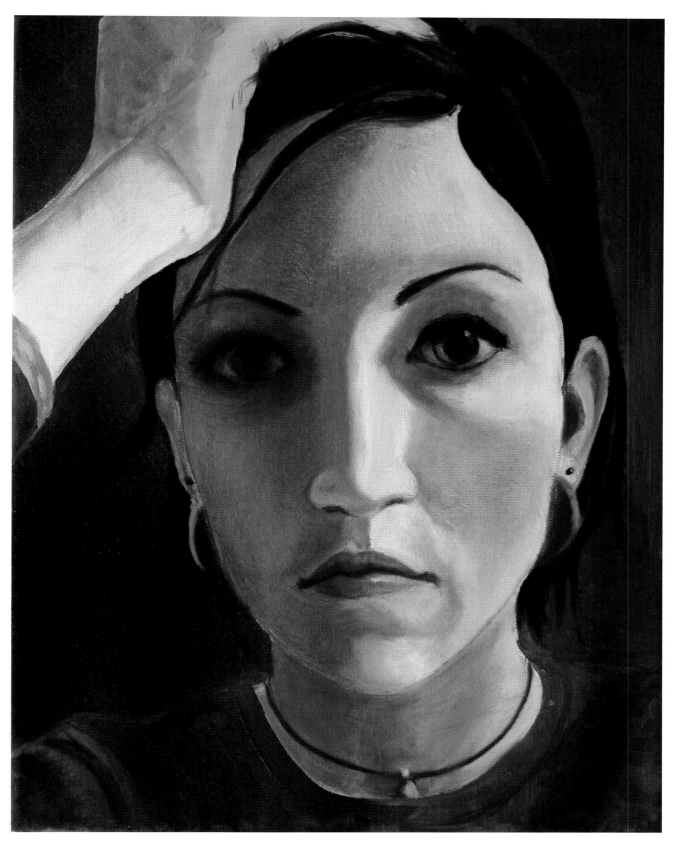

Holly Soros
Oil on canvas

This portrait of Holly Soros is a somewhat psychological interpretation, with her eyes just slightly averted from the viewer. The hand on her head suggests support and creates an interesting composition as well.

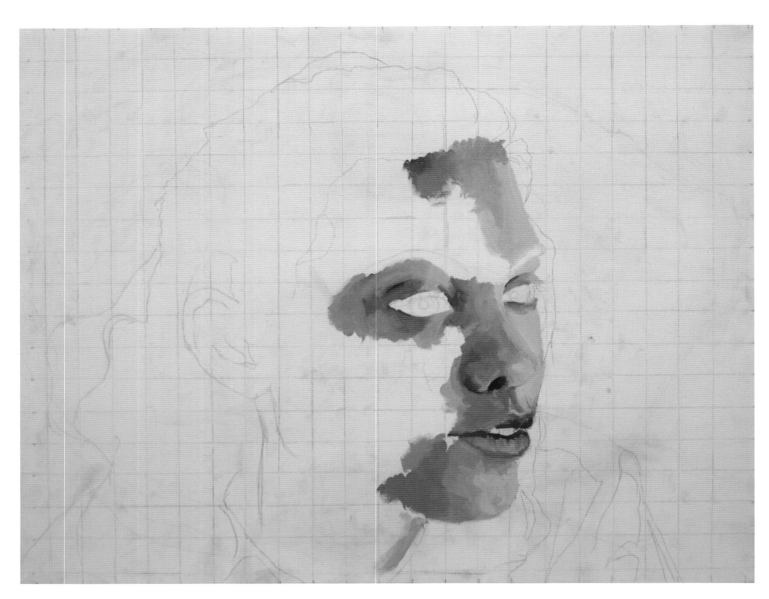

At this stage of a student self-portrait by Rebecca Claire Stephens, a grid was used to get the proportions correct. The grid is drawn on a photograph, which is then enlarged on the canvas using each of the squares as a sort of mini viewfinder.

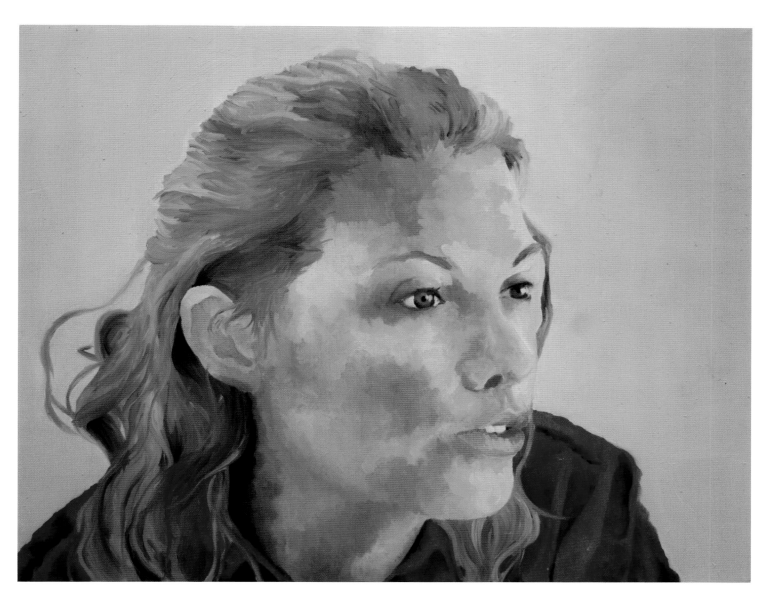

Rebecca Claire Stephens
Oil on canvas

Completed self-portrait by Rebecca Claire Stephens. Note how the same tones of colour are used for every aspect of her canvas, and how the lower part of her face is set off by the reddish colour of her shirt.

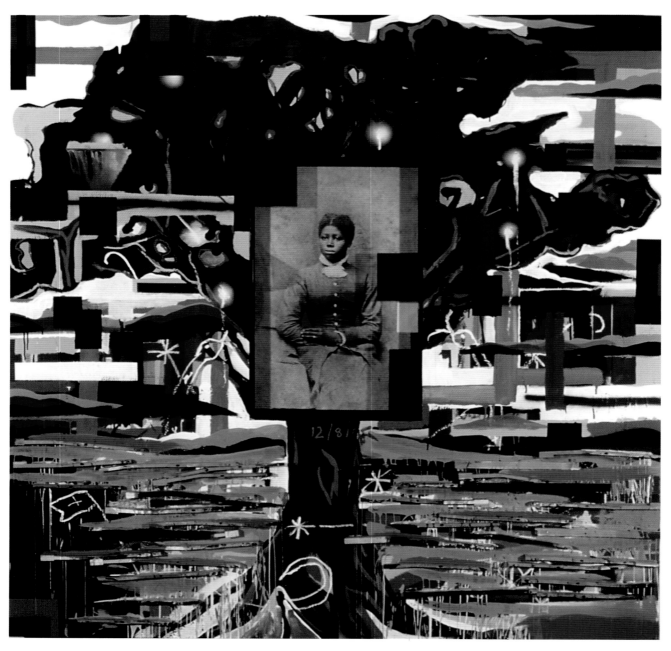

Radcliffe Bailey
One of Four Corners
2005
Photograph and mixed media
on panel
90 x 90 in. (228.6 x 228.6 cm)
Solomon Projects, Atlanta,
Georgia

This is one of four paintings with the same title, each of which stands alone yet forms a part of the whole. Bailey's painting combines paint, photography and other media to create a grand sense of space. The very personal iconography of the imagery focuses on family and time. The photograph of the seated woman, along with a blue-tinted colour scheme, presents a mood of both sadness and dignity at once. The cool colours retreat visually, but the contrast keeps the image floating up front. The tree imagery further adds to the centrality of the stance of the woman.

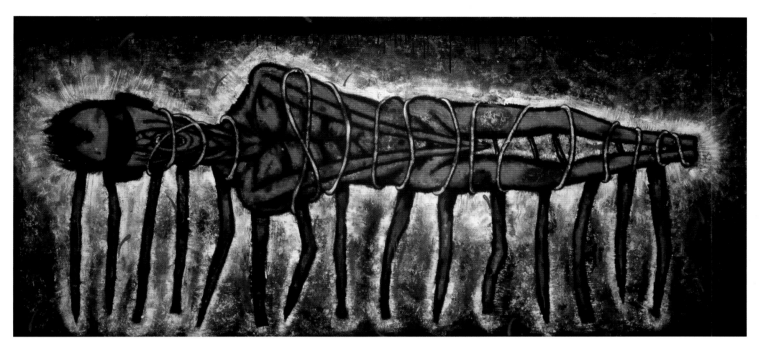

Luis Cruz Azaceta
*Homage to Latin-American
Victims of Dictators, Oppression,
Torture, and Murder*
1987
Acrylic on canvas
77 ½ x 168 in. (196.8 x 426.7 cm)
Courtesy of George Adams
Gallery, New York

The intent of Azaceta's political title is more than
amplified through the painting's imagery, with the
symbolic sacrificial figure bound and controlled.
The use of a cool blue background colour serves to
project the figure even closer into the foreground.

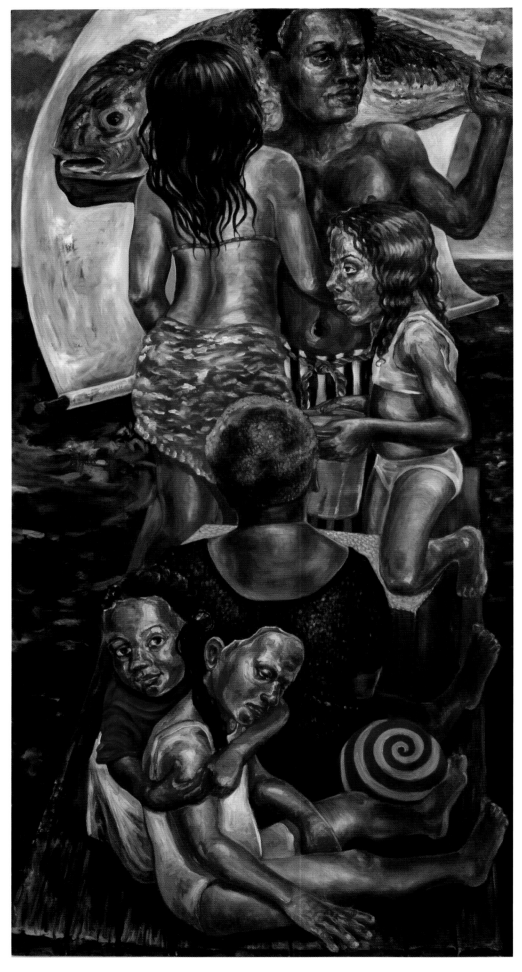

Stefanie Jackson
The Raft is not the Shore
2006
Oil on canvas
72 x 36 in. (182.8 x 91.4 cm)
Courtesy of the artist

In the tradition of heroic painting, Stefanie Jackson depicts images inspired by the recent flooding and storm damage that occurred in New Orleans in 2005. The message is also about the many faces of disaster and how those people affected keep their emotional wits together. The closed-in feeling of the composition heightens the sense of urgency, though Jackson does not present an easy way out—rather, she forces the viewer to look on helplessly, almost with a sense of collusion.

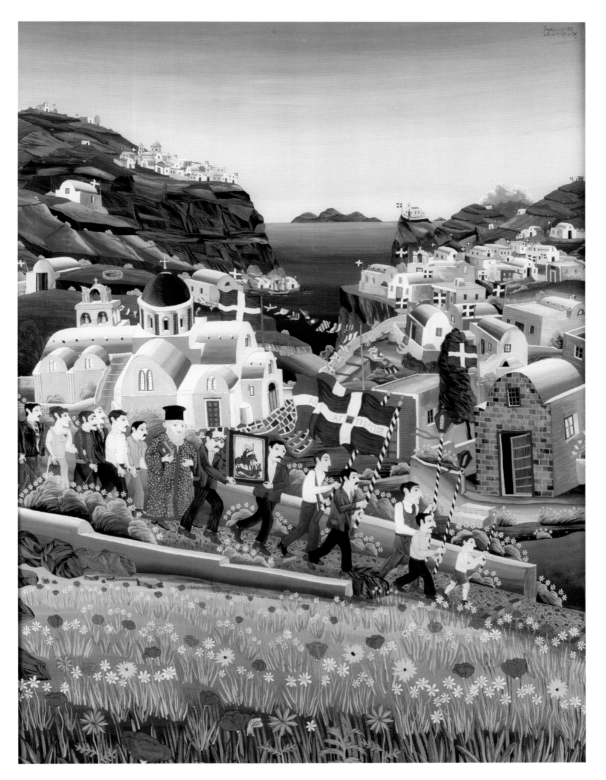

Antonios von Santorinios-Santorinakis
Four Seasons on Santorini— Spring
1980
Acrylic on glass
23 x 31 ½ in. (60 x 80 cm)
Private collection

Four Seasons on Santorini—Spring is an imaginative interpretation of a landscape with figures. Colour usage is closer to local colour, which is colour that is unaffected by light and dark. In your painting assignments thus far, you have been exposed to full-range colour that is very much dependent on the natural environment. Here, the background at times appears to be closer than it possibly could be, the result of bright contrast and heavy details, which is normally how we view items that are closer to us.

Abstraction

So far, you have been introduced to painting from a traditional and representational point of view. We will now explore pure abstraction by looking at some recent paintings by students. Studying closely the paintings of others, observing what you like and do not like and making notes about the way in which certain effects are achieved will help you to formulate your own ideas of how to approach your own abstract painting. Remember that you have already been encouraged to use an abstract design quality when using the viewfinder—the cropping makes some imagery visually unclear and random. How and why artists choose abstraction is as varied and personal as any other choice and it sometimes requires a leap of faith to move from representative to nonobjective, or abstract, imagery. You should consider what you are aiming for in an abstract painting and how best to articulate that aim on the canvas.

Madeline Edwards
Oil on canvas

Student Madeline Edwards combines four separate canvases to create a whole, with imagery that mimics nature. Each panel could very well exist as a stand-alone painting as well.

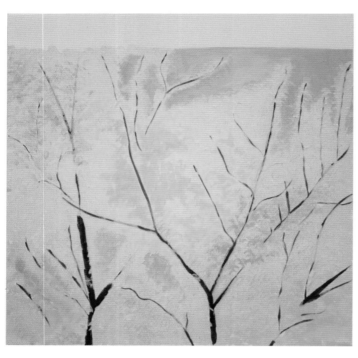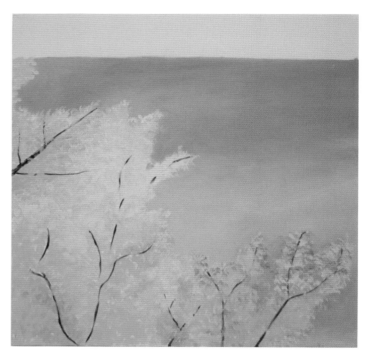

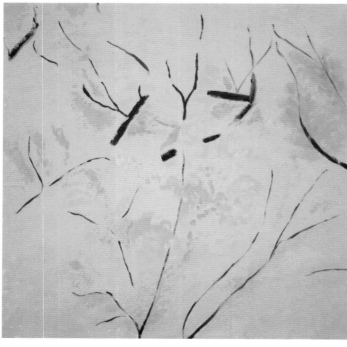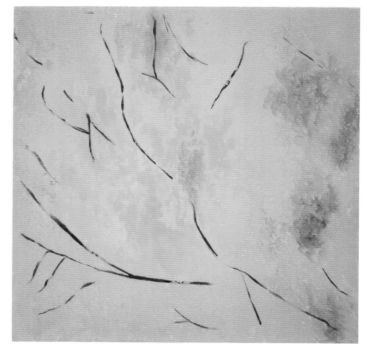

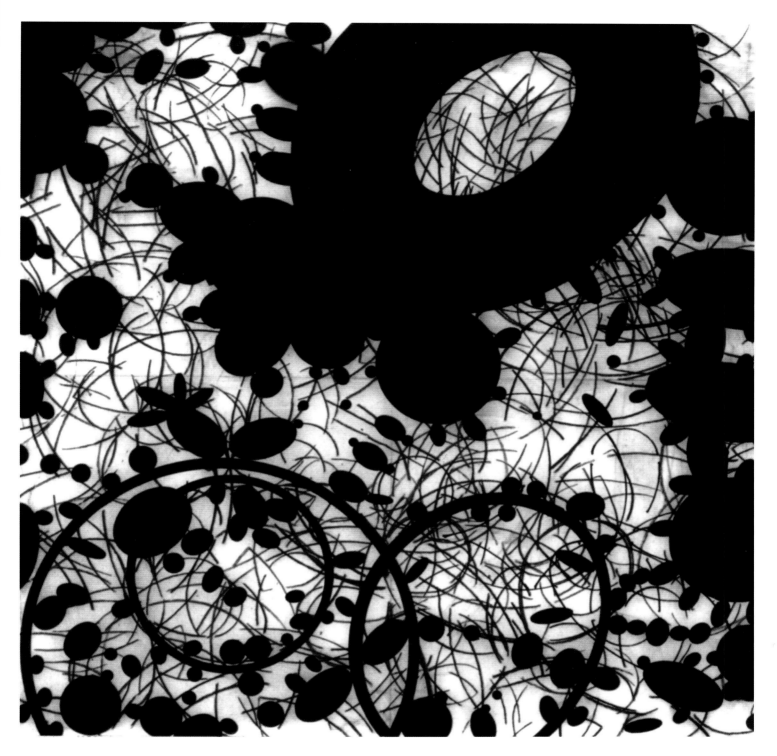

Clarence Morgan
Subliminal Memory
2003
Acrylic, pencil and ink on Mylar
59 x 59 in. (149.8 x 149.8 cm)
Courtesy of the artist

Clarence Morgan's painting is accentuated by both deep and shallow illusory space. His distillation of colour and pervasive use of spheres and elliptical shapes further create a powerful space, which transcends the edges of the canvas, giving an illusory sense of weight and spaciousness.

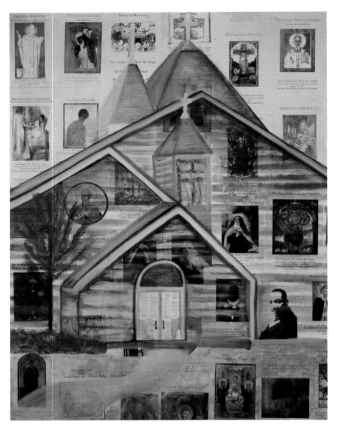

Krista Franks
Oil paint, paper, transfers and acrylic paint on canvas

Student Krista Franks uses the motif of the church to create a tableau of faith. She combines paint, news clippings and transfers, repeating the shapes above the steeple for emphasis. She has also used text that visually and literally continues the narrative.

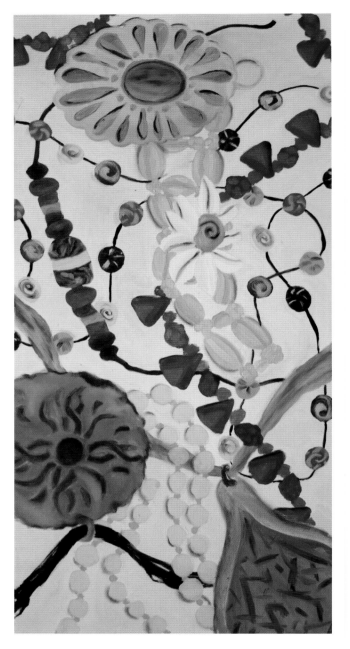

Miriam Rowe
Oil on canvas

This abstract oil painting by student Miriam Rowe is based on an interpretation of necklaces and other pieces of jewellery. The abstract quality comes from the way in which positive/ negative overlaps create interesting visual tensions and patterns throughout the painting.

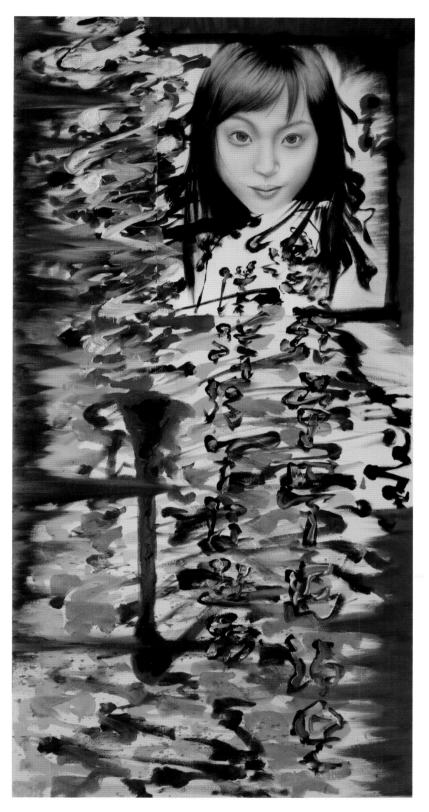

David Yeom
Oil on canvas with graphite

Student David Yeom creates a painting within a painting. His use of graphite to render the face is in direct visual opposition to the gestural painting techniques used throughout the painting. There is an almost textlike sensibility to the painting.

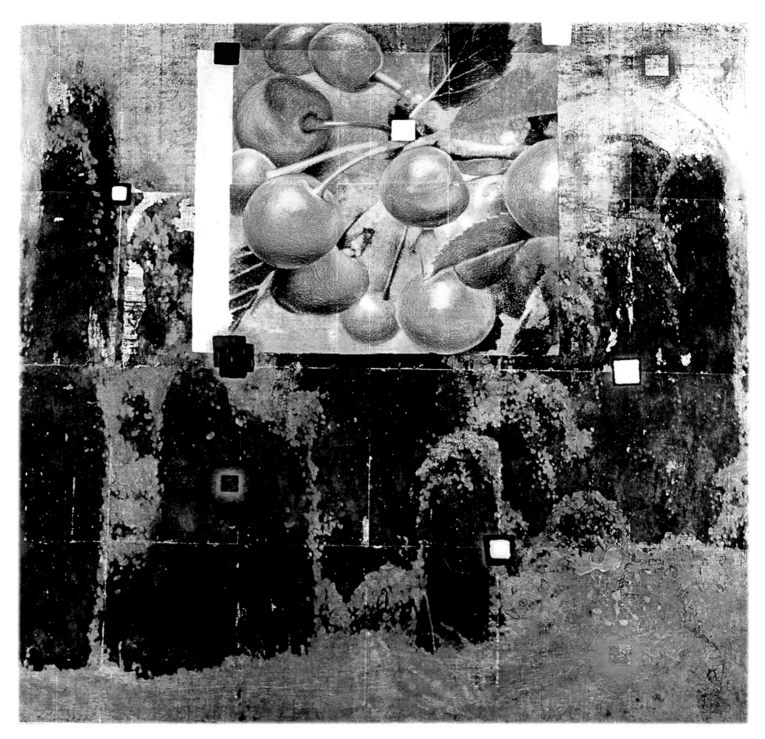

John Rudel
Kudzu Berries
2006
Acrylic paint, inkjet transfers
and coloured pencil on canvas
42 x 42 in. (106.6 x 106.6 cm)
Courtesy of the artist

Kudzu Berries appears to pay homage to the ubiquitous plant that threatens to take over the southern region of the United States. The abstraction of the landscape brings into focus the abstract qualities in the natural world. In his use of new materials to weave a tapestry of overgrown vines, the artist treats his subject matter with unexpected respect.

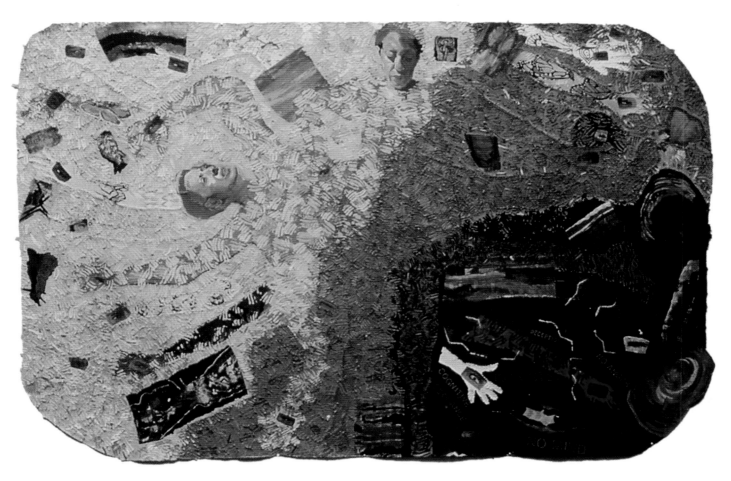

Howardena Pindell
Autobiography: The Search:
Chrysalis/Meditation:
Positive/Negative
1988–99
Acrylic, tempera, oil stick, cattle
markers, paper and polymer
photo transfer on canvas
72 x 112 in. (182.8 x 284.5 cm)
Courtesy of the artist

Howardena Pindell's *Autobiography* combines
straight abstraction with representation to create
a vast environment of overlapping identities, the
provocative and personal separation of colour from
the bright yellow of the sunlight perhaps signifying
openness versus the right-hand side of doubt. This
is underscored by the repetition of her face, which
is more prominent on the left side of the painting.

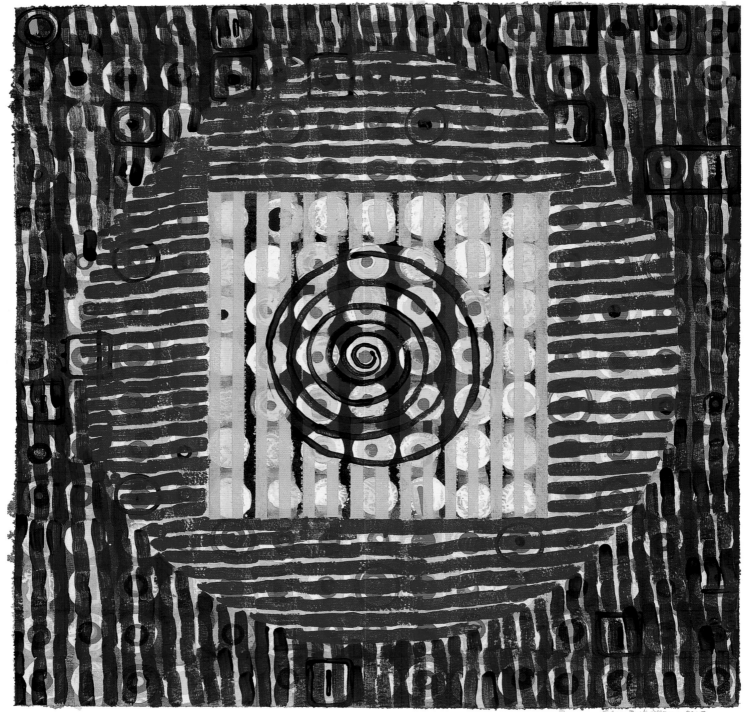

Arlene Burke Morgan
#8
2005
Acrylic on paper
15 x 15 in. (38 x 38 cm)
Courtesy of the artist

Arlene Burke Morgan's acrylic painting on watercolour paper is lush, with both the properties of water and the opaque imagery of the acrylic ensuring that it is rich in colour and design. Morgan's illusory tactile texture creates an intricate web of symmetry. The basic circle-within-square motif creates a push-pull visual competition between each section.

If one considers nontraditional modes of expression, and you may, the ability to be fearless and take risks is most often strengthened by the basics. Breaking the rules as you learn them is simply an extension of this knowledge. The accidental mark, the so-called mixing of the wrong paint, should not need to be seen in this light at all. The lines between old and new fade with each generation of artists and the variables of taste. When I meet with a painting class for the first time, a good part of my introduction and explanation of my teaching philosophy centres on the concept of how we as a class, and myself as the instructor, will learn and acquire all sorts of knowledge from each other continuously as part of a type of compact. This transcends the instruction that a student should expect when signing up for a class. Consciously or not, every class is its own entity and no two groups will be taught in the same matter. This lifelong learning is something to be strived for and treasured.

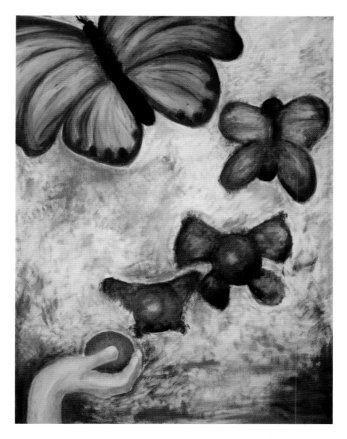

Abbie Morris
Oil on canvas

Abstract painting of a ball being thrown from a hand and changing into a butterfly. Student Abbie Morris shows how a picture of transformation can create a feeling of movement.

"We work in the dark—we do what we can—we give what we have. Our doubt is our passion and our passion is our task. The rest is the madness of art".

Henry James, *The Middle Years*, 1893

Critiques
Health and Safety

Incorporating Critique and Self-critique

Over the years, I have always found it helpful to think of the current work that I am doing as my best. I say this because it usually is. You may improve tremendously over time, but the improvements will likely be incremental, so your current work will be your best at any given time. This sense of self-satisfaction is realistic, as you cannot know what kind of improvements lie ahead. To continue to grow as an artist and achieve this incremental improvement, the beginner will need to find ways to advance his or her skill level and at the same time have some criteria for measuring success. If one is attending a school, the opportunities for improvement and influence are built in.

One very important aspect of the class experience is critique. Critique can take the form of a solitary instructor's review or a group critique; the latter is the way in which I like to involve my students. In a group critique, artists attempt to analyze a painting through examination of the finished results. The two questions that sum up this search are *What is working?* and *What could use improvement?* For some, the term "critique" has negative connotations, which is why the very thought may induce a natural defensiveness. I rather prefer to treat group critique as an affirmative and collective self-help session. So aside from the positive responses from friends and family, based on the fact that you can make a painting of subject matter that is recognizable to the viewer, there is another layer of commentary that can help you grow. When first starting out, hearing these supportive comments is in itself a validation.

What is self-critique?

After leaving a class, or even if you are self-taught, the next step, if one is to consider painting in a more serious fashion, is the question of soliciting an informed critical voice to respond to your paintings. In some communities there are artists' circles (communities of visual artists) who may choose to meet weekly and discuss each other's work in a supportive atmosphere. For those who either do not have access to such a group or are not ready for this type of critique, it would be helpful in the meantime to try to learn to assess your own work. Usually, students are much harder on themselves than anyone else is when it comes to critique. There is often a tendency to disparage their own work before anyone can say anything. Artists both new and old still have an involuntary need to protect their creations.

Critique is simply a way of understanding what you have accomplished in a painting. As in group critique, so in self-critique it is still necessary first to understand the most successful aspects of your work and then to look for what needs improvement. Critique is simply a way of understanding what you have accomplished in a painting. Over the course of a painting assignment in a class, beginners will usually have group critiques at every stage of the painting, from sketch to completion. In self-critique this is no less important. When you are making a preparatory sketch on the painting surface, this is the first opportunity to critically observe your start. Your critique can be based on whether you have a correct interpretation of your subject matter, if that is what you wish. But what exactly does "correct" mean in this situation? You are not taking a photograph, so it must be you who provides that the answer. Although critique is subjective, when you judge your own work, you should be aware of your own criteria and expectations.

What purpose should it serve?

At its most basic, critique, when done well, should help beginners to advance their painting skills and encourage them to take the risks needed to advance to the next level. First and foremost, beginners should judge themselves at their current level, rather than against any professional painters they may admire. Remember, these artists had their own beginnings and their own struggles, as will you. In that spirit, it is important to like what you are doing even as you struggle to do it. In each new painting you create, there will be some improvement from the last and there will always be something important about each experience that is carried forward.

How can critique encourage rather than discourage?

When describing the nature of critique to my painting students, I speak of affirmation, support, honesty, clarity, and, most importantly, brevity. I believe it is particularly helpful to speak about the most positive aspects of a painting as a way of affirming the effort and encouraging continuation. Being honest in critique is sometimes hard, but should be seen as a gift. In a group critique, giving critique freely will guarantee the favour being returned. Brevity in critique forces the speaker to be clear and to the point.

When you observe your own work, follow the same advice and consider what you think is good and which areas you need to work on. In many cases, the improvements may not show until you have made several more paintings. If you create ten paintings over a period of time, some will be weak and some strong. Your successful efforts will be built on earlier struggles. You must have the patience to learn, and to work through the normal frustrations that arise in every learning experience. Even as a professional artist, I still believe I work in a state of hopeful doubt. My past experiences are not an assurance of a great painting, only a knowledge that the ability is there.

General Health and Safety Issues for Painting and Woodshop Studios

Whether you are painting at home in a spare room or in a dedicated studio, it is important to observe basic safety protocols.

Oil and acrylic paints

— Oil paints are for the most part toxic in nature, and the most hazardous of the paint colours are those containing cadmium. Although acrylic paint is much less toxic, you should at the very least assume that it is not completely safe.

— If at all possible, it is advisable to develop the habit of painting with gloves on, either cloth or surgical (latex). This will prevent absorption of chemicals through your pores.

— Avoid eating or drinking in your studio area. Eating a sandwich while painting makes it that much more likely that you will accidentally ingest some paint.

— Do not leave paints in direct sunlight.

— To prevent fumes from building up in your studio, save leftover paint in closed containers, or the whole palette can be covered in plastic wrap of some sort. Always replace the caps on your paint tubes.

— Wash your hands (including under your fingernails) after a painting session.

Turpentine and other toxic chemicals

— Before working with chemicals, always read the labels for further information.

— Turpentine (gum or odourless) is highly toxic, whether through ingestion, skin contact, or inhalation, and when used requires good ventilation. Odourless turpentine only masks the danger. If working at home, try to dedicate one area for your workshop and work near an open window. If you intend to have a separate studio space, try to choose one with high ceilings and windows on both sides for cross-ventilation, or use an electric fan while the window is open for a complete change of air.

— Basic poison precautions for turpentine and other toxic chemical exposure are given below. It would also be advisable to call your local poison control centre in case of contact or ingestion.

— Painting mediums should be kept in airtight glass containers and securely covered when not in use. This simple precaution will prevent fumes from building up within your environment.

— Do not leave mediums or turpentine in direct sunlight.

Turpentine and other toxic chemical exposure precautions

— If swallowed, do not induce vomiting.

— Flush eyes with water for fifteen minutes.

— Wash hands thoroughly with soap and water.

— If inhaled heavily, get fresh air.

— In case of contact or ingestion, call your local poison control centre.

Tools and equipment

— When using spotlights for still life painting, use the lowest wattage possible as a fire precaution.
— When using extension cords, make sure they are heavy-duty, and take care in placing them around your working area.
— When cleaning your palette, use your paint scraper carefully. They are usually made with a razor held in place with a metal or plastic holder. The blades can break, so it is advisable to wear safety goggles. Always push the paint away from your body, keeping your hands out of the path of the blade.

General health advice

— If you are pregnant or have other health issues such as a compromised immunity, please contact a health care professional.
— Take regular breaks to go outside for fresh air.
— Supervise children in your studio.
— Keep your pets away from your studio at all times.
— Clean up completely after a painting session.

Woodshop safety

When you decide it is time to build your own stretchers, you will need to use electric power tools. This is perhaps the most dangerous part of painting preparation. You must respect the power of these tools to do harm, so do not get too comfortable with them.

— Goggles, dust mask and earplugs are essential.
— Make sure that all woodshop areas are properly ventilated.
— Always keep the floors free of excess wood shavings to prevent slipping.
— If you are new to these tools, you *MUST* first get training, and afterward work with a partner. The buddy system protects you both if there is an accident.
— To prevent entanglements, do not wear loose clothing or have your hair hanging loosely while cutting.
— Before you cut, always check where your fingers are. All it takes is one moment of careless distraction for a serious accident.
— If the wood you are about to cut has rough knots in the grain, you may want to choose another piece, as the blades can at times kick back when they meet a knot.
— Clean up completely after painting and/or working in a woodshop.

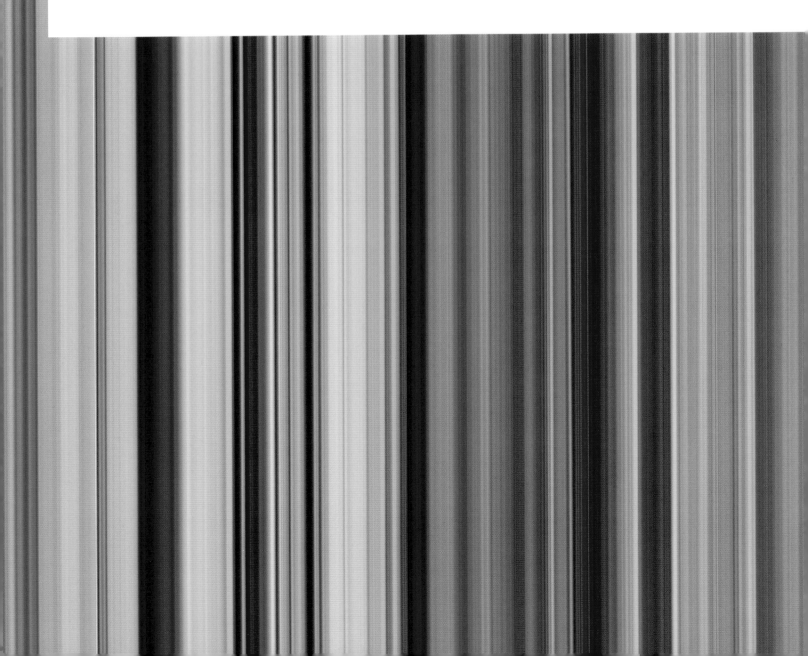

Glossary
Further Reading

Glossary

A

absorbent ground *See* ground.

abstraction A work of art using nonobjective imagery, i.e., objects or images that may derive from the visible world but that do not imitate a recognisable subject.

acrylic A type of paint made with synthetic resin as the medium to bind the pigment (colour) rather than natural oils. It is fast-drying and water-soluble.

advancing colour An optical phenomenon by which deep, warm colours, such as yellow and orange, appear to move toward the foreground of the picture plane. *See also* retreating colour.

alla prima painting *See* wet on wet.

atmospheric perspective The method used by an artist to show distance and/or atmospheric effects, such as dust or clouds, by soft-edged, hazy painting.

B

blending Mixing paint to create subtle gradations from light to dark, or from one colour to another. This technique can be used wet on wet, or with glazing and scumbling. This is the basis for shading in most paintings.

body colour *See* gouache.

bright brush *See* brush.

bristle A hair used for brush tips, traditionally from hogs, though now also made from nylon. Stiffer than sable hair (*see* sable), the rough quality of bristle hair makes it a good choice for scumbling and "drawing" with the brush.

brush You should always use different brushes for oil and acrylic. There are five main types of brush: The round brush has long hairs tapered to a point, with a round ferrule. The flat brush is flat with long hairs and makes the placement of paint more manageable, as it does not leave a raised edge on either side of the brush mark. The filbert brush is flat, oval-shaped and fairly thick; one of the best all-around brushes for painting. The bright brush is flat with short hairs. The fan brush is, as its name suggests, fan-shaped. It can be both flat or thick and fluffy, is especially soft and comes in a variety of hairs. It is generally used to blend areas where the colour has been applied and softer edges are required. This is a finishing brush, usually reserved for the finishing touches. *See also* ferrule.

brush-cleaning jar Glass or metal container with a metal coil or netting at the bottom, which prevents the brush from touching the residue of old, dissolved paint.

brushwork The characteristic way an artist brushes paint onto the surface.

C

canvas Type of flexible material support for use in either oil or acrylic painting. The two main types are linen and cotton duck. Linen is high-quality, expensive and has an irregular surface. Cotton duck is a cheaper option and has a more even, machine-woven surface.

cast shadows When a light source strikes an object, it casts a shadow similar to the shape of the object. The density and shape of a cast shadow depend on the brightness of the light source and its closeness to the object. The different positions of the light will affect the shape, tone and size of the cast shadow.

charcoal A drawing instrument made by charring thin pieces of wood in a furnace. It can also be in the form of compressed charcoal, which is powdered charcoal mixed with a binding substance and compressed into sticks. It can be used both for finished drawings and for preliminary sketches. Charcoal comes in shades from white to black.

chiaroscuro A shading technique that uses the contrasts between lights and darks for dramatic effect. It is based on five principles of shading: the lightest light, the shaded area, the core (the darkest part of the shaded area), reflected light and cast shadow. It comes from the Italian words for "clear" and "dark."

chroma The relative intensity or purity of a colour when compared to greyness or lack of colour.

chromatic chart A method of displaying the different types of chromatic grey.

chromatic grey, or chromatic neutral A grey created by mixing colours that are opposite each other on the colour wheel, which will have a colour bias or a distinct colour to it.

collage The technique (and the name given to the finished work) in which the artist glues scraps of materials such as paper, metal, plastic, found objects, etc., to a painting or drawing surface. Sometimes also combined with painting or drawing.

colour bias In chromatic greys, or neutrals, the colour emphasis is determined by more weight being given to one colour than the other in the mixing process. For example, red mixed with its complement, green, will produce a grey that is more red or more green depending on the relative quantities of red and green paint that you add.

colour temperature Reds, yellows, oranges and red-violets are generally described as warm colours. Blues, greens and violets are considered cool colours. Warm and cool are relative terms and one colour can have warm and cool shades: for example, a yellow with a hint of green is a cool yellow. *See also* advancing colour, retreating colour.

colour wheel A system designed to show the properties of colour. In this book, we use the Johannes Itten colour wheel. Itten's standard colour wheel illustrates the primary colours: red, yellow and blue. The larger colour wheel consists of three sections: primary colours, secondary colours (formed by mixing pairs of primary colours) and tertiary colours (formed by mixing adjacent primary and secondary colours). *See also* primary colours, secondary colours, tertiary colours.

E/F G H

complementary colours
Colours directly opposite each other on the colour wheel. For example, red's complementary colour is green. By mixing complementary colours together, chromatic neutrals (greys) are produced.

composition The process of arranging the forms of two- or three-dimensional visual art into a unified whole by means of elements and principles of design, such as line, shape, colour, balance, contrast, space etc., for the purposes of formal clarity and artistic expression.

content The meaning with which you imbue your chosen subject matter.

cool colours *See* colour temperature.

cotton duck *See* canvas.

encaustic A method of painting that uses pigments melted with wax and fixed or fused to the painting surface with heat.

fan brush *See* brush.

fat over lean, or thick over thin
A rule important to remember when painting in layers, especially with oil paint. "Fat" paint is paint that contains more oil (such as paint straight out of the tube), while "lean" paint has a lower oil content (such as paint mixed with turpentine). If your last layer of paint dries more quickly than your first layer, this will lead to problems such as cracking in the finished painting. Fat over lean means that earlier layers of paint should be leaner, so that the first coats dry faster. When using a painting medium that speeds up the drying time, a good rule is to add a drop or two less for each layer. Each subsequent layer should be thicker and fatter than the one before it.

ferrule The section of the paint brush between the handle and the hairs that holds the hairs in place. It is generally made of metal.

figure/ground relationship
The relationship between the shape in the picture, whether object or person and the space between the shapes and on which the shapes rest in a painting.

filbert brush *See* brush.

film (paint film) A layer of paint once it has been applied to a canvas.

flat brush *See* brush.

fresco Traditional form of painting using watercolour on the wet plaster of a wall or ceiling.

full-range colour painting A way of painting that uses a full range of colour from beginning to end; painting with colour as one sees it naturally, using the whole colour wheel and all tints, shades and chromatic greys in between.

gesso An undercoating medium used on the painting surface before painting to prime the surface. Usually a white, chalky, thick liquid.

gesso-prepared hardboard
Wood or masonite board prepared with gesso for use as a painting surface.

glazing A technique by which transparent colours are applied over a dry underpainting. Many glazes may be layered to create particular colour effects. Each layer of dried paint, or glaze, must be more flexible than the previous one, so the principle of fat over lean must be used. *See* fat over lean, or thick over thin.

gouache An opaque, water-soluble paint.

ground The surface on which you paint, often a coating (gesso) rather than support, unless the support is paper. An absorbent ground pulls in or absorbs paint rather than letting it sit on the surface.

harmony The art of bringing together all the design elements of a painting in the right proportions so as to create an image that is easy to view.

hide The covering ability of paint.

horizon line The point in a perspective drawing or painting where the vanishing points converge. *See* vanishing point.

hue The name of a colour, such as blue or red-orange. Another word for colour.

Glossary

L

landscape A work of art showing the outdoors, comprising any one element of nature, landforms, weather conditions or humanity. Also used to describe a rectangular page orientation where the longer axis is horizontal.

linear perspective The representation of an image as perceived by the eye, so that objects are painted smaller the further they are away from the viewer and elements are foreshortened to cater to different angles of viewpoint. There are three main types of linear perspective:
One-point perspective—the artist is standing at the centre of the scene and there is a single point at which the lines and figures converge to a vanishing point.
Two-point perspective—the artist is standing at an angle to the scene and the lines and figures will converge in two different points.
Three-point perspective—the artist is viewing the scene from above or below, adding yet another vanishing point at the top or bottom of the painting.

linen See canvas.

Liquin Brand name for an oil painting medium that helps create a smooth, glossy surface, thickens oil paint and speeds up its drying time.

local colour The actual colour of an object or surface, unaffected by the quality of the light, reflected colour, or other factors.

luminosity Describes a surface, which shines, glows and has a lustrous and glassy finish.

M

masking fluid Clear, latex-rubber fluid applied to any areas of a painting (acrylic or watercolour) that the artist wants to protect from paint. It can then be peeled off to reveal an untouched area.

monochromatic Describes the use of one colour that is tinted by white and shaded with black. This is generally used for the underpainting, prior to glazing with full colour.

muddy colour In general, a colour that is unclear or has a greyish or brownish tone—a form of chromatic grey. It may not be needed for your red apple overall, yet it may play a role in creating a cast shadow or a reflection on the apple.

N/O

negative space The area or space around an object or arrangement of objects in a painting or drawing that creates a visual shape or pattern. Negative space drawing involves concentrating on the background, leaving the object white.

oil A type of paint made with natural oils, such as linseed, walnut, or poppy, as the medium to bind the pigment. Oil paints dry slowly, allowing the artist time to blend the colours and rework the paint.

one-point perspective See linear perspective.

opacity A paint's resistance to light. A more opaque paint will not allow images or colours in the layers of paint underneath it to show through.

P

painting cups Small cups in which to collect leftover paint to prevent it from drying out between painting sessions.

painting medium Agent mixed with oil or acrylic paint to affect its behaviour. Mediums can change the gloss, drying time, levels of transparency and the final film of the painting.

palette A flat surface on which to mix paint colours, such as piece of glass or wood or a ceramic tray.

palette cup A circular metal cup used for saving leftover paint after a day's work, designed to clamp on to the palette.

palette knife A metal knife with a wooden handle for mixing paint on a palette, and for applying or removing paint.

pastel A coloured chalk made of powdered pigment bound together with a water-based gum and moulded into small sticks.

peephole viewfinder See viewfinder.

picture plane Any flat surface on which to start a painting, e.g., paper or canvas.

pigment Substance that imparts colour to other materials. In paint, the pigment is a powder that, when mixed in liquid, imparts colour to a painted surface.

R

S

Pointillism A technique used by neo-Impressionist painters, where tiny dots of pure colour are blended in the viewer's eye. See p. 9 for an example by Seurat.

portraiture A work of art depicting a person, usually concentrating on the face and its expression. Also "portrait format" is also used to describe a rectangular page orientation where the longer axis is vertical.

primary colours Red, yellow and blue. These colours cannot be formed by the mixing of any other colours and are the foundation from which other colours are created. *See also* colour wheel, secondary colours, tertiary colours.

reflected colour The colour of one object reflected in another object.

rendering as you go A loose description of the technique of finishing whole areas of the painting in a piecemeal fashion.

retarder A medium added to acrylic paint to slow down the drying time.

retreating (or receding) colour An optical phenomenon by which cooler colours, such as blues and greens, appear to retreat, or recede, on the picture plane. *See also* advancing colours.

round brush *See* brush.

sable A natural animal hair traditionally used for brush tips. It is soft and pliable, leaving a smooth surface finish.

scumbling A method of glazing in which very thin layers of wet colour are applied to a dried paint film by moving trace amounts of paint around the surface with a stiff-bristled brush. Also known as wet on dry. See Chapter 4 for a full discussion of this technique.

secondary colours The three colours formed by mixing together the primary colours: orange (red plus yellow), green (blue plus yellow) and violet-purple (blue plus red). *See also* colour wheel, primary colours, tertiary colours.

shade The darker colour of a given hue resulting from the addition of black or another dark colour. A shade is always darker than the colour that comes straight from the tube. *See also* tint.

sheen The way light can stream and brighten up an area and create a luster on the surface.

simultaneous contrast An optical phenomenon that can occur when two different colours are placed next to each other, producing a heightened contrast, which intensifies the difference between them. Each colour seems brighter than when viewed alone. A shimmering effect is also sometimes produced.

still life A work of art depicting inanimate objects.

stretcher A frame, usually wooden although sometimes made of metal, on which a canvas is stretched and attached.

subject matter The elements that you choose to include in your painting, chosen as a result of many decisions such as preference, ease and interest, and other personal influences.

support (painting support) The actual material or surface on which a painting is created, usually canvas, paper or wood.

Glossary

T

tempera Painting method in which finely ground pigment is mixed with a solidifying base such as albumen, sap or glue. The name distemper is given to the method when a glue base is used.

tertiary colours The six colours formed by mixing together adjacent primary and secondary colours: red-orange, red-violet, yellow-green, yellow-orange, blue-green and blue-violet. *See also* colour wheel, primary colours, secondary colours.

three-point perspective *See* linear perspective.

tint The lighter colour of a given hue resulting from the addition of white or another light colour. A tint is always lighter than the colour that comes straight from the tube. *See also* shade.

tone The lightness or darkness of a colour in terms of black to white; for example, light or dark red, or light or dark grey.

tooth Grained but even texture of canvas. Tooth allows the attachment of succeeding layers of paint.

transparency The degree to which a layer of paint allows light to pass through, revealing the previous layers.

transparent colours Colours that have less hide, used for glazing or in conjunction with thicker paints.

turpentine For use in mixing the oil paint medium.

two-point perspective *See* linear perspective.

U/V

underpainting Traditional stage in Venetian painting using a monochrome or dead colour as a base for composition.

value The relative lightness or darkness of a visual space. Value in colour is defined as the relative gradations between the darkest and lightest tones. Adding white tints a colour lighter, whereas adding black creates a darker shade. Examples: dark blue or pale red-orange.

value patterns The shape of patches of colour on the surfaces of the subject matter. On a shiny silver ball, the shapes of the colours reflected in its surface will conform to its circular quality. Paying attention to these shapes will help in controlling the composition, and painting these shapes along with the outside lines of the object will help you to identify your colour combinations.

vanishing point The point in a perspective drawing or painting to which the lines and figures seem to converge.

varnish A mixture used to bring a particular shine to a painting once it has dried. As well as its protective properties, it helps to brighten the painting surface and brings out the darks and lights in dramatic contrast.

Venetian painting technique A style of painting that originated in Venice and was prominent from the fourteenth to the sixteenth centuries. It is a method of glazing that uses a number of fixed steps, and relies on the colour Venetian red both for toning the painting surface and for the underpainting itself. See Chapter 5 for a full description of this technique.

viewfinder A handheld frame that helps in editing a composition by putting a border around the chosen subject matter. This border represents the outside edges of the painting surface. A viewfinder can be constructed by cutting the centre out of a piece of paper or cardboard. By cutting out the centre of a piece of paper in roughly the same dimensions, you will have a handheld viewfinder. A peephole viewfinder, made of white card and with a smaller hole in the centre, is designed to isolate individual colours, either on the painting palette or in the subject matter itself, by blocking out the other colours.

viscosity The thickness and body of paint.

W

wet on dry *See* scumbling.

wet on wet, or alla prima painting A technique in which the painting is worked while the paint is still wet. Wet paint is blended into wet paint, and the painting is often completed in one session, or can be worked on in layers. See Chapter 2 for a full discussion of this technique.

Further Reading

Jim **Aims**, *Color Theory Made Easy*, New York: Watson-Guptill, 1996

Josef **Albers**, *Interaction of Color*, New Haven, CT: Yale University Press, 1975

Neil **Ardley**, *The Science Book of Color*, San Diego, CA: Harcourt Brace Jovanovich, 1991

Tim **Armstrong**, *Colour Perception*, Stradbroke, Norfolk: Tarquin Publications, 1991

Julian **Bell**, *What is Painting? Representation and Modern Art*, London and New York: Thames and Hudson, 1999

Faber **Birren**, *Color and Perception in Art*, New York: Van Nostrand Reinhold, 1976

Gerald **Brommer**, *Emotional Content: How To Create Paintings That Communicate*, Verdi, NV: International Artist,and Newton Abbot, Devon: David and Charles, 2003

Manlio **Brusatin**, *A History of Colors*, Boston, MA: Shambhala, 1991

Dawson W. **Carr** and Mark Leonard, *Looking at Paintings: A Guide to Technical Terms*, Malibu, CA: J. Paul Getty Museum, 1992

Alan **Chong** (ed.), *Rembrandt Creates Rembrandt: Art and Ambition in Leiden 1629–1631* (exhibition catalogue), Zwolle, The Netherlands: Waanders, 2000

Susan P. **Compton**, *Chagall* (exhibition catalogue), New York and London : Harry N. Abrams, 1985

Bill **Creevy**, *The Oil Painting Book: Materials and Techniques for Today's Artist*, New York: Watson-Guptill, 1994

Joseph **D'Amelio**, *Perspective Drawing Handbook*, New York: Tudor, 1964; New York: Van Nostrand Rheinhold, 1984; New York: Dover Publications, 2003

Luigina **De Grandis**, *Theory and Use of Color*, New York: Harry N. Abrams, 1986

François **Delamare** and Bernard Guineau, *Colors: The Story of Dyes and Pigments*, New York: Harry N. Abrams, 2000

Maurice **de Sausmarez**, *Basic Design: The Dynamics of Visual Form*, London: Studio Vista and New York: Reinhold, 1964; revised edition with a foreword by Gyorgy Kepes, London: Herbert Press and New York: Van Nostrand Reinhold, 1983; second revised edition, London: A & C Black, 2002

Helene W. **Eckstein**, *Color in the 21st Century*, New York: Watson-Guptill, 1991

James **Elkins**, *What Painting Is: How to Think about Oil Painting using the Language of Alchemy*, New York and London: Routledge, 1999

Edith Anderson **Feisner**, *Colour: How to Use Colour in Art and Design*, London: Laurence King Publishing and as *Color Studies*, New York: Fairchild Publications, 2000; revised edition, 2006

Victoria **Finlay**, *Color: A Natural History of the Palette*, New York: Ballantine Books, 2002

Mark David **Gottsegen**, *The Painter's Handbook*, revised and expanded edition, New York: Watson-Guptill, 2006

Barbara **Haskell**, *The American Century: Art & Culture 1900–1950*, New York: W.W. Norton, 1999

Cynthia Newman **Helms** (ed.), *Diego Rivera: A Retrospective* (exhibition catalogue), New York: W.W. Norton, 1986

Hayden **Herrera**, *Frida: A Biography of Frida Kahlo*, London and New York: Harper & Row, 1983; London: Bloomsbury,1998

Linda **Holtzchue**, *Understanding Color*, New York: Van Nostrand Reinhold, 1995

David **Hornung**, *Colour: A Workshop for Artists and Designers*, London: Laurence King Publishing; and as *Color: A Workshop Approach*, New York: McGraw-Hill, 2004

Robert **Kaupelis**, *Experimental Drawing*, London: Pitman and New York: Watson-Guptill, 1980

Michael D. **Kinerk** and Dennis W. Wilhelm, *Popcorn Palaces: The Art Deco Movie Theatre Painting of Davis Cone*, New York: Harry N. Abrams, 2001

Margaret **Krug**, *An Artist's Handbook: Materials and Techniques*, London: Laurence King Publishing and New York: Harry N. Abrams, 2007

Trevor **Lamb** and Janine Bourriau, *Color: Art and Science*, Cambridge and New York: Cambridge University Press, 1995

Samella **Lewis**, *Art: African American*, New York: Harcourt Brace Jovanovich, 1978; revised edition as *African American Art and Artists*, Berkeley: University of California Press, 1990; third edition, 2003

John **Lidzey**, Jill Mirza, Nick Harris and Jeremy Galton, *Color Mixing for Artists*, New York: Barrons, 2002

Judy **Martin**, *Dynamic Color Drawing*, Cincinnati, OH: North Light Books, 1989

Ellen **Marx**, *Optical Color and Simultaneity*, New York: Van Nostrand Reinhold, 1983

Guy C. **McElroy**, Richard J. Powell, and Sharon F. Patton, with an introduction by David C. Driskell, *African-American Artists 1880–1987: Selections from the Evans-Tibbs Collection* (exhibition catalog), Seattle: University of Washington Press, 1989

Otto G. **Ocvirk**, *et al. Art Fundamentals: Theory and Practice*, tenth edition, New York: McGraw-Hill, 2006

José María **Parramon**, *Color Theory*, New York: Watson-Guptill, 1988

Emma **Pearce**, *Artists' Materials: Which, Why, and How*, London: A & C Black, 1992

Stephen **Pentak** and Rich Roth, *Color Basics*, Belmont, CA: Wadsworth, 2004

Richard **Pumphrey**, *Elements of Art*, Upper Saddle River, NJ and London: Prentice Hall, 1996

Tom **Rockwell**, *The Best of Norman Rockwell, 1894 –1978*,London: Courage and Philadelphia, PA: Running Press, 1988; revised edition, 2005

Ogden **Rood**, *Modern Chromatics*, New York: Van Nostrand Reinhold, 1973

Hans **Schwarz**, *Color for the Artist*, New York: Watson-Guptill, 1968

Pip **Seymour**, *The Artist's Handbook: A Complete Professional Guide to Materials and Techniques*, London: Arcturus, 2003

Ray **Smith**, *An Introduction to Oil Painting*, New York: Dorling Kindersley, 1993

Alvia J. **Wardlaw**, with essays by Edmund Barry Gaither, Alison de Lima Greene, and Robert Farris Thompson, *The Art of John Biggers: View from the Upper Room* (exhibition catalogue), New York: Harry N. Abrams, 1995

Kurt **Wehlte**, *The Materials and Techniques of Painting*, translated by Ursula Dix, New York: Van Nostrand Reinhold, 1975

Michael **Wilcox**, *Color Theory for Oil Colors or Acrylics*, New York: Watson-Guptill, 1983

Philip **Yenawine**, *Colors*, New York: Museum of Modern Art, 1991

Paul **Zelanski** and Mary Pat Fisher, *Color*, fifth edition, Upper Saddle River, NJ: Prentice Hall, 2006

Index
Picture Credits

Index

Page numbers in **bold** refer to illustrations and subjects mentioned in illustration captions.

Index

Picture Credits

Laurence King Publishing, the authors and the picture researcher wish to thank the institutions and individuals who have kindly provided photographic material. Collections are given in the captions alongside the illustrations. Sources for illustrations not supplied by museums or collections, additional information and copyright credits are given below. Numbers are figure numbers unless otherwise indicated.

While every effort has been made to trace the present copyright holders, we apologise in advance for any unintentional omission or error and will be pleased to insert the appropriate acknowledgement in any subsequent edition.

All photographs by Robin Dana unless marked otherwise.

The following abbreviations have been used:
L left
R right
T top
B bottom

6 Courtesy Idelle Weber and Bill Massey;
7 © Laurin Ramsey;
9 © Photo Josse, Paris;
12 Courtesy of George Adams Gallery, New York;
13 © Photo Josse, Paris;
14 © Quattrone, Florence;
15 © Quattrone, Florence;
16 Courtesy of the artist;
17 © Kelly Smith;
18 Courtesy of George Adams Gallery, New York;
19 Image © 2007 Board of Trustees, National Gallery of Art, Washington (1937.1.44);
20 © Jessica Schramm;
21 © Vincenzo Pirozzi, Rome, fotopirozzi@inwind.it;
22 (3 drawings) Advanced Illustrations Ltd.;
23 © Photo Josse, Paris;
24 Courtesy Idelle Weber and Bill Massey;
25 Bridgeman Art Library, London;
26 Bridgeman Art Library, London;
27 Photo Curtis Publishing;
30 © James Morris, London;
31 © Photo Josse, Paris;
33 Private Collection;
34 Gallery Henoch, New York;
37 Courtesy of George Adams Gallery, New York;
41 Courtesy of George Adams Gallery, New York;
43 © 2004 Pacita Abad Art;
45 Roger Fawcett-Tang;
46T © David Zoellick;
46B © Kimberley Perry;
47 © Krista Franks;
50 © Zeke Paull;
52T Roger Fawcett-Tang;
52B © Laurin Ramsey;
53 © Alexander Shute;
55TR Rylan Steel
60 Courtesy of George Adams Gallery, New York;
61 Courtesy of the artist and the Woodward Gallery, New York;
62 © Kelly Smith;
66–67 steps 1 and 6 Rylan Steel;
70 Courtesy of the artist and the Woodward Gallery, New York;
73T © Brittany Gabey;
73B © Jasmin Kern;
74 © Miriam Rowe;
75 © Miriam Rowe/photo Rylan Steel
76 © Christin McMurray/photo Rylan Steel
77BR © Brittany Gabey;
79L © Photo Josse, Paris;
79R Courtesy of George Adams Gallery, New York;
80L&R Bridgeman Art Library, London;
81 © Craig McPherson, courtesy of Forum Gallery, New York;
82 Rylan Steel;
83T © Kari Ann Gertz;
83B © Jasmin Kern;

85 Courtesy of George Adams Gallery, New York
88 © Photo Josse, Paris;
89 © Elizabeth Baek;
91 © Brittany Gabey;
93 © Brittany Gabey;
96 © Studio Fotografico Quattrone, Florence;
97 © Patrimonio Nacional, Madrid;
98 © Photo Josse, Paris;
99 Museo National de San Carlos, Mexico City;
101 Courtesy of the artist and the Cumberland Gallery, Nashville;
104 © Brittany Gabey;
105 © Brittany Gabey;
106 (2 photographs) Rylan Steel
107 © Brittany Gabey;
110 © Elizabeth Baek;
111 Courtesy of the artist;
114–15 © Cameraphoto Arte, Venice;
116 Courtesy of the artist;
117 Courtesy of the artist and the Cumberland Gallery, Nashville;
119 © Brittany Gabey;
121 © Brittany Gabey;
122 (6 photographs) Rylan Steel;
123 © Brittany Gabey;
124 © Ashley Long;
125 © Brittany Gabey;
128 © Photo Josse, Paris;
129 © Vincenzo Pirozzi, Rome;
130 © Krista Franks;
131 Courtesy George Adams Gallery, New York;
134 Private Collection. Image courtesy of George Adams Gallery, New York;
136T&B © John Lutz;
137T&B © Amanda Henke;
138 © Fotografica Foglia, Naples;
139 © Studio Fotografico Quattrone, Florence;
140 Collection Walker Art Center, Minneapolis;
141 Photo Kerry Ryan McFate;
142 © Diane Edison;
143 © Diane Edison;
144 Courtesy of the artist and the Cumberland Gallery, Nashville;
146–47 © & photos David Zoellick;
148T © Elizabeth Baek;
148B © Tyler Brantley;
149 © Holly Soros;
150–51 © Rebecca Claire Stephens;
152 Solomon Projects, Atlanta, Georgia;
153 Courtesy of George Adams Gallery, New York;
154 Courtesy of the artist;
155 Bridgeman Art Library;
156 © Madeline Edwards;
157 Courtesy of the artist;
158L © Krista Franks;
158R © Miriam Rowe;
159 © David Yeom/photo Rylan Steel;
160 Courtesy of the artist;
161 Courtesy of the artist;
162 Courtesy of the artist;
163 © Abbie Morris.